Unity on the Global Left

This book brings together a collection of essays by progressive global activists in response to Samir Amin's call for a new global organization of progressive workers and peoples. Amin's proposal is applauded, criticized and reformulated by these scholar-activists who are all proponents of ways forward toward a more egalitarian world society.

Samir Amin, a leading scholar and co-founder of the world-system tradition, died on August 12, 2018. Just before his death, he published, along with close allies, a call for 'workers and the people' to establish a 'fifth international' to coordinate support for progressive movements. Amin, an Egyptian economist, was an intrepid intellectual and organizer of popular movements whose scholar activism provided inspiration to the global justice movement. The essays in this volume are by other prominent scholar activists who praise, critique and reconfigure Amin's proposal in order to help humanity confront the contemporary crisis of global capitalism and move toward a more egalitarian global society.

The chapters in this book were originally published in the journal, *Globalizations*.

Barry Gills is Editor in Chief of *Globalizations* journal and Founding Editor of the Rethinking Globalizations book series (Routledge). He is a member of the Global Extractivisms and Alternatives Initiative (EXALT), and the Peoples Sovereignty Network.

Christopher Chase-Dunn is Distinguished Professor of Sociology and Director of the Institute for Research on World-Systems at the University of California, Riverside, USA. He is the author of *Social Change: Globalization from the Stone Age to the Present* (with Bruce Lerro) and *Global Struggles and Social Change* (with Paul Almeida).

Rethinking Globalizations

Edited by Barry K. Gills, University of Helsinki, Finland and Kevin Gray, University of Sussex, UK.

This series is designed to break new ground in the literature on globalization and its academic and popular understanding. Rather than perpetuating or simply reacting to the economic understanding of globalization, this series seeks to capture the term and broaden its meaning to encompass a wide range of issues and disciplines and convey a sense of alternative possibilities for the future.

Reglobalization
Edited by Matthew Louis Bishop and Anthony Payne

Unity on the Global Left
Critical Reflections on Samir Amin's Call for a New International
Edited by Barry K. Gills and Christopher Chase-Dunn

The Interface of Domestic and International Factors in India's Foreign Policy
Edited by Johannes Dragsbaek Schmidt and Shantanu Chakrabarti

Questioning the Utopian Springs of Market Economy
Damien Cahill, Martijn Konings and Adam David Morton

Between Class and Discourse: Left Intellectuals in Defence of Capitalism
Boris Kagarlitsky

Challenging Inequality in South Africa
Transitional Compasses
Edited by Michelle Williams and Vishwas Satgar

The Redesign of the Global Financial Architecture
State Authority, New Risks and Dynamics
Stuart P. M. Mackintosh

Authoritarian Neoliberalism
Philosophies, Practices, Contestations
Edited by Ian Bruff and Cemal Burak Tansel

Migration, Civil Society and Global Governance
Edited by Carl-Ulrik Schierup, Branka Likic-Brboric, Raúl Delgado Wise and Gülay Toksöz

For more information about this series, please visit:
https://www.routledge.com/Rethinking-Globalizations/book-series/RG

Unity on the Global Left

Critical Reflections on Samir Amin's Call
for a New International

Edited by
Barry Gills and Christopher Chase-Dunn

Routledge
Taylor & Francis Group

LONDON AND NEW YORK

First published 2021
by Routledge
2 Park Square, Milton Park, Abingdon, Oxon OX14 4RN

and by Routledge
52 Vanderbilt Avenue, New York, NY 10017

Routledge is an imprint of the Taylor & Francis Group, an informa business

British Library Cataloguing in Publication Data
A catalogue record for this book is available from the British Library

ISBN: 978-0-367-55222-0 (hbk)
ISBN: 978-0-367-55225-1 (pbk)
ISBN: 978-1-003-09248-3 (ebk)

Typeset in Minion Pro
by Newgen Publishing UK

Publisher's Note
The publisher accepts responsibility for any inconsistencies that may have arisen during the conversion of this book from journal articles to book chapters, namely the inclusion of journal terminology.

Disclaimer
Every effort has been made to contact copyright holders for their permission to reprint material in this book. The publishers would be grateful to hear from any copyright holder who is not here acknowledged and will undertake to rectify any errors or omissions in future editions of this book.

Contents

Citation Information

The chapters in this book were originally published in the *Globalizations*, volume 16, issue 7 (August 2019). When citing this material, please use the original page numbering for each article, as follows:

Chapter 1
In search of unity: a new politics of solidarity and action for confronting the crisis of global capitalism
Barry Gills and Christopher Chase-Dunn
Globalizations, volume 16, issue 7 (August 2019), pp. 967–972

Chapter 2
Climate justice and sustained transnational mobilization
Paul Almeida
Globalizations, volume 16, issue 7 (August 2019), pp. 973–979

Chapter 3
Samir Amin and the challenges of socialist transformation in senile capitalism
Carlos Eduardo Martins
Globalizations, volume 16, issue 7 (August 2019), pp. 980–984

Chapter 4
The twenty-first century revolutions and internationalism: a world historical perspective
Sahan Savas Karatasli
Globalizations, volume 16, issue 7 (August 2019), pp. 985–997

Chapter 5
On Samir Amin's call for a Fifth International
Valentine M. Moghadam
Globalizations, volume 16, issue 7 (August 2019), pp. 998–1005

Chapter 6
The rational kernel within Samir Amin's mythological shell: the idea of a democratic and pluralist world political party
Heikki Patomäki
Globalizations, volume 16, issue 7 (August 2019), pp. 1006–1011

Chapter 16

Capital has an Internationale and it is going fascist: time for an international of the global popular classes

William I. Robinson

Globalizations, volume 16, issue 7 (August 2019), pp. 1085–1091

Chapter 17

On heeding the lessons of the past and adapting them to the present: a strategy for an effective Fifth International

Michael Tyrala

Globalizations, volume 16, issue 7 (August 2019), pp. 1092–1101

Chapter 18

Eurocentrism, state-centrism and sexual self-determination in the construction of a global democratic organization

Teivo Teivainen

Globalizations, volume 16, issue 7 (August 2019), pp. 1102–1108

Chapter 19

Rethinking Samir Amin's legacy and the case for a political organization of the global justice movement

Bonn Juego

Globalizations, volume 16, issue 7 (August 2019), pp. 1109–1115

Chapter 20

Building a new international is necessary and urgent

Carlos Serrano Ferreira

Globalizations, volume 16, issue 7 (August 2019), pp. 1116–1123

Chapter 21

*The kick off**

Mamdouh Habashi

Globalizations, volume 16, issue 7 (August 2019), pp. 1124–1127

For any permission-related enquiries please visit:
www.tandfonline.com/page/help/permissions

Notes on Contributors

Biko Agozino is Professor of Sociology and Africana Studies, Virginia Tech. He was Director of Administration at the Directorate for Literacy, organizing free literacy classes for workers in Nigeria, and was Associate Editor of the free *Mass Line: The Liberation Journal*, with Eskor Toyo as Editor. He was involved in the formation of the Labour Party, in alliance with organised labour, that campaigned for the restoration of democracy in Nigeria in the 1980s until the military dictatorship banned the party. He was a founding member of the International Governing Council of the Center for Democracy and Development that advocated against authoritarian rule in West Africa. He is currently a member of the Democratic Socialists of America. He is the author of *Black Women and the Criminal Justice System: Towards the Decolonisation of Victimisation* (1997, republished by Routledge in 2018) and of *Counter-Colonial Criminology: A Critique of Imperialist Reason* (2003), among other works. His film, 'Shouters and the Control Freak Empire' won the Best International Short Documentary at the Columbia Gorge Film Festival, USA, 2011.

Paul Almeida is Professor of Sociology at the University of California, Merced. He regularly teaches courses in environmental sociology, social movements, and globalization. Almeida's research centres on the efficacy of collective action at the local, national and global levels of social and political life. He has empirically examined the timing and distribution of dozens of large-scale campaigns whereby ordinary citizens and excluded social groups mobilized to protect themselves from the loss of vital necessities such as health care, pensions, public water services/utilities, environmental quality and social citizenship rights. He is a two-time Fulbright Fellowship Recipient and received the 2015 Distinguished Scholarship Award from the Pacific Sociological Association for his book, *Mobilizing Democracy: Globalization and Citizen Protest* (2014). His most recent book is *Social Movements: The Structure of Collective Mobilization* (2019).

Rebecca Álvarez is Assistant Professor of Sociology at New Mexico Highlands University. Her research interests include political economy, global social movements and gender violence. She is the author of *Vigilante Gender Violence: Social Class, the Gender Bargain, and Mob Attacks on Women Worldwide* (2020).

Samir Amin (Arabic: سمير أمين) was Egyptian-French Marxian economist, political scientist and world-systems analyst. He was born on September 3, 1931 and he died on August 12, 2018. Amin was born in Cairo, the son of an Egyptian father and a French mother (both medical doctors). He spent his childhood and youth in Port Said where he attended a French high school. From 1947 to 1957 he studied in Paris, gaining a diploma in political science (1952) before graduating in statistics (1956) and economics (1957). After arriving in Paris, Amin joined the French Communist Party (PCF), but he later distanced himself from Soviet Marxism and associated himself for some time with Maoist circles. In 1980 Amin became a director of the Third World Forum in Dakar. He was also active in the World Social Forum and an intrepid protagonist in the global justice movement.

Patrick Bond is Professor of Government at the University of the Western Cape and Honorary Professor of Geography at the University of the Witwatersrand in Johannesburg, South Africa. Recent co-edited, co-authored and sole-authored books include *BRICS and Resistance in Africa* (2019); *BRICS: An Anti-capitalist Critique* (2015); *South Africa: The Present as History* (2014) and *Elite transition: From Apartheid to Neoliberalism in South Africa* (2014). He works closely with social, environmental and economic justice movements.

Christopher Chase-Dunn is Distinguished Professor of Sociology and Director of the Institute for Research on World-Systems at the University of California, Riverside, USA. He is the author of *Social Change: Globalization from the Stone Age to the Present* (with Bruce Lerro) and *Global Struggles and Social Change* (with Paul Almeida).

Radhika Desai is Professor at the Department of Political Studies, and Director, Geopolitical Economy Research Group, University of Manitoba, Winnipeg, Canada. She has just started her third term as President of the Society for Socialist Studies. She is the author of *Geopolitical Economy: After US Hegemony, Globalization and Empire* (2013), *Slouching Towards Ayodhya: From Congress to Hindutva in Indian Politics* (2nd rev. ed., 2004) and *Intellectuals and Socialism: 'Social Democrats' and the Labour Party* (1994), a *New Statesman and Society* Book of the Month. Her edited or co-edited books are: *Karl Polanyi and Twenty-first Century Capitalism* (2020, with Kari Polanyi Levitt), *Revolutions, a Special Issue of Third World Quarterly* (2020, with Henry Heller), *Russia, Ukraine and Contemporary Imperialism, a special issue of International Critical Thought* (2016), *Theoretical Engagements in Geopolitical Economy* (2015), *Analytical Gains from Geopolitical Economy* (2015), *Revitalizing Marxist Theory for Today's Capitalism* (2010) and *Developmental and Cultural Nationalisms* (2009). Her articles and book chapters appear in international scholarly journals and edited volumes. With Alan Freeman, she co-edits the Geopolitical Economy book series and the Future of Capitalism book series.

Carlos Serrano Ferreira is Vice-coordinator of the Laboratory of Hegemony and Counter-Hegemony Studies at the Federal University of Rio de Janeiro (LEHC – UFRJ), Head of the Department of Latin American Studies at the Institute for Innovative Development (Moscow) and researcher at the Interdisciplinary International Relations Study Laboratory (Lieri – UFRRJ). He is a PhD candidate in Political Science at the Higher Institute of Social and Political Sciences of the University of Lisbon (ISCSP-UL). He previously worked as a professor at the Department of Political Science at UFRJ (2015–2017) and as Assistant Executive Secretary and Researcher at the UNESCO / UNU Chair and Network on Global Economy and Sustainable Development – REGGEN (2009–2013). He is scholarship holder of the UNESCO ULHT Chair 'Education, Citizenship and Cultural Diversity' (Lisbon). He has held leading positions in student, union and party organizations in Brazil.

Barry Gills is Editor in Chief of *Globalizations* journal and Founding Editor of the Rethinking Globalizations book series (Routledge). He is member of the Global Extractivisms and Alternatives Initiative (EXALT), and the Peoples Sovereignty Network.

Andrej Grubacic is Professor and Chair of Anthropology and Social Change at California Institute of Integral Studies-San Francisco. He works with the Social Science Departments at Rojava University and Mesopotamia Academy of Social Sciences. He is the author and co-author of several books, including *Don't Mourn, Balkanize: Essays After Yugoslavia* (2011), *The Staughton Lynd Reader* and *Living at the Edges of Capitalism: Adventures in Exile and Mutual Aid*.

Mamdouh Habashi is a member of the board of the Arab and African Research Centre and Vice President of the World Forum for Alternatives. He is Co-founder of the Egyptian Socialist Party and since 2015 head of the international office of the SPA Socialist Alliance Party. He has written widely on political Islam; the European left and the Arab-Israeli conflict; and problems of democracy and secularization in the Arab countries.

Bonn Juego is a postdoctoral researcher and university teacher at the University of Jyväskylä, Finland. He has been granted visiting research fellowships at the City University of Hong Kong and the University of Copenhagen and has lectured on global political economy at the University of Helsinki. Prior to pursuing a PhD at Aalborg University, he worked for the Manila-based secretariat and coordination of the Asia-Europe People's Forum.

Boris Kagarlitsky was a dissident in the Soviet times and in 1990–1993 a deputy to Moscow Soviet (provincial council) till it was dissolved by President Boris Yeltsin in a coup d'etat in 1993. He is currently a Professor at Moscow Higher School of Social and Economic Sciences and Editor of internet journal *Rabkor*.

Sahan Savas Karatasli is Assistant Professor of Sociology at University of North Carolina, Greensboro. His broad research areas are international political economy, global sociology, labour unrest and nationalism. Karatasli's research on historical capitalism received many awards including PEWS Best Faculty Article Award and Theda Skocpol Dissertation Award by the American Sociological Association.

Carlos Eduardo Martins has a degree in Sociology and Politics from the Pontifical Catholic University of Rio de Janeiro (1990), a Master's degree in Business Administration from Getúlio Vargas Fundation (1996) and a PhD in Sociology from the University of São Paulo (2003). He is Associate Professor at the Institute of International Relations and Defense (IRID/UFRJ), Professor of the Permanent Framework of the Post-Graduation Program in International Political Economy (PEPI/UFRJ), Coordinator of the Laboratory of Studies on Hegemony and Counter-hegemony (LEHC / UFRJ), and Researcher of CLACSO WGs (the Regional Integration and United States).

Francine Mestrum has a PhD in Social Sciences and has worked at a number of European institutions and several Belgian universities. Her research concerns the social dimension of globalisation, poverty, inequality, social protection, public services and gender. She is an active member of the International Council of the World Social Forum and of the International Organising Committee of the Asia Europe People's Forum. She is the author of several books (in Dutch, French and English) on development, poverty, inequality and social commons. She is the founder of the global network of Global Social Justice and currently works on a project for social commons. www.socialcommons.eu

Valentine M. Moghadam is Professor of Sociology and International Affairs at Northeastern University, Boston, and former Director (Jan. 2012–July 2017) of the International Affairs Program. Born in Tehran, Iran, she was previously Professor of Sociology and Director of Women's Studies at Purdue University and Illinois State University; a section chief at UNESCO in Paris, where she led policy-oriented research on gender equality and development in the Social and Human Sciences Sector; and a senior researcher at the United Nations University's WIDER Institute in

Helsinki, Finland, where she coordinated the research program on women and development. Her areas of research include globalization, transnational social movements and networks, comparative revolutions, and women and gender relations in the Middle East and North Africa. She is the author of many journal articles and books, including *Modernizing Women: Gender and Social Change in the Middle East* (1993, 2003, 2013) and the award-winning *Globalizing Women: Transnational Feminist Networks* (2005). Her current research focuses on varieties and gender dynamics of populisms, outcomes of the Arab Spring protests, and feminist movements.

Heikki Patomäki is Professor of World Politics at University of Helsinki. His research interests include philosophy and methodology of social sciences; peace research; economic theory; global political economy, justice and democracy; and futures studies. His most recent book is *Disintegrative Tendencies in Global Political Economy: Exits and Conflicts* (2018).

William I. Robinson is Professor of Sociology and Global Studies at the University of California at Santa Barbara. Among his recent books are *Global Capitalism and the Crisis of Humanity* (2014), *Into the Tempest: Essays on the New Global Capitalism* (2018), and *The Global Police State* (2020). His professional website is http://robinson.faculty.soc.ucsb.edu/ and his Facebook blog is https://www.facebook.com/WilliamIRobinsonSociologist/.

Leslie Sklair is Emeritus Professor of Sociology at the London School of Economics. His work in the last few decades has focused on the transnational capitalist class, capitalist globalization, the culture-ideology of consumerism, architecture and cities and, most recently, how these connect with the Anthropocene. He is co-ordinating an international research project on how the Anthropocene is being reported in mass media in local languages all over the world with a team of 45 volunteer researchers. His edited book on the project (*The Anthropocene in Global Media: Neutralizing the Risk*) will be published by Routledge at the end of 2020.

Teivo Teivainen is Researcher and Lecturer at the Ibero-American Centre, University of Helsinki since 1991. From the beginning of 2001 he has been Adjunct Associate Professor of Development Studies at the University of Helsinki. He has worked as Visiting Scholar at the State University of New York at Binghamton in 1988 (Sociology Department) and 1994 (Fernand Braudel Centre), and as Visiting Researcher at the Peruvian Research Centre Desco throughout the 1990s. He is an active consultant and cooperates with various social movements. His publications include books and articles on democracy, economic policies, integration, global institutions and human rights. Apart from the issues related to the world-system as a whole, the main geographical focus of his publications is Latin America where he has done field work in most countries of the continent.

Michael Tyrala is Postdoctoral Fellow at the Institute for Emerging Market Studies of the Hong Kong University of Science and Technology. His research interests lie at the intersection between international relations, political economy and historical sociology. He focuses on the global offshore nexus between high net worth individuals, multinational enterprises, tax havens and the professional intermediaries that facilitate their interactions; on the political, economic and socio-cultural forces that struggle against this nexus; and on the impacts of these struggles on the structural dynamics that constitute the capitalist world-economy. His professional experience includes traineeships at NATO Allied Command Transformation and the European Economic and Social Committee, and in 2016, he completed an internship with the Trade Union Advisory Committee to the OECD, during which he drafted two official publications on reforming the international tax system. Shortly after, he was awarded the 2016 TTN Tax Prize. His two current research projects are centred on incorporating offshore wealth extraction into the conceptual and analytical toolbox of world-systems analysis, and on examining the complex roles of India and China in global tax governance.

Owen Worth works in the Department of Politics and Public Administration at the University of Limerick. His recent book, *Morbid Symptoms: The Global Rise of the Far Right* has been published by Zed Books (2019). He is also the author of *Rethinking Hegemony* (2015), *Resistance in the Age of Austerity* (2013) and *Hegemony, International Political Economy and Post Communist Russia* (2005) and has written numerous articles in and around the area of Global Politics.

In search of unity: a new politics of solidarity and action for confronting the crisis of global capitalism

Barry Gills and Christopher Chase-Dunn

ABSTRACT
This essay is an introduction to a Special Forum by critical scholar-activists responding to the late Samir Amin's call for the establishment of a new political vehicle that would be capable of uniting diverse progressive and revolutionary movements consisting of the workers and peoples of the whole world. The purpose of this vehicle would be to confront and radically transform a global capitalist order in deep crisis. The authors of these essays tend to agree that Amin was a profound contributor to the global justice movement, and to the reformulation of Marxism to address the evolution of global capitalism and imperialism that took place in the late twentieth and early twenty-first centuries. However, some are critical of Amin's stance. The essayists differ about whether they see Samir Amin's proposal for the establishment of a global party as a good or bad idea. Among those who think it is a good idea there are differences regarding the organizational nature and issue focus of the proposed organization. There are also different attitudes toward the institution of the nation-state and regarding the sources of progressive revolutionary political forces in the contemporary world. We briefly review the main issues under contention.

Samir Amin, a leading scholar and co-founder of the world-systems tradition, died on August 12, 2018. Just before his death, he published, along with close allies, a call for 'workers and the people' to establish a 'fifth international' [https://www.pambazuka.org/global-south/letter-intent-inaugural-meeting-international-workers-and-peoples] *to coordinate support to progressive movements. To honor Samir Amin's invaluable contribution to world-systems scholarship, we are pleased to present readers with a selection of essays responding to Amin's final message for today's anti-systemic movements. This forum is being co-published between* Globalizations [https://www.tandfonline.com/rglo], *the* Journal of World-Systems Research [http://jwsr.pitt.edu/ojs/index.php/jwsr/issue/view/75] *and* Pambazuka News [https://www.pambazuka.org/]. *Additional essays and commentary can be found in these outlets.*

The time has come to unite the hundreds of struggles, campaigns, networks, movements and organizations that are combating the different ways transnational corporations (TNCs) are appropriating our destinies … people's rights have been systematically violated, the Earth and its resources destroyed, pillaged and contaminated, and resistance criminalized, while corporations continue committing economic and ecological crimes with impunity … to confront corporate power and the system that protects and benefits TNCs, it is urgent and necessary to give a systematic response. We need to unite our experiences and our struggles, learn collectively from our victories and our failures and share our analysis and strategies …

'Call to International Action', www.stopcorporateimpunity.org

Samir Amin was a lifelong and indefatigable protagonist of the cause of socialism, independence and justice for peoples of the Global South. Like many earlier revolutionaries, he saw the Global North as a nexus of imperialism in which the movements of workers and peoples had been compromised by their favoured position in the modern world-system. Amin was an Egyptian economist who spent much of his early life in Paris, before moving to Dakar, Senegal where he directed the Third World Forum. He died on August 12, 2018 and there have been many tributes to the man and his work.[1] Samir Amin was one of the principal founders of the world-system perspective that emerged in the 1970s as a prominent critique of modernization theory. His analysis provided a new focus on the hierarchical nature of the international economy. He argued the need for progressive movements and national regimes in the Global South to 'delink' from the chains of imperialism in order to establish more self-reliant and independent forms of economic and political development (Amin, 1990). He advocated a new polycentric world order to supersede the hegemony of the global North and the continued legacy of centuries of colonialism. Amin's version of the world-system perspective was more influenced by his Marxist perspective and less by the Braudelian school which was prominent in the work of Immanuel Wallerstein and his followers. Amin's extensive knowledge of the history of North Africa, especially the work of Ibn Khaldun, enabled him to theorize the comparison between the modern capitalist world-system and earlier 'tributary' systems (Amin, 1980a, 1991). He offered a widely influential early critique of Eurocentric world history (Amin, 1989). Amin (1980b) was a pioneer in the study of contemporary global class relations, a predecessor of the theorists of global capitalism who emerged in the 1990s, some of whom are contributors to this Special Forum.

In this brief introduction we cannot possibly fully review the extraordinary *ouvre* of Samir Amin. What we can do is indicate the present context of his urgent call for global action and unity and discuss the essays contributed here by critical scholar-activists[2] addressing Samir's call for the establishment of a global organization to mobilize progressive social forces and people's movements into a new global struggle to move humanity towards a just, democratic and collectively rational global commonwealth (Amin, 2008). As we write, the global climate change crisis is accelerating and deepening, threatening increasing environmental and social calamity. Vast sums continue to be spent on the military apparatus, on wars and preparations for wars, including possible nuclear confrontation. Democratic political culture is perceived to be on the defensive globally, as the trend towards authoritarianism intensifies. Yet, there is also an upsurge in the spirit of resistance. Rebellion is in the air again, in places as diverse as Armenia, Sudan, Hong Kong, Russia and many more. A new popular mobilization to demand urgent action to arrest global warming is fast gaining momentum. We may conclude that we live in revolutionary times. It is a time for rebellion. A time for renewed struggle for radical transformation of the dominant global system.

This engagement with Amin's proposal is motivated by both long-standing conditions of global injustice and by a series of recent developments that suggest a greater need for urgency and solidarity. The World Social Forum process, though still holding promise, is seemingly in need of either reinvention or replacement. The Latin American Pink Tide has now entered a new phase of crises, wherein authoritarian and right-wing regimes are arising. Numerous right-wing, populist, nationalist and even neofascist movements and parties have emerged in Europe. The new radical progressive and anti austerity parties that emerged in Spain and Greece have been either defeated or obstructed by the neoliberal policies of the European banking system. Internationalist cosmopolitanism, in both neoliberal and progressive forms, is increasingly challenged by nationalist and populist movements. Some progressives have concluded that the large global demonstrations that were the template for the global justice movement in the 2000s are no longer a sufficient response. The search for new forms of organization and action to unite progressive and democratic forces throughout the world in order to effectively address mounting local, regional and global crises is now an ever more urgent concern.

Samir Amin was an active participant in the World Social Forum (WSF) process as recounted in several of the essays; including those by Teivo Teivainen and Patrick Bond. Critique of the perceived limitations of the WSF is a recurrent theme in the essays. The need to reinvent its process is argued by Alvarez and Chase Dunn, who offer a critical account of the limitations of horizontality and loose organizations. Patrick Bond highlights the gap between top-down intellectual formulations and manifestos and bottom-up strategic narratives, and criticizes the WSF for the lack of coherent ideology. He, and Bonn Juego point to the need to strengthen the connection between a new international as an organization and active social struggles and mass social movements. William Robinson offers a critical view of the refusal of the WSF to adopt a political programme and he advocates a new structure that includes both progressive political parties and social movements, to create a new model of transnational revolutionary struggle. Desai points to Amin's criticism of 'Proudonist economics and network politics' while calling for a renewed emphasis on anti- imperialist resistance and active pursuit of socialist economic reconstructions. Juego also stresses the limitations of the past network structure of both new social movements and the WSF. The systemic unity of capitalism should be recognized and the radical response needs to be one with global coordination amongst diverse social forces and forms of struggle in a 'continuous dialogue' and active coalition building.

Amin himself tried to influence the WSF to move away from the model of a discursive arena and evolve toward a more structured organization that would adopt consensual positions and undertake coordinated campaigns. The struggle between those in the leadership who wanted to maintain the WSF as an inclusive 'open space' for diverse social movements, and those like Amin and others who wanted to move in the direction of a more structured political organization reflected a strong current in the culture of the Global Left that emerged in the World Revolution of 1968.[3] This tension has been described as one between horizontalism (loose networks of equals) and verticalism (hierarchical organizational command and control structures), discussed in the Alvarez and Chase Dunn essay. Amin and other proponents of greater organizational coherence have not advocated creating hierarchical control structures. As reviewed in the essay by Sahan Karatasli, the Global Left has alternated between more and less hierarchical forms of organization since the middle of the nineteenth century. The belief that communist parties are always internally undemocratic is a widely held myth, but the New Left critique of the Old Left and the demise of the Soviet Union has confirmed this belief in the minds of a majority of contemporary progressive activists. Any effort to found a capacious progressive global political organization must contend with this perception. These and related issues are analysed in historical and contemporary context by Boris Kagarlitsky. He argues that it was the defeat of the global left that stimulated rapid increases in corruption and in decay amongst the dominant capitalist classes; aggravating all the contradictions and problems the system faced. Kagarlitsky argues that it was the failures of both revolutionary and reformist alternatives to the rule of capital that have been the key factors affecting the decay of the bourgeois order.

The contributions to the forum diverge around whether they endorse or criticize Amin's proposal for a new international. Most of the contributors endorse the basic idea of the need for some type of new global umbrella organization that would unite diverse movements across global South and

North and seek coalitions amongst diverse struggles. The imperative for creating a new form of global organization includes the threat posed by the accelerating global climate change crisis, increasing global inequality and concentration of wealth in oligarchic circles, and the imminent threat of rising nationalist, right wing populist and authoritarian movements and regimes. Mamdouh Habashi, a fellow Egyptian and close ally of Amin within the World Forum for Alternatives (which was founded by Samir Amin to bring together radicals and revolutionaries from across the globe) uses his essay to explain the reasons a new organization must be established and to outline a series of key questions concerning its aims and constitutional structures.[4] Alvarez and Chase Dunn elaborate on the 'diagonal' model of transnational revolutionary organization, which aims to synthesize horizontality with verticalism and practice democratic collective decision-making.

The rise of twenty-first century forms of fascism is a threat acknowledged by many of the essays. Ferreia's essay points to the danger of populism and the dilution of class into a 'fascist mass'. He stresses the vital role of the proletariat in building a new international and a unitary articulation of a socialist transition. Robinson explicitly invokes the idea of constructing a broad anti-fascist front on transnational scale. Mestrum calls for a transition that combines social and environmental justice with a campaign against fascism, while Agozino insists on recognition of the links between racism, imperialism and patriarchy on world scale. Alvarez and Chase Dunn advocate naming the predations of the transnational corporate class and the neo-fascist and populist global Right as the enemy.

There are other important issues at play in the essays. Some authors contest the very idea of global organizing, claiming that the only sensible approach is to focus on the creation of local sustainable communities that can confront the problems of the Anthropocene (Leslie Sklair; Andrej Grubacic). These same authors see the state, as well as capitalism, as a necessarily repressive institution that must be abolished. Grubacic explains Abdullah Ocalan's reconceptualization of the nation as a diverse community of freely associating cooperators, challenging the more predominant existing versions of both nations and states. Amin, it should be noted, was a proponent of progressive nationalism and the use of state power by workers and farmers for purposes of mobilizing a more egalitarian and self-reliant political economy. While leftist global cosmopolitans are usually critics of nationalism and the nation-state as institutions, Amin contends that these institutions can be reconfigured as valuable tools for organizing socialist national polities and an anti-imperialist world society. Worth's essay takes exception to Amin's analysis of progressive nationalism as a reversion back to existing national frameworks, and he deploys Rosa Luxemburg's critique of the dangers of 'left nationalism'. Worth contends that any new international should be geared towards new transnational conditions and move beyond the traditional forms and aspirations of twentieth century socialism. Robinson strongly insists on the need for both a transnational analysis and transnational forms of resistance. In contrast, Desai, like Amin, sees the need to emphasize the role played by the state, whether as an arena for progressive reconstruction of the productive economy or as an element in imperialism. She criticizes the past role of Western Marxism and the Western left. Agozino calls for the centrality of race and gender issues and the inclusion of the indigenous peoples of the world in a New International.

Our authors also differ about where, geographically, they see the main contemporary contradictions and the most fertile locations for organizing. Amin is often regarded as a 'Third Worldist', meaning that he saw a primary role for the Global South. He also emphasized the importance of agrarian social relations in the Global South as the main fulcrum of revolution, with small farmers as the key agents of socialist revolution. As the most exploited and oppressed sector of the global system, the small farmers and workers of the Global South would be the most revolutionary agents that would challenge and transcend global capitalism by organizing self-reliant national societies. This conviction led to his sometimes taking on quite controversial positions in support of national regimes in the Global South.

Some of the contributors to this Special Forum on Amin's call for a 5th International are globalists, in the sense that they advocate Global North/South coordinated action. However, Michael Tyrala argues that progressive outcomes are more likely to emerge and to have wide consequences if a world party concentrates on the Global North. This position is also implied by Heikki Patomaki's critique of Samir's stance. Patomaki advocates the formation of a world party along the lines of the campaign for democracy within the European Union that has been organized by Diem25. Patomaki also claims that Amin's analysis of global capitalism is stuck in the twentieth century, failing to comprehend the important developments that have emerged more recently. But Carlos Martins presents a clear picture of how Amin adapted Marxian analysis to understand the neoliberal globalization project (Amin, 1997).

Some contributors stress the need to emphasize social and political issues which they argue cannot be excluded. Teivainen questions why the issue of LGBT rights was invisible in Amin's formulation of the foci of the new global instrument he was proposing. Paul Almeida and Leslie Sklair claim that the global environmental catastrophe will be the crucial pivot around which the contemporary progressive movements should and must organize. Valentine Moghadam confronts the difficult problem of the distinction between 'progressive' and 'counterhegemonic,' an important issue that any future global political party of the Left must confront. She sees Jihadist conservatism as part of the Global Right even though it is counterhegemonic.

In concluding this brief introduction, we hope the readers of this Special Forum will explore the many issues implied by Samir Amin's call for a new international. The debate has begun. The form, procedures, and aims of a new international are yet to be determined. This set of contributions is one step closer to the goal. The times are exceptional and the threats to the future health and well being of all humanity are mounting. It is time to seek new forms of unity.

Notes

1. A 59 minute film with English and French sub-titles about his life and contributions to popular struggles is available at https://mronline.org/2019/03/29/samir-amin-the-organic-intellectual/. Another full-length video about Samir Amin's life has been made by Aziz Fall. It is titled 'Samir Amin: The Organic Internationalist' (71 minutes, English-French), https://www.youtube.com/watch?v=mKBJNpTU1Jw.
2. The contributors to the Amin/5th forum are mainly from more recent generations of scholar-activists. Samir Amin was part of the generation that came of age before and during the World Revolution of 1968. He and Immanuel Wallerstein, Terence Hopkins, Andre Gunder Frank and Giovanni Arrighi founded and developed the world-system perspective. Except for Wallerstein, that generation has passed along with many others who helped elaborate the prehension of the modern world-system. Gunder Frank passed in 2005, Janet Abu-Lughod in 2013; Walter Goldfrank in 2017, Anibal Quijano, Teotonio dos Santos and Samir Amin in 2018. The contributors to this Special Forum on Amin/5th International are from the second, third and fourth generations (see Table of Contents).
3. Surveys of activists attending the World Social Forums in Porto Alegre (2005) and in Nairobi (2007) found that the attendees were about evenly divided between those who favored the open forum and those who favored a more structured organization (Chase-Dunn, Aldecoa, Breckenridge-Jackson, & Herrera, 2019).
4. Mamdouh Habashi (habashi.mamdouh@gmail.com) has called for a kickoff meeting of the 5th international proposed by Samir Amin to be held in Nepal in early November of 2019. The title of the meeting is 'Building an alliance of the progressive forces and the oppressed people'.

Disclosure statement

No potential conflict of interest was reported by the authors.

References

Amin, S. (1980a). *Class and nation, historically and in the current crisis*. New York, NY: Monthly Review Press.

Amin, S. (1980b). The class structure of the contemporary imperialist system. *Monthly Review, 31*(8), 9–26.

Amin, S. (1989). *Eurocentrism*. New York, NY: Monthly Review Press.

Amin, S. (1990). *Delinking: Towards a polycentric world*. London: Zed Press.

Amin, S. (1991). The ancient world-systems versus the modern capitalist world-system. *Review, 14*(3 (Summer)), 349–385.

Amin, S. (1997). *Capitalism in the age of globalization*. London: Zed Press.

Amin, S. (2008). Towards the fifth international? In Katarina Sehm-Patomaki and Marko Ulvila (Eds.) *Global political Paties* (pp. 123–143). London: Zed Press.

Chase-Dunn, C., Aldecoa, J., Breckenridge-Jackson, I., & Herrera, J. (2019). Anarchism in the Web of transnational social movements. *Journal of World-Systems Research, 25*(2). Retrieved from http://jwsr.pitt.edu/ojs/index.php/jwsr/index

Democracy in Europe Movement 2025 (Diem25). Retrieved from https://diem25.org/

Climate justice and sustained transnational mobilization

Paul Almeida

ABSTRACT

Samir Amin's final essay called for the creation of a new international organization of progressive social forces. Here I review evidence from twenty-first century transnational movements germane for understanding the likelihood of the emergence of such an international organization and the issues and sectors most likely to facilitate coalitional unity. More specifically, the ecological crises identified by Amin in the form of global warming and climate change have created an unprecedented global environmental threat capable of unifying diverse social strata across the planet. The climate justice movement has already established a global infrastructure and template to coordinate a new international organization for confronting neoliberal forms of globalization. Pre-existing movement organizing around environmental racism, climate justice in the global South, and recent intersectional mobilizations serve as promising models for building an enduring international organization that will represent subaltern groups and have a substantial impact on world politics.

Samir Amin, a leading scholar and co-founder of the world-systems tradition, died on August 12, 2018. Just before his death, he published, along with close allies, a call for 'workers and the people' to establish a 'fifth international' [https://www.pambazuka.org/global-south/letter-intent-inaugural-meeting-international-workers-and-peoples] to coordinate support to progressive movements. To honor Samir Amin's invaluable contribution to world-systems scholarship, we are pleased to present readers with a selection of essays responding to Amin's final message for today's anti-systemic movements. This forum is being co-published between Globalizations *[https://www.tandfonline.com/rglo],* the Journal of World-Systems Research *[http://jwsr.pitt.edu/ojs/index.php/jwsr/issue/view/75] and* Pambazuka News *[https://www.pambazuka.org/]. Additional essays and commentary can be found in these outlets.*

Introduction

The transition to the neoliberal form of global capitalism in the late twentieth century corresponded with a variety of novel forms of resistance at the local, national, and international levels of political life (Almeida & Chase-Dunn, 2018). Neoliberalism produces new models of unequal development (Amin, 1976) between the capitalist core and periphery as well within nation states along with a host of tensions and threats motivating popular movements. These struggles will likely intensify as we move into the third decade of the new millennium. At the local level, collective action centres on everyday forms of resistance and grassroots struggles over racism, land grabbing, mining and mega development projects (Almeida, 2019). At the national level, opposition to neoliberalism manifests in the form of social movement campaigns against a bundle of economic liberalization policies that include austerity cuts, free trade agreements, privatization, de-regulation, and labour flexibility laws (Silva, 2009; Walton & Seddon, 1994). At the transnational level, opposition to international capital is most pronounced in the global economic justice movement, the World Social Forums, and, increasingly, the movement for Climate Justice, which is the focus of this essay.

In past decades, sociologists theorized that global capitalist accumulation would create its own self-induced limits through the depletion of natural resources, pollution, and environmental destruction (Gould, Pellow, & Schnaiberg, 2004; Rudy, forthcoming; Schnaiberg, 1980). Amin (2018) also referred to the ecological crisis of the twenty-first century in his final essay. James O'Connor (1988) conceptualized these processes as the 'second contradiction of capitalism', a contradiction in addition to the capitalist crisis of overproduction. In this perspective, advanced forms of capitalist accumulation undermine the necessary material requisites for systemic reproduction by destroying the ecological bases for continuous and expanded industrial activities on a global scale, leading to a crisis of underproduction. More recently, scholars contributing to these debates incorporate carbon emissions and global warming as an 'ecological rift' caused by global capitalism (Foster, Clark, & York, 2011; Moore, 2015).

The most recent scientific reporting suggests that the outlook for continued global warming is dire. Instead of a reduction in carbon emissions since 2017, there was a global increase of 1.6% in 2017 and 2.7% in 2018. (Dennis & Moody, 2018). Moreover, the past four years (2015–2018) have seen the warmest documented mean global temperatures on record, while the twenty warmest years on record have occurred over the past twenty-two years (World Meteorological Organization, 2018). The environmental challenge of global warming and climate change produced by neoliberal capitalism in the twenty-first century has also generated a massive transnational movement – the movement for climate justice. Environmental justice and climate justice combine threats of environmental degradation with concerns about inequality and the larger impacts on people with fewer resources and disadvantaged populations (Bullard, 2005; Pellow, 2017).

Ecological threats provide a major incentive for collective action in that failure to mobilize in the present will likely lead to worsening environmental conditions (Almeida, 2018; Johnson & Frickel, 2011). Earlier conservation movements (often involving more privileged social strata) organized in waves of environmentalism since the late nineteenth century against ecological threats associated with the expansion of industrial capital (Gottlieb, 1993). The movement to resist the environmental threat of climate change traces its origins back to the late 1980s and early 1990s. In the late 1980s, climate scientists and environmental NGOs started to push international organizations and nation states to take action based on meteorological and atmospheric studies that demonstrated a clear trend in global warming and its likely negative consequences. The United Nations established the Intergovernmental Panel on Climate Change (IPCC) to begin scientific discussions about how to reduce greenhouse gas emissions (Romm, 2018). Concurrently, a global network of environmental NGOs emerged to pressure the U.N. to propose a binding international climate accord – the Climate Action Network (CAN) (Brecher, 2015). During the United Nations Earth Summit on sustainability in Rio de Janeiro, Brazil in 1992, the United Nations Framework Convention on Climate Change (UNFCC) was established as an intergovernmental forum to work on reducing global warming (Caniglia, Brulle, & Szasz, 2015). In 1995, the UNFCC forum also set up annual meetings to move toward a global climate treaty to decrease carbon emissions – the Conference of Parties (COP). Throughout the 1990s and early 2000s the global climate movement to reduce greenhouse gases was concentrated in advanced capitalist countries and largely worked through the institutional channels of these U.N. bodies via the participation of environmental NGOs. This period has been referred to as 'mobilization from above' (Brecher, 2015).

Beginning in the mid-2000s, the climate justice movement became more contentious, organizing rallies and marches across the globe. The use of more non-institutionalized tactics rose in tandem with the lack of progress within the U.N. system to enforce past agreements and hold countries accountable for CO2 emissions. Already by 2005 the mass climate justice movement could mobilize simultaneous demonstrations in cities across several continents. The climate justice movement peaked in 2014 and 2015 by holding global days of protest in most of the world's countries and mobilized another large campaign in September of 2018 (Almeida, 2019). The movement has gained tremendous momentum in 2019 with the rise of Extinction Rebellion and Fridays for the Future promoting hundreds of actions across the globe. This global reach marked the transnational climate justice movement as one of the most extensive social movements on the planet.

The emphasis here is on the organizational infrastructure that has made the transnational climate justice movement so extensive and its prospects for future mobilization and lasting and effective coordination of popular organizations and movements. I examine the role of the global economic justice movement and the anti-war movement in providing the organizational and experiential bases for planetary mobilization against climate change. These are empirically based assessments to understand the likelihood of building a sustained international organization of progressive and subaltern forces along the lines envisioned by Amin (2018).

The global justice movement

The global justice movement took off in the late 1990s shortly after the establishment of the World Trade Organization (WTO) in 1996. The movement quickly developed an innovative organizational template for mobilizing mass protests on a transnational level. The coordinating template involved mobilizing a series of actions at the focal conference/summit/financial meetings while simultaneously holding dozens of solidarity actions across the globe (Almeida & Lichbach, 2003). This transnational organizing model is referred to by activists as a 'global day of action' (Wood, 2004). The global justice movement was a response to the neoliberal form of global capitalism that had been taking shape since the 1980s with a heavy emphasis on free trade and deregulation of social protections. The emerging global justice movement began to take advantage of the rise of internet communication technologies (ICTs). Beginning with international financial meetings in Europe in the late 1990s and the 1999 WTO conference in Seattle (Smith, 2001), the global organizational template was widely adopted. Indeed, by the turn of the twenty-first century the global justice movement had organized over 15 transnational campaigns per year with over 200,000 participants (Lichbach, 2003).

The organizational template invented by the global justice movement involves holding a large set of protests at the site of an international event along with simultaneous solidarity protests around the world (Almeida & Lichbach, 2003). By the early 2000s, the global justice movement had expanded the simultaneous protests to every continent. This would become the main form of transnational opposition to global capitalism in the twenty-first century (Wood, 2012). After the WTO meetings in Seattle, at least a half dozen global days of protest took place between 2000 and 2003. These included the IMF/World Bank meetings in Prague in September 2000, the G8 conference in Genoa in 2001, the WTO ministerial in Doha, Qatar in November 2001, and the fifth WTO Ministerial in 2003 in Cancun, Mexico (Juris, 2008). The global justice movement brought a wide coalition of different groups into their global days of action campaigns – youth, labour unions, human rights, environmentalists, LGBTQ groups, indigenous activists, feminists, peace, anarchists and etc. They united around the idea of protecting social citizenship and environmental rights that had been granted by nation-states in the twentieth century and now were under threat from neoliberal deregulation.

The global justice movement spilled over into the global anti-war movement in 2003 with demonstrations against the U.S. invasion of Iraq[1] and into the climate justice movement by the mid-2000s (Fisher, 2007; Hadden, 2014). At the same time, the issues and networks involved in the global justice movement continued via the World Social Forum process and ongoing mass demonstrations outside G20 meetings, as well as the global day of action in October of 2011 at the height of the Occupy Wall Street campaign. If there is to be a sustained progressive international movement in the twenty-first century it will probably coalesce around the climate justice movement and will further develop and augment the global days of action template.

Networks of transnational activists began to piece together the first Global Days Action to reduce carbon emissions in 2005 and 2006. These global networks came out of the alter-globalization and anti-war movements of the early 2000s to now battle climate change (Bond, 2012). They were joined by coalitions such as the Campaign against Climate Change and the transnational environmental NGOs such as Friends of the Earth and Greenpeace (Foran, 2014). By 2009, the climate justice movement reached 92 nations in the days of global action leading up to COP 15 in Copenhagen with the assistance of more assertive coalitions such as Climate Justice Action and Climate Justice Now! and greater representation from the Global South.[2] In the 2010s, web-based NGOs such as 350.org and Avaaz took a leadership role as brokers in coordinating the large mobilizations in 2014 and 2015 leading up to the Paris Climate Agreement. The 2014 and 2015 global days of climate action reached up to 75 percent of all countries on the planet with at least 1.5 million participants. Fridays for the Future and Extinction Rebellion are currently sustaining similar campaigns across the globe.

The increasing participation from countries across the world in the transnational climate justice actions, including from the global South, is remarkable. This loosely coupled global infrastructure provides a basis for future rounds of progressive collective action. The next steps for solidifying this infrastructure would be to continue to coordinate global summits and forums with representatives from the participating groups in the global days of action. Past examples of this approach include the World People's Summit on Climate Change and the Rights of Mother Earth held in Bolivia in 2010 following the worldwide mobilizations associated with COP 15 (Smith, 2014) and the World Social Forums. The Bolivia Summit called for ecological reparations for the Global South and an immediate and drastic reduction in carbon emissions.

Perhaps most pressing would be to increase the rate of summits and forums that bring together representatives from the climate justice coalition. The impressive scale of the transnational mobilizations over the past ten years is still limited by the vast amount of time between the launching of global days of action campaigns, even though much traditional organizing takes place on the ground in the interim periods. To overcome the 'flash activism' nature of these campaigns and to build the necessary level of solidarity among diverse groups, classes, and sectors for a long-term and capacious anti-systemic movement (Amin, 1990; Ciplet, Timmons Roberts, & Khan, 2015), climate justice activists will need to continue to find avenues and mechanisms for more frequent forums and mobilizations that can maintain and accelerate the momentum of a truly planetary movement.

The increasing intensity of climate change as an existential threat does create relatively more favourable conditions for international unity and avoids the sectarianism and fragmentation discussed by Amin (2018) in previous attempts at building a socialist *internationale* or permanent global organization of progressive sectors and groups. The threat is imminent and global, providing urgency and aligning common interests, the basic building blocks of sustained collective action (Almeida, 2019). At the same time, a number of pre-existing social and economic divisions will need to be given heightened recognition to build enduring transnational coalitions across the lines of race, class, gender, and colonial status. The environmental justice movement against ecological racism (Bullard, 2005), the Cochabamba Climate Change conference (Bond, 2012), and the current mass mobilizations fostering intersectional alliances (Luna, 2016; Terriquez, Brenes, & Lopez, 2018) offer some of the most promising models to incorporate within the larger global climate justice movement. With global warming disproportionately harming billions of the world's poor and excluded by global capital, the climate justice movement cannot continue to be directed by relatively privileged strata in the global North or South. Chase-Dunn and Reese (2007) also demonstrate that previous progressive parties organized on a global scale were initially able to coordinate simultaneously in the global periphery and capitalist core with membership from a variety of social sectors, including peasants and the urban working-class. The transnational climate justice alliance may also build internal cohesion by mobilizing against the xenophobia, authoritarianism, and climate change deniability of rightwing populism.

Notes

1. One of the largest protests in world history took place on 15 February 2003 against the impending U.S. invasion of Iraq. Nearly 800 cities in eighty countries participated against initiating a war on Iraq using the Global Days of Action template.
2. The terminology of the world-system perspective divides the Global South into the periphery and the semiperiphery.

Disclosure statement

No potential conflict of interest was reported by the author.

References

Almeida, P. D. (2018). The role of threat in collective action. In D. Snow, S. Soule, H. Kriesi, & H. McCammon (Eds.), *Wiley- Blackwell companion to social movements* (2nd ed., pp. 43–62). Oxford: Blackwell.
Almeida, P. D. (2019). *Social movements: The structure of collective mobilization*. Berkeley: University of California Press.

Almeida, P. D., & Chase-Dunn, C. (2018). Globalization and social movements. *Annual Review of Sociology, 44,* 189–211.

Almeida, P. D., & Lichbach, M. I. (2003). To the internet, from the internet: Comparative media coverage of transnational protest. *Mobilization, 8*(3), 249–272.

Amin, S. (1976). *Unequal development: An essay on the social formations of peripheral capitalism.* New York, NY: Monthly Review Press.

Amin, S. (1990). The social movements in the periphery: An end to national liberation? In S. Amin, G. Arrighi, A. Gunder Frank, & I. Wallerstein (Eds.), *Transforming the revolution: Social movements and the world-system* (pp. 96–138). New York, NY: Monthly Review Press.

Amin, S. (2018). It is imperative to reconstruct the Internationale of workers and peoples. *International Development Economic Associates (IDEAs).* July3, 2018. Retrieved from http://www.networkideas.org/featured-articles/2018/07/it-is-imperative-to-reconstruct-the-internationale-of-workers-and-peoples/

Bond, P. (2012). *Politics of climate justice: Paralysis above, movement below.* Cape Town: University of Kwa Zulu Natal Press.

Brecher, J. (2015). *Climate insurgency: A strategy for survival.* Boulder, CO: Paradigm.

Bullard, R. (2005). *The quest for environmental justice: Human rights and the politics of pollution.* San Francisco, CA: Sierra Club Books.

Caniglia, B., Brulle, R., & Szasz, A. (2015). Civil Society, social movements, and climate change. In R. Dunlap & R. Brulle (Eds.), *Climate change and Society* (pp. 235–268). Oxford: Oxford University Press.

Chase-Dunn, C., & Reese, E. (2007). The world social forum: A global party in the making? In K. Sehm-Patomaki & M. Ulvila (Eds.), *Global political parties* (pp. 53–92). London: Zed Press.

Ciplet, D., Timmons Roberts, J., & Khan, M. R. (2015). *Power in a warming world: The new global politics of climate change and the remaking of environmental inequality.* Cambridge, MA: MIT Press.

Dennis, B., & Moody, C. (2018). 'We are in trouble.' Global carbon emissions reached a new record high in 2018. Washington Post, December 5, 2018.

Fisher, D. (2007). Taking cover beneath the anti-bush umbrella: Cycles of protest and movement-to-movement transmission in an era of repressive politics. *Research in Political Sociology, 15,* 27–56.

Foran, J. (2014). 'Get it done!' The global climate justice movement's struggle to achieve a radical climate treaty. Unpublished ms. University of California, Santa Barbara, Dept. of Sociology.

Foster, J. B., Clark, B., & York, R. (2011). *The ecological rift: Capitalism's war on the earth.* New York, NY: New York University Press.

Gottlieb, R. (1993). *Forcing the Spring: The transformation of the American environmental movement.* New York, NY: Island Press.

Gould, K. A., Pellow, D. N., & Schnaiberg, A. (2004). Interrogating the treadmill of production: Everything you wanted to know about the treadmill but were afraid to ask. *Organization & Environment, 17*(3), 296–316.

Hadden, J. (2014). Explaining variation in transnational climate change activism: The role of inter-movement spillover. *Global Environmental Politics, 14*(2), 7–25.

Johnson, E. W., & Frickel, S. (2011). Ecological threat and the founding of US national environmental movement organizations, 1962–1998. *Social Problems, 58*(3), 305–329.

Juris, J. (2008). *Networking futures: The movements against corporate globalization.* Durham: Duke University Press.

Lichbach, M. I. (2003). The anti-globalization movement: A new kind of protest. In M. G. Marshall & T. R. Gurr (Eds.), *Peace and Conflict 2003* (pp. 39–42). College Park, MD: Center for International Development and Conflict Management, University of Maryland.

Luna, Z. T. (2016). 'Truly a women of color organization': Negotiating sameness and difference in pursuit of intersectionality. *Gender and Society, 30*(5), 769–790.

Moore, J. W. (2015). *Capitalism in the web of life: Ecology and the accumulation of capital.* London: Verso Books.

O'Connor, J. (1988). Capitalism, nature, socialism a theoretical introduction. *Capitalism Nature Socialism, 1* (1), 11–38.

Pellow, D. N. (2017). *What is critical environmental justice?* London: Polity Press.

Romm, J. (2018). *Climate change: What everyone needs to know.* Oxford: Oxford University Press.

Rudy, A. (Forthcoming). On misunderstanding the second contradiction thesis. *Capitalism, Nature, Socialism.*

Schnaiberg, A. (1980). *The environment: From surplus to scarcity*. Oxford: Oxford University Press.

Silva, E. (2009). *Challenges to neoliberalism in Latin America*. Cambridge: Cambridge University Press.

Smith, J. (2001). Globalizing resistance: The battle of Seattle and the future of social movements. *Mobilization*, 6(1), 1–21.

Smith, J. (2014). Counter-hegemonic networks and the transformation of global climate politics: Rethinking movement-State Relations. *Global Discourse*, 4(2–3), 120–138.

Terriquez, V., Brenes, T., & Lopez, A. (2018). Intersectionality as a multipurpose collective action frame: The case of the undocumented youth movement. *Ethnicities*, 18(2), 260–276.

Walton, J., & Seddon, D. (1994). *Free markets and food riots: The politics of global adjustment*. Oxford: Blackwell Publishers.

Wood, L. J. (2004). Breaking the bank & taking to the streets: How protesters target neoliberalism. *Journal of World-Systems Research*, 10(1), 69–89.

Wood, L. J. (2012). *Direct action, deliberation, and diffusion: Collective action after the WTO protests in Seattle*. Cambridge: Cambridge University Press.

World Meteorological Organization. (2018). *WMO provisional statement on the state of the global climate in 2018*. New York, NY: United Nations.

Samir Amin and the challenges of socialist transformation in senile capitalism

Carlos Eduardo Martins

ABSTRACT
This article intends to point out strategic dimensions of the thought of Samir Amin. It highlights his analysis of capitalism, of the world system in which it is articulated, and of ways to overcome them in the twenty-first century. He also approaches his reflections on the construction of a V international and his criticisms of those that preceded it.

Samir Amin, a leading scholar and co-founder of the world-systems tradition, died on August 12, 2018. Just before his death, he published, along with close allies, a call for 'workers and the people' to establish a 'fifth international' [https://www.pambazuka.org/global-south/letter-intent-inaugural-meeting-international-workers-and-peoples] *to coordinate support to progressive movements. To honor Samir Amin's invaluable contribution to world-systems scholarship, we are pleased to present readers with a selection of essays responding to Amin's final message for today's anti-systemic movements. This forum is being co-published between* Globalizations [https://www.tandfonline.com/rglo], *the* Journal of World-Systems Research [http://jwsr.pitt.edu/ojs/index.php/jwsr/issue/view/75] *and* Pambazuka News [https://www.pambazuka.org/]. *Additional essays and commentary can be found in these outlets.*

Samir Amin's reflections on the importance of the creation of a Fifth International, gathered principally in his article, *Pour la Cinquième Internationale*, published first in 2006, reveal the vitality of his thought manifested along several driving axes. Among them, we can point to the analysis of the long-term trends of capitalist globalization, particularly in the form it assumes in its neoliberal stage; the anti-systemic movements that are constituted to resist its expansion or to defeat and overcome it; the potentialities, limits and failures of the earlier Internationals; and the projects that are oriented toward the transition to socialism in the twenty-first century in short, medium and long-term perspective.

Amin points out that capitalism constitutes a polarizing world system whose central contradiction, capital versus labour, is cross-cut by other contradictions that act in a distinct direction – the main ones being imperialism versus the self-determination of peoples and the sovereignty of national states. These contradictions fragment the unity of workers in their struggles with capital. Other contradictions also include the growing division of labour, which drives the heterogeneity of workers within and between national states, acting to reinforce the fragmentation of the workers. The success of capital in the fight against workers is specifically articulated in the forms of geospatial specialization and dispersion of labour, but this advantage is not linear, progressive or definitive. It presents itself, cyclically, subject to the political and social actions of the workers who, through the national and international articulations of their class struggles guided by their material, subjective and civilizing interests, can partially restrain or destroy it by means of combined rebellions, reforms and revolutions.

As the senility of the capitalist world-system advances, the spaces for intervention of the struggles of labour against capital expand. Senility is linked to a double condition: the combination of the advance of monopolization and centralization of capital; and the growing loss of its political and ideological hegemony to lead globalization and national interests, which becomes a project of domination. The workers Internationals were attempts to respond to the globalization of capital. Though partial victories were achieved and to some extent imposed the political economy of labour on the bourgeoisie, were neutralized, absorbed and defeated by the restructuring of capitalism and its world power arrangements.

According to Amin, the main reason for the polarization in the capitalist world-system is that of the contradiction between the law of value that operates on a national scale and that, which operates on a world scale. While the first law of value refers to the purest and most abstract forms of the capitalist mode of production by competitively integrating the circulation of capital and commodities and labour power, the second refers to the concrete forms in which it operates in the world space, where it restricts the circulation of workforces. This contradiction between political and economic forces is inherent in capitalism, which cannot function without the existence of capitalist states, resulting in the concrete polarization of the mode of production in centres and peripheries on a world scale. Amin established these theses in his publications in the 1970s, such as the *Accumulation à la echelle mondialle* (1970), *l'echange inegal et la loi de la valeur* (1973), and they are developed in more recent works devoted to the analysis of neoliberal globalization as *Les dèfis de la mondialialization* (1996) and *Obscolescent capitalism* (2003).

For Amin one can only speak of a capitalist world system since the 1800s, despite its mercantilist precedents from 1500, when the specific basis of its productive forces in the centre was established. This happened with the industrial revolution, the proletarianization of the labour force and the beginning of the construction of a new international division of labour on a world scale that was driven by European imperialism and the British hegemony during the nineteenth century. Amin contends that the thesis of Immanuel Wallerstein and Giovanni Arrighi, (inspired by Fernand Braudel) which posits the existence of a *Modern world system and Historical capitalism* from the sixteenth century onwards, is dissociated from the concept of mode of production, dehydrating it too much. Amin seeks to articulate the concept of mode of production for analysing the world system, conceiving these as two articulated and contradictory levels of the construction of existing capitalism.

The polarization of the capitalist world in the centre and periphery leads to distinct monopolistic structures and divisions of labour in the functioning of the development of productive forces and the internationalization of class struggles. Initially, the form of the division of labour in the capitalist world economy was to allocate industrial production to the centres, and agricultural products and raw materials to the peripheries. However, the Russian, Chinese and Mexican revolutions, the resurgence of protectionism in the world economy and policies of import substitution in Latin America, the decolonization of the European colonial empires in Africa and Asia, and the rise of the United States established important changes between the years 1930 and 1980. Industrialist projects in the USSR and China were juxtaposed with the industrialization projects of some peripheral bourgeoisies which, even within the framework of dependence, reached a certain degree of national autonomy. From the 1980s onward, however, the neoliberal offensive, the collapse of the USSR and the imposition of the Washington Consensus on Latin America, Africa and Eastern Europe dismantled much of this autonomy and reoriented the industrial bourgeoisies of the peripheral countries toward the position of bourgeoisie buyers. These turned to primary-export activities or to the generation of parts and components, as well as extractive mining, land speculation or usurious income through public debt. Amin asserted, however, that socialist China could sustain its autonomy and challenge the prominence of American Atlanticism because of the depth of reforms implemented during the Maoist period, which defined land ownership as public.

The neoliberal globalization project established a period of senile capitalism centred on five monopolies: new technologies, the monetary standard and international financial flows, access to the planet's natural resources, the media and weapons of mass destruction. However, its obsolete character reveals itself in several dimensions: in the plutocracy that directs it and uses money to transform democracy in low-intensity democracy based on consensus about private property, deepening inequality and imposing limits on emancipations; in the destruction of peasant property and the planetary ecosystem, which threaten the survival of humanity and produce the unlimited conversion of labour, land and the biomes into commodities; and in the decline of the American and European imperialisms, which produces risks of militaries conflicts. Confronting this senile neoliberal capitalism requires a new internationalism that articulates action around social progress, democratization and the construction of a multi-centred world system.

In his review of the earlier Internationals Amin emphasizes that the Fifth International must rescue from the First its critical spirit and its diversity of visions. He points out that democracy must demand the right to move toward socialization through innovation, subversion and rupture with the sacredness of private property. The Fifth International must reject the theses, which, since the Second International, have claimed a party monopoly of theory over the social movements and the masses. Socialism must be seen as a set of long, medium and short-term transitions in which both theory and practice articulate with each other to produce gradual convergences. The Fifth International should encompass a broad spectrum of social forces representing political parties and social movements that are acting against capitalism, imperialism and inequality and for the emancipation of human beings from the oppressions of gender, ethnic-racial and sexual orientations. But in order to do so, it will be necessary to overcome the limited social base achieved by the previous Internationals. The First represented only segments of the European industrial male proletariat; the Second, their political parties; the Third, the direction of the national liberation movements; the Fourth, the small avant-garde groups.

To achieve this broad spectrum of mobilization, Amin argues that the Fifth International must have its axis of gravity around the establishment of the international centre-left, capable of gathering around them revolutionaries and reformists who not only struggle against neoliberalism, but for democratic and social advances, for a multipolar world and for the ecological management of the planet. He sees in the World Social Forums a beginning of this articulation, from which neoliberal and imperialist forces should be eliminated. He points out that there is no reason to suppose that the reformist movements will not learn from their mistakes, even though he acknowledges that some of them probably never will. What favours this optimistic perspective is the extension of the victims of the centralization and monopolization of capital that reaches large populations of the core countries, reducing the asymmetry between the victims of imperialism and capitalism. This asymmetry constituted the social basis for the working classes and their political organizations and trade unions to support the imperialism from which they benefited through the international redistribution of surplus value. Such a scenario could lead the progressive forces of social democracy and the identity movements in the core countries to escape being captured by the logic of imperialism and capitalism. For the national liberation movements of the Global South, which would form an important part of the Fifth International, the fundamental challenge is to deepen its link with democracy and the socialization of power, articulating them with the anti-imperialist, decolonial and anti-capitalist struggles.

The articulated action of the world left is fundamental for combatting the rise of forces to the right of neoliberal globalization, which seek to compensate for the destructive effects of monopolization and centralization of capital, supporting the deepening of imperialist logic. Amin points out that the contradictions of the neoliberal globalization project are linked to the rise of neofascism. Neofascists intend to use the power of the state to monopolize privileges and to destroy the competitive pressures arising from the emergence of new poles of economic power, migratory flows of workers, and democratic and emancipatory demands in the context of senile capitalism and the decline of American hegemony. Neofascism is linked to religious, social, ethnic and tribal dimensions that prioritize cultural battles and intolerance of diversity, neglecting the economic battles and conflicting material interests in the capitalist world system. As such, they serve not only the decadent sectors of the northwestern Atlantic power centres, but also the buyer bourgeoisie of the periphery that seeks to monopolize political power and increase its ability to mediate access to assets, natural resources, sources of energy and labour. Very dangerous are the American right sheltered in the Republican Party, and the jihadist currents of Islam.

Amin contends that the central struggle in the capitalist world system in the twenty-first century is the struggle between socialism and capitalism. It develops within each State according to its specificities, partly determined by its place in the hierarchies of the international division of labour. In this sense, the simple ascent of China and East Asia in opposition to Atlantic imperialism does not guarantee a transition to socialism, because the Chinese state is permeated, albeit in its own way, by the same conflict that develops in the world system. The overall transition to socialism, if established, will be the result of a broad set of social and political forces that will be articulated at several levels – micropolitical, local, national, world regional. and global. The socialist project is a planetary civilizational project manifested in multiple dimensions: economic, political, social, cultural and environmental. Its construction involves the contradictory and dialectical combination of struggles for political power and for culture, which must preserve their relative autonomy. It should be founded on solidarity, limiting competition, replacing competitive advantages with cooperative advantages for the establishment of a multicentered system based on peace, negotiation and law.

Samir Amin leaves us a vast and consistent body of thought for meeting the challenges of the twenty-first century. He developed Marxist categories to formulate an analysis of real capitalism, as it exists, in the world-system it engendered. We can disagree with several of its aspects, such as the role it confers on the global mobility of the workforce in determining international value transfers and world polarization, the absence of the concept of scientific-technical revolution to analyse the senility of contemporary capitalism, or their refusal to extend the concept of the capitalist world-system until the fifteenth or sixteenth century, as Wallerstein and Arrighi do (Martins, 2011).

Notwithstanding, he gives us a set of valuable interpretations and questions of great theoretical and analytical importance for the task of transforming the contemporary world towards human emancipation.

Disclosure statement

No potential conflict of interest was reported by the author.

References

Amin, S. (1970). *Accumulation à la echelle mondialle*. Paris: Antrophos.
Amin, S. (1973). *L'exchange inegal et la loi de la valeur*. Paris: Antrophos.
Amin, S. (1996). *Les defís de la mondialization*. Paris: L'Harmattan.
Amin, S. (2003). *Obsolescent capitalism*. London: Zed Books.
Amin, S. (2006). *Pour la cinquième internationale*. Paris: Temps de cerise.
Martins, C. E. (2011). *Globalização, dependência e neoliberalismo na América Latina*. São Paulo: Boitempo.

The twenty-first century revolutions and internationalism: a world historical perspective

Sahan Savas Karatasli

ABSTRACT

In his essay, 'It is imperative to reconstruct the Internationale of workers and peoples', Samir Amin (2018) suggested that in order to 'deconstruct the extreme centralization of wealth and the power that is associated with the system', we should seriously study 'the experience of the worker Internationales [...], even if they belong to the past. This should be done, not in order to "choose" a model among them, but to invent the most suitable form for contemporary conditions'. In this paper, I will follow Amin's suggestion and provide a brief examination of the past experiences of first Internationales in the nineteenth century, and conditions that produced them, with an eye to the present moment. By comparing the political climate of the early twenty-first century to analogous comparable periods in world history, I will argue that today we need two distinct forms of global political organizations. First one should serve as a horizontal 'movement of movements' that reflects the spontaneous and creative energy of mass movements from below; the second one should serve as a hierarchically organized international party which points out, brings to front and represents the global and long-term interests of the movements against their local/ short-term interests.

Samir Amin, a leading scholar and co-founder of the world-systems tradition, died on August 12, 2018. Just before his death, he published, along with close allies, a call for 'workers and the people' to establish a 'fifth international' [https://www.pambazuka.org/global-south/letter-intent-inaugural-meeting-international-workers-and-peoples] *to coordinate support to progressive movements. To honor Samir Amin's invaluable contribution to world-systems scholarship, we are pleased to present readers with a selection of essays responding to Amin's final message for today's anti-systemic movements. This forum is being co-published between* Globalizations [https://www.tandfonline.com/rglo], *the* Journal of World-Systems Research [http://jwsr.pitt.edu/ojs/index.php/jwsr/issue/view/75] *and* Pambazuka News [https://www.pambazuka.org/]. *Additional essays and commentary can be found in these outlets.*

Since the turn of the twenty-first century, we have been experiencing rapid intensification of revolutionary situations, social revolts and rebellions on a global scale (Badiou, 2012; Chase-Dunn & Nagy, 2019; Karatasli, Kumral, Scully, & Upadhyay, 2014; Mason, 2012; Therborn, 2014; Žižek, 2012).

This is not an ordinary wave of social unrest. It belongs to one of the major world historical waves of mobilization (see Silver & Slater, 1999) which has the *potential* to transform political structures, economic systems and social relations. Recent research shows that the frequency and the geographical spread of social unrest around the world in the post-2008 era are exceptionally high, making it one of the major waves of social mobilization in the long twentieth century (Karatasli, Kumral, & Silver, 2018). Furthermore, the number of revolutionary situations in the 2010–2014 period are almost equal to the 1915–1919 period (Beissinger, 2018). Hence structural and objective conditions of another round of world-historical transformation seem to be almost as fertile as it was a century ago.

There are also other interesting similarities between the current moment and the early twentieth century that might help us make sense of the current era we are living in. For instance, similar to the early twentieth century, the major wave of social revolts and revolutions that we have experienced in the twenty-first century has been taking place in synchrony with interlinked political-economic and geopolitical crises on a world scale (Fominaya, 2017; Karatasli, 2018; Wallerstein, 2012). In the previous era, the intensification of economic and geopolitical crises that spanned roughly from 1870 to 1940s had undermined the foundations of the British world-hegemony and gave birth to the U.S. world hegemony, which transformed the way historical capitalism operated (Arrighi, 1994). Today, since the 1970s, we have been experiencing similar interlinked crises in economic and geopolitical spheres, which have been undermining the U.S. world hegemony, and signalling that capitalism can no longer operate in the way it used to do. Hence from such a world-historical perspective, it can be argued that we are living in a period analogous to the 'chaos' phase of the decline of the British world-hegemony in the early twentieth century (Arrighi & Silver, 1999). Moreover, like the early twentieth century, the rise of social unrest in twenty-first century has widely been interpreted as a counter-movement to the rise of self-regulating markets and commodification (Burawoy, 2012; Fraser, 2017; see Polanyi, 1944). Both periods reversed the previous trends of trade globalization and unleashed a period of de-globalization in the world-economy (Alvarez & Chase-Dunn, 2018; also see Chase-Dunn & Gills, 2005). In both periods, world-wide social mobilization was accompanied by nationalist movements that started to challenge existing territorial maps of the world (Karatasli, 2018), and were followed by the rise of far-right groups and parties around the world (Chase-Dunn & Nagy, 2019). We can easily extend the list of such similarities.

Focusing only on similarities, however, will conceal the radical differences between the socio-political climates of these two periods. One major difference is that in the early twentieth century many of these revolutionary situations produced revolutionary outcomes. Put differently, while the communist, socialist and national liberation movements in the early twentieth century failed to fulfil their promises in the long run, they were spectacularly successful in the short and medium run (Arrighi, Hopkins, & Wallerstein, 2012). Especially the success of the 1917 Bolshevik revolution in Russia and the rising tide of proletarian revolutions and national liberation movements went beyond the preceding historical examples of the 1871 Paris commune and 1905 revolutions by demonstrating that the exploited, the oppressed and the excluded could take power, establish their own states, invent new modes of governments and successfully defend it against the ruling classes and imperialist states. In short, despite all of their shortcomings, the revolutions that took place in the early twentieth century were unprecedented world-historical achievements.

Today the picture we see, however, is quite different. The overwhelming majority of revolutionary situations that could potentially transform the world have failed to make their bids for such a change. Neither the occupy-type anti-austerity movements in Europe and North America nor the Arab Spring in the Middle East and North Africa nor the rising labour militancy and pro-democracy movements in East Asia have so far made an impact compared to the revolts and revolutions of the early twentieth century (Springborg, 2011). Of course, we should be careful in this assessment because this period is not yet over. We will probably continue to see rounds of interconnected waves of social unrest in years to come as the crisis of the U.S. world hegemony further unfolds. Moreover, we should keep in mind that success is a relative and highly subjective term for evaluating social movement outcomes. From a certain perspective, it has been argued that the movements of the early twenty-first century have already been very successful in 'changing the subject' (Milkman, Luce, & Lewis, 2013) by turning attention – for the first time in a long while – to the issues of capitalism, class, inequality and democracy. Likewise, it has been suggested that these movements have been extremely successful in demonstrating that spontaneous, horizontal and leaderless movements can be very effective in opening spaces 'for people to voice their concerns and desires' (Sitrin, 2012). While these observations are correct, they employ a very low threshold for assessing social change. Despite their contribution to turning attention to these issues, the progressive counter-movements in the twenty-first century have not slowed down or reversed Polanyi's (1944) market-ization pendulum in a way that would reduce the rate of commodification of land, labour and money. Of course, rising protests and conflicts have overturned governments in many places such as Tunisia, Egypt, Libya, Yemen and Ukraine. Yet, in none of these places (probably except for Kurds in Rojava[1]), have movements representing the exploited, the oppressed and the excluded sections of the society managed to take power. In most cases, movements in the twenty-first century ended up replacing one type of authoritarianism for another type. Even according to bourgeois-democratic standards, we have been experiencing a major failure.

Divergent trends of the 'Marxist Century' and the 'American Century'

I argue that the differential outcomes of the revolutionary waves of 1915–1919 and 2010–2014 have their roots in the asymmetrical evolution of the ideological and organizational structures of social movements in the course of what Arrighi (1990) called the 'Marxist Century' (i.e. the long nineteenth century) and the 'American Century' (i.e. the long twentieth century). Today, the dominant tendency is to explain these divergent trends as an outcome of a switch from vertical to horizontal organizational structures in social movements (Mason, 2012; Sitrin, 2012). While this distinction is not altogether wrong, it does not capture the essence of the problem. The issues at stake are more complex than verticalism and horizontalism.

Divergent trends in these two long centuries can better be understood by examining the different attitudes of movements towards 'voluntarism' and 'spontaneity' (Gramsci, 1971, pp. 196–205) in the two centuries. In the early nineteenth century, vertically organized revolutionary movements in Europe – such as *the Carbonari* and the various proto-communist organizations founded by Buonarroti, Barbes and Blanqui after the example of Babeuf's *Conspiracy of the Equals* – were voluntarists (see Draper, 1986, pp. 123–127; Greene, 2017). Their approach to revolution took into account neither objective conditions (e.g. structural opportunities for mobilization, class relations, crises in political, social or economic spheres) nor the dynamics of spontaneous mass movements. Voluntarists believed that revolution 'required the conscious intervention of a revolutionary elite through an act of will' (Greene, 2017, p. 109) and its success was function of organizational strength. Accordingly, many of these voluntarist organizations proclaimed the exact date of their revolutionary insurrection months (or sometimes years) in advance regardless of the fertility of objective conditions.

In the course of the nineteenth century, however, revolutionary organizations gradually moved away from such unqualified voluntarism. Especially those inspired by Marxism tried to counter-balance their voluntarist heritage by seriously considering dynamics of the spontaneous mass movements. For Marxists, the proletariat was the main force of revolution. On the one hand, Marx and Engels argued, under capitalism 'the modern labourer […] sinks deeper and deeper below the conditions of existence of his own class. He becomes a pauper, and pauperism develops more rapidly than population and wealth' (Marx & Engels, 1848, p. 233; also see Marx, 1867, Ch. 25). On the other hand, capitalism gives an end to isolation of labourers, brings them together in large factories and increases contact, cooperation and coordination among workers, and thus strengthens and empowers the proletariat (Marx & Engels, 1848, p. 233; also see Marx, 1867, Chs 13–15). Therefore, through simultaneously plunging the proletarians into misery and strengthening them, 'the bourgeoisie produces […] its own gravediggers' (Marx & Engels, 1848, p. 233). Moreover, the periodic crisis tendencies of capitalism produces periodic upheavals among its gravediggers, preparing the preconditions for a proletarian revolution.

Despite these observations, however, Marx and Engels did not believe that the proletariat could make a global revolution without an external intervention by the communists. This is why the dominant tendency in the Marxist left during the second half of the nineteenth century was not a gradual switch from 'voluntarism' to 'spontaneity', but rather to a synthesis of these. Hierarchically organized formerly voluntarist revolutionary organizations now saw their task as to *guide* and to strategically *intervene* the horizontally organized spontaneous mass movements for the success of the world revolution. Of course, there has never been a progressive consensus regarding on the nature and form of this 'intervention' and hence the role of communists in a workers' revolution. Should the communists be a part of these mass movements and try to convince them from within or should they bring them consciousness from outside? Could they ride the tide of these mass movements to come to power? The practices of different organizations – ranging from the Communist League (1846–1852) and the International Workingman's Association (1864–1876), from the Socialist International (1889–1916) to the Communist International (1919–1943) – reveal different attitudes on these issues. Yet, most communists agree on the minimal formulation that Marx and Engels laid out in the *Communist Manifesto*. According to this formulation:

> The Communists are distinguished from the other working-class parties by this only: 1. In the national struggles of the proletarians of the different countries, they point out and bring to the front the common interests of the entire proletariat, independently of all nationality. 2. In the various stages of development which the struggle of the working class against the bourgeoisie has to pass through, they always and everywhere represent the interests of the movement as a whole. (Marx & Engels, 1848)

Marx and Engels's explanation of *pointing out, bringing to front* and *representing* the global and long-term interests against national and immediate interests is a shorthand formula for the role they ascribed to a communist party. In its more general form, this formula suggests that communists should struggle to *expand mass movements' spatial, temporal and substantive horizons*; which means to unite struggles in different geographies, movements with different immediate priorities and groups with substantive problems together in the pursuit of a unified revolution. For this reason, in contrast to purely *voluntarist* organizations which largely ignore the dynamics of spontaneous mass movements, the communists should use their associational power (1) to coordinate localized and spontaneous struggles in different sectors and geographies into united national struggles aiming at taking over state power and abolishing private property, and (2) then to coordinate national struggles in different parts of the world into a united international struggle aiming at spreading the revolution to all over the world.

While an advanced version of their strategy, implemented by Bolsheviks, played a key role in the success of the 1917 revolution and triggered a revolutionary wave, structural conditions of such synthesis gradually dissolved in the course of the 'American' century. Parallel to the uneven spatial development of the capitalist world-system, the two interlinked tendencies Marx and Engels observed in the case of the conditions of the proletariat in England in the nineteenth century (i.e. immiseration on the one hand, and empowerment on the other hand) developed unevenly across the core and the (semi)peripheral regions in the twentieth century (Arrighi, 1990). While empowerment and strengthening of the working classes were more prominent in industrial capitalist 'core' countries, immiseration and pauperization remained the dominant tendency in '(semi)peripheral' regions of the Global South. This uneven development deeply influenced internationalist revolutionary organizations' ability to find a synthesis of 'spontaneity' and 'voluntarism'.

In advanced capitalist countries of the Global North, labour movements turned out to be strong enough to pressure capitalist business-government complexes for economic redistribution and partial extension of their social and political rights. Also directly benefiting from post-1871 wave of new imperialism, labour aristocracies in core regions did not feel the necessity of a revolution. Especially after the 1917 Revolution and the 1929 economic depression, the bourgeoisie in Western Europe and North America also found such partial welfare redistribution to working classes as a useful strategy to maintain their rule. Under these conditions, existing revolutionary organizations could not mobilize 'spontaneous' energy of the masses for a revolution to overthrow the state and capital. These structural conditions pushed some of these organizations to become reformist working class parties that defend the national interests of the labour aristocracies, and some of them to remain as left-wing sectarian and ineffective groups that are largely isolated from broader masses and mass politics.

In peripheral regions of the Global South, where immiseration of the masses and the legitimacy crisis of the ruling classes were more prominent, the revolutionaries of different varieties managed to take state power but failed to fulfil their promises (Arrighi et al., 2012). For one thing, instead of bringing the proletariat to power, the communists and the revolutionary cadres had to take power themselves in the name of people. Likewise, especially after the dissolution of the *Communist Internationale*, communist regimes in the Global South did not proliferate through new waves of social revolutions by 'soviets' or 'communes'. Expansion of communism in the Global South after the 1940s was a variant of what Gramsci (1971, pp. 104–107) called as 'Piedmont-type function in passive revolutions' where states (or armies) acted on behalf of social classes. Expansion of communism during the 'American century' mostly occurred through the defeat of national/imperial armies by socialist armies established by existing communist regimes or by indigenous armies controlled by communist parties that were formed during the national liberation against Axis powers (Arrighi, 1990, p. 45). Furthermore, as victories of the Old Left gained momentum, instead of coordinating the spontaneous mass movements into a unified global revolution, the Old Left mainly ignored, suffocated and repressed these movements in most locations when they got to power under the pretext of protecting their national and 'revolutionary' interests.

Faced with such betrayal both in the West and the rest of the world, instead of trying to re-balance degrees of *spontaneity* and *voluntarism* to simultaneously get rid of capitalism and bureaucratic socialist or national states that were formed by the Old Left, the New Left rejected the voluntarist heritage completely. Hence, from the second half of the twentieth century to present, horizontally connected spontaneous mass movements gradually became the norm (Robinson & Tormey, 2009; Sitrin, 2012). Efforts to guide, coordinate and intervene in mass movements were seen as authoritarianism or, at best, arrogance (Arrighi et al., 2012, p. 102). This emphasis is important because the failure of the post-2008 wave of social unrest is not a failure of the masses who took the streets, occupied squares and challenged governments and economic institutions. These movements proved that they are *still* extremely powerful agents of world revolution both in the Global North and in the Global South. The failure belongs to the Global Left, which was not able to appear in its historical mission to guide, coordinate and strategically intervene in these mass movements for the success of a world revolution. Without such intervention, the *spatial, temporal and substantive horizons* of spontaneous mass movements remained insufficient to transform the world. For instance, the temporal horizons of most of the movements in the post-2008 wave of social unrest were minimal without any plans beyond the short run. Hence most of the activists who occupied and emancipated 'squares and parks' all over the world did not know what to do next, were not prepared for it, or were not even interested in that question. Similarly, the spatial horizons of many movements have also been very narrow. According to the trends we have been observing from 1968 onwards, we can see that many localized struggles have less and less interest in taking state power (Sitrin, 2014, p. 256), and many struggles operating at the *national* level – e.g. those who want to take state power through electoral or other means – are not interested in such a 'universal revolution'.

Do we need a global political organization in the twenty-first century?

If the political landscape of the early nineteenth century was dominated by voluntarist movements that were preoccupied with the subjective conditions of revolutions without paying attention to dynamics of spontaneity and the objective conditions, the contemporary landscape in the twenty-first century is dominated by spontaneous movements and activists who do not trust or find much value in political organizations that have a clear vision of the necessary steps for a world revolution. Hence, what is absent today – in comparison to the early twentieth century – are the global political communist organizations who can coordinate, guide and strategically intervene in these mass movements through a synthesis of *voluntarism* and *spontaneity* without committing the errors of the early twentieth century communists. Do we need a global political organization (i.e. an *Internationale)* in the twenty-first century as Samir Amin (2018) has proposed? My answer is *no! We need two of them*!

In order to understand what the term '*two Internationales*' refers to, we first need to understand a conceptual ambiguity in the way that we think about Internationales. Today we have a tendency to count Internationales as the First, the Second, the Third and so on. This practice did not exist in the late nineteenth century and is quite misleading for two main reasons.

First, what we call as the First, Second and Third were not the same types of global-level organizations. For instance, aiming to bring together trade unions with political parties, socialists with anarchists, English Owenites with French Proudhonists and Blanquists, Bakunin and his followers with Mazzini's followers and Garibaldi, Marx with Irish and Polish nationalists, the International Workingsmen's Association (i.e. the 'First Internationale') was more similar to contemporary World Social Forums in the context of the nineteenth century than the 'Communist International' (i.e. the 'Third Internationale'), which acted as a *communist world party* (also see Amin, 2008). In direct contrast to all other global or national level political organizations of the Left, the groups that composed the First Internationale had an exceptional degree of diversity and autonomy. As Hal Draper rightly observed '[t]here has never been any socialist organization, national or international, that rivalled it in this respect' (Draper, 1990, p. 151). Despite the enormous autonomy the First Internationale provided to its sections, however, it was not completely horizontal. Because it had an organizational decision-making structure that was rather similar to the *diagonal vessel form of* organization that combines horizontalism and verticalism (Alvarez & Chase-Dunn, 2018).

Second, contrary to what is widely assumed, the history of *the Internationales* in the communist movement does not start with the formation of the 'First International' in 1864 [which was the name later given to the 'International Workingsmen's Association' (1864–1876)]. An embryonic form of *International* had already been realized when an ex-Blanquist organization founded by German emigres called *Bund der Gerechten (the League of the Just)* merged with the Brussels *Communist Correspondence Committee, which put forward* a new variant of socialism led by Karl Marx and Friedrich Engels. The *Communist League* (1846–1852) – for which the famous *Communist Manifesto* was written – was already an *Internationale*. As a report by *the League*'s central authority – Schapper, Bauer, and Moll (1847) – made clear, before the outbreak of the 1848 revolutions, *the Communist League* was organized in Switzerland, France, Belgium and Sweden, and was in the process of organizing in America, Norway, Germany and Holland. The Preamble of the *Manifesto of the Communist Party*, explained that *the League* was composed of 'communists from various nationalities'. Hence they needed to publish the Manifesto in a number of languages including English, French, German, Italian, Flemish and Danish (Marx & Engels, 1848). Because of its *International* nature, the *Manifesto* declared the League's political stand in various parts of the world including England, America, France, Switzerland, Poland and Germany in its final chapter. This practice was consistent with the template of communist organization that Marx and Engels provided in the Manifesto. This suggests something quite interesting about the nature of communist organizations. *They are, by definition, global level political organizations.* Communists' claim to defend general/long-term interests against particularistic/short-term interests does not come merely from their ideology but more importantly from the global character of their organization.

In direct contrast to the International Workingmen's Association, *the Communist League* was a hierarchical, homogenous world party in an embryonic form. While the International Workingmen's Association tried to include the broadest possible alliance of the Left, the Communist League tried to do its best to distinguish itself from all other variants of socialism in the nineteenth century as they explained in Chapter III of the Communist Manifesto. Regarding structure and political claims, it resembled the *Communist Internationale* founded by the Bolsheviks, although not in size and strength. However, unlike the *Bolshevik Third Internationale*, *the Communist League* did not have the size, organizational capacity, connections with mass movements and experience to effectively intervene in the 1848 revolutions. Hence, it quickly failed. That's why, today, the *Communist League* itself is little known except for its political vision as explained in the Manifesto. In many ways, the International Workingmen's Association was the diametrical opposite of the *Communist League*.

In the twenty-first century we need both kinds of global level political organizations (horizontal and vertical). But we should be careful not to confuse their purposes. The horizontal should serve as a 'movement of movements' at global, national and local levels. The primary goal and the basic principle of this *Internationale*, as Marx (1872) had put it in a speech to the International Workingmen's Association, should be forging *solidarity*. This horizontal *Internationale* should struggle to counter capital's, states' and all other existing racial, ethno-religious, patriarchal and other historical orders' tendency to divide the masses, and force them to compete with each other and exclude them. This movement of mass movements should be as inclusive as possible, representing the broadest possible spectrum of progressive democracy forces, and bringing together associations of workers, peasants, ethnic and racial minorities, environmentalists, oppressed genders and sexualities, to name a few. It should consist of trade unions, mass associations, workers cooperatives, environmentalist organizations, human rights associations, transnational and local movements, feminist organizations, progressive political parties as well as individual activists. In short, it should aim to include any movement which is organized around concrete grievances caused by activities of states, capital or other historical racial, religious, patriarchal orders as long as their activities do not contradict with the general purpose of 'resisting against capital's, states' and other historical orders' efforts to divide and exclude masses' and 'forging solidarity'. Because of the diversity of elements it aims to bring together, this Internationale must be ideologically heterogeneous. By coordinating with, learning from and forging solidarity with each other this movement of mass movements should reflect, boost and spread the spontaneous and creative energy of the masses from below. In addition to this, however, we also need a global world party analogous to *the Communist League*, which the Bolsheviks reinvented in the early twentieth century. In contrast to the horizontally connected, ideologically heterogeneous and eclectic 'movement of mass movements' this global communist party should be vertically organized and ideologically homogeneous and coherent. In order to avoid Eurocentric biases, it should be organized in all regions of the world and have a strong representation from the Global South. This party should not see itself as a rival of the 'movement of mass movements' but, on the contrary, should aim to further enhance and extend the movement of movements' networks at local, national and global levels. It should especially pay attention to strengthening the movement of movements' ties with the most exploited, oppressed and excluded sections of each nations, as consistent with the minimal formula suggested in the Manifesto. In each nation, the world party should aim to bring these organized masses from below to power (rather than coming to power itself). By *pointing out, bringing to front* and *representing* the general and long-term interests of people's revolution against the particularistic and immediate interests that naturally arise out of the spontaneous and heterogeneous nature of mass movements, it should struggle to overcome tendencies that would prevent the abolition of private property and the dismantling the bourgeois character of each state. Likewise, it should actively defend the right of national self-determination against great-nation chauvinism and defend and advance the rights and liberties of all ethnic, racial, and sexual minorities and oppressed groups against counter-tendencies that may appear in an extremely heterogeneous mass movements. While propagating the necessity of a global revolution for emancipation, it should defend the idea that the exploited, the oppressed and the excluded sections of each country must, in Marx and Engels' words, 'first settle matters with their own bourgeoisie' (Marx & Engels, 1848). When the mass movements from below become strong enough to produce a backlash from right-wing groups and neo-fascists, it should defend mass forces of democracy and take all precautions to defeat this reaction. Last, but not the least, when a revolution occurs in a particular region of the world, this global political party should defend and spread the revolution with an eye to its universal and long-term interests. Hence, it should aim to spread the social revolution worldwide until the revolutionary wave gains a global character.

Spreading a revolution is important for two reasons: First, it is the only way to defend a revolution without sacrificing its revolutionary character. As Marx observed *'this is the great lesson of the French Commune, which fell because none of the other centers – Berlin, Madrid, etc. – developed great revolutionary movements comparable to the mighty uprising of the Paris proletariat'* (Marx, 1872). This statement should not be read from an economistic perspective. It does not imply that revolutions will fail unless they are accompanied by revolutions in advanced capitalist countries. The reverse is also correct. As Marx once asked Engels:

> The difficult question for us is: on the Continent the revolution is imminent and will immediately assume a socialist character. Is it not bound to be crushed in this little corner, considering that in a far greater territory the movement of the bourgeoisie is still in the ascendant? (Marx, 1858)

The answer to this question, without hesitation, should be 'yes'. This is precisely why the communist party must assume a 'global' character.

Secondly, in an interconnected capitalist world-economy, the exploited, the oppressed and the excluded groups in a particular country or region *cannot* 'emancipate' themselves unless those in all other countries and regions are emancipated. This was because 'emancipation', for communists, means something more than a revolution in a particular geography. It requires taking over *all* objective forces of production and regulation developed by historical capitalism and the bourgeoisie states, and radically transforming social and class relations that constitute them in a way that would give an end to the class-based, economic, social and political contradictions they produce on a global scale. However, the experience of the twentieth century shows that the *methods* used to spread the revolutions matter. For this global revolution to be emancipatory, communists should bring the exploited, the oppressed and the excluded masses to power through social revolutions, and should not try to rely on 'Piedmont-type functions' (where states or armies act of behalf of people) to expand the domain of communist regimes.

Towards an anarchist or a second Marxist twenty-first century?

If the analysis about the political climate in the twenty-first century presented above is accurate, then we should expect disproportionately more people to agree with the first part of the proposal (formation of a movement of mass movements at local, national and global levels) than the second part (formation of a world communist party). This is necessarily so because, while the first part of the proposal is broad and inclusive, the second part requires an agreement about the fundamental premises of communism as well as limitations of spontaneous mass movements. Yet, since especially the last quarter of the long American century has unmade all ideological and organizational experience and heritages that the communist revolutionaries had gained in the course of the long Marxist century, today, even a minimal agreement on such premises has become extremely rare.

Likewise, when we look at the actual historical development toward the realization of these two *Internationales*, we can easily see a divergence. Despite all its failures and shortcomings, something close to a 'movement of movements' has already been taking place in recent decades (see Cox & Nilsen, 2007). The ups and downs we see in the development of this process since the turn of the twenty-first century should not be demoralizing for its proponents because these cycles eventually reflect the tempo and pace of spontaneous mass movements from below. Yet, except for small circles of revolutionaries, there is no serious and visible effort to establish a world communist party; and even the most sympathetic circles are rather skeptical regarding the idea. Hence, we are further away from the realization of a world communist party than a movement of movements.

These divergent tendencies suggest that if contemporary trends do not change in the near future, the twenty-first century might be closer to an 'anarchist century' than a 'second Marxist century'. The current tendencies in social movements in the twenty-first century already point out this trend. I must note that the anarchism we observe today is a new political formation and most activists do not openly embrace this title. This new anarchism is neither similar to Blanqui nor to Bakunin in the nineteenth century. The new anarchist movements are not preoccupied with taking over state power (as was the case with Blanqui) or destroying it (as was the case with Bakunin). They are usually quite hostile toward vertical organizational structures and voluntarism which were strategically used both by Blanqui and Bakunin in different ways. If we really work to find historical analogies, in many respects, the new anarchism of twenty-first century is an eclectic mix of Proudhon's utopian vision towards 'transformation of societies from within' and creating a 'new society within the shell of the old' (preformism) with Bernstein's revisionist socialist motto that 'movement is everything'. In contrast to Proudhon, however, today, together with the legacies of communism, almost all utopian visions – both their anarchist and socialist variants – have vanished. In most cases, they have been replaced by visions of re-establishing 'welfare states', which started to look like a utopia for many. This is one of the key differences between the current moment and the early nineteenth century.

Despite all differences between these two centuries, however, there is one key similarity that is fundamental. As explained above, the early nineteenth century provided the preconditions for the rise of Marxism and led to the formation of a series of Internationales. Similarly, despite all the disadvantages already mentioned, the current waves of social revolts and revolutions and 'new anarchism' has also been preparing the structural preconditions of a second Marxist revival, including the opportunities to bring together those who recognize the necessity of a world party. To understand this link, it is important to note that, in the nineteenth century, the idea of international or global political organizations was not confined to the communist organizations but was also embraced by liberals, anarchists and even nationalists. Even before the establishment of the First International in 1864, from Buonarroti to Weitling, from Blanqui to Mazzini, from Bakunin to Marx and Engels, all different strands of revolutionary and reformist opposition in Europe shared some ideal of internationalism. They key factor for the rise of internationalism in the nineteenth century was the defeat of the French Revolution and the revolutionary waves it triggered. Especially after the Bourbon Restoration of 1815, there was a shared feeling of defeat by liberals and radicals who believed in the ideals of *liberté, égalité, fraternité*. Dissolution of the Napoleonic army produced thousands of ex-Napoleonic officers spread all around Europe who were ready to take part in emerging secret organizations to realize the ideals of the French Revolution. While Carbonari style organizations were spreading all around Europe, the Concert of Europe and the Holy Alliance between autocratic monarchies and empires of Europe (i.e. Prussia, Austria and Russia) were constantly repressing any kind of liberal, anarchist, nationalist or socialist opposition. Activists who faced collective oppression by the Holy Alliance *intuitively* grasped that their resistance and their cause had to transcend the narrow boundaries of local organizations and their countries. Internationalism and the need for an effective international political party were not abstract ideals but matters of necessity.

In short, the revolutionary organizations that shaped the Marxist century did not emerge out of the thin air. They emerged when revolutionaries who were serious about overcoming obstacles before the revolution seriously considered the limitations of their strategies, organizational structures and ideologies, and came together with those who had similar concerns. For instance, Karl Schapper, the revolutionary who convinced and recruited Marx and Engels into the organization that eventually became the 'Communist League' (McLellan, 1995, pp. 150–151), was a former member of Mazzini's 'Young Germany' and 'Young Europe' organizations (Wittke, 1950, p. 22), and later a member of the *Bund der Geaechteten* (i.e. League of Outlaws) and its offshoot *Bund der Gerechten (League of the Just)* (McLellan, 1995, pp. 150–151). He fought side by side with Blanqui's *Société des saisons* in May 1839 uprising in Paris (Wittke, 1950, p. 29) and became comrades with revolutionaries as diverse as Mazzini, Weitling, Marx and Engels. Schapper's life is an example of revolutionaries of the era who were constantly struggling to overcome the limitations of their revolutionary activities to invent something better (McLellan, 1995, pp. 150–153; Wittke, 1950, pp. 22, 29, 97–105).

This analysis is critically important because the series of defeats and failures we have been experiencing in this most recent wave of social revolts and revolutions make the current moment very similar to the early nineteenth century. The major difference is that instead of 'voluntarism', in this century 'spontaneity' has become the norm. Hence, activists who really want to overcome the limits of current social movement strategies will need to re-introduce the 'organized subjective will' into this 'spontaneity' to find a new synthesis, without committing the errors of the early twentieth century communists. Objective conditions for such synthesis are more fertile today than the previous century. In contrast to the 'American' twentieth century where 'immiseration' and 'strengthening' tendencies of the global proletariat took place in different world geographies, today we see a convergence in these two trends. As the crisis of the U.S. world hegemony deepens, together with the middle classes, labour aristocracies in core regions that were formed during the long twentieth century are losing their privileges and gradually dismantling. Together with the precaritization of the labour in the Global North, we also see the formation of new working classes in the Global South. As the post-2008 wave of revolts and revolutions show, the exploited, the oppressed and the excluded sections of societies in the Global North and South have already been taking the streets and facing serious obstacles towards producing a better future. What is missing are coordinated efforts to *organize* these masses effectively at local, national and global on the one hand, and to *point out, bring to front* and *represent* the global and long-term interests of the movement on the other hand. If we can succeed at these fronts, the twenty-first century can be a second and successful Marxist century.

Note

1. The Kurds in Rojava, who were a part of this most recent revolutionary wave, have managed to produce a completely different outcome. Using the revolutionary opportunities produced by the Syrian Arab Spring and the Syrian internationalized civil war, Kurds took up arms, gained de facto control of their territory and have started to transform the social, economic and political relationships in their region.

Acknowledgements

I would like to thank Corey Payne and Christopher Chase-Dunn for their very valuable comments, suggestions and feedback on earlier drafts of this paper.

Disclosure statement

No potential conflict of interest was reported by the author.

References

Alvarez, R., & Chase-Dunn, C. (2018). Forging a diagonal instrument for the global left: The vessel. Retrieved from https://irows.ucr.edu/papers/irows130/irows130.htm. Retrieved from https://www.tandfonline.com/globalizations/aminforum/alvarez

Amin, S. (2008). Towards the fifth international? In K. Sehm-Patomaki & M. Ulvila (Eds.), *Global political parties* (pp. 123–143). London: Zed Books.

Amin, S. (2018). It is imperative to reconstruct the *Internationale* of workers and peoples. Retrieved from https://mronline.org/2018/08/23/it-is-imperative-to-reconstruct-the-internationale-of-workers-and-peoples

Arrighi, G. (1990). Marxist century, American century: The making and remaking of the world labour movement. *New Left Review I/179* (pp. 29–64).

Arrighi, G. (1994). *The long twentieth century: Money, power and the origins of our times*. London: Verso.

Arrighi, G., Hopkins, T. K., & Wallerstein, I. (2012). *Antisystemic movements*. London: Verso.

Arrighi, G., & Silver, B. (1999). *Chaos and governance in the modern world system*. Minneapolis: University of Minnesota Press.

Badiou, A. (2012). *Rebirth of history: Times of riots and uprisings*. London: Verso.

Beissinger, M. R. (2018). The urban advantage in revolution. Retrieved from https://scholar.princeton.edu/mbeissinger/home

Burawoy, M. (2012). Our ivelihood is at stake – we must pursue relationships beyond the university. *Network*, *111*, 27–30.

Chase-Dunn, C., & Gills, B. (2005). Waves of globalization and resistance in the capitalist world system: Social movements and critical global studies. In R. P. Appelbaum & W. I. Robinson (Eds.), *Critical globalization studies* (pp. 45–54). New York, NY: Routledge.

Chase-Dunn, C., & Nagy, S. (2019). Global social movements and world revolutions in the twenty-first century. In B. Berberoglu (Ed.), *The Palgrave handbook of social movements, revolution, and social transformation* (pp. 427–446). Cham: Palgrave Macmillan.

Cox, L., & Nilsen, A. G. (2007). Social movements research and the 'movement of movements': Studying resistance to neoliberal globalisation. *Sociology Compass, 1*(2), 424–442.

Draper, H. (1986). *Karl Marx's theory of revolution Vol III: The 'dictatorship of the proletariat'*. New York, NY: Monthly Review Press.

Draper, H. (1990). *Karl Marx's theory of revolution Vol IV: Critique of other socialisms*. New York, NY: Monthly Review Press.

Fominaya, F. C. (2017). European anti-austerity and pro-democracy protests in the wake of the global financial crisis. *Social Movement Studies, 16*(1), 1–20.

Fraser, N. (2017). A triple movement? Parsing the politics of crisis after Polanyi. In M. Burchardt & G. Kirn (Eds.), *Beyond neoliberalism* (pp. 29–42). Cham: Palgrave Macmillan.

Gramsci, A. (1971). *Selections from the prison notebooks*. New York, NY: International Publishers.

Greene, D. E. (2017). *Communist insurgent: Blanqui's politics of revolution*. Chicago, IL: Haymarket Books.

Karatasli, S. S. (2018). Political economy of secession: Global waves of state-seeking nationalism, 1492 to present. In A. Bergesen & C. Suter (Eds.), *The return of geopolitics* (pp. 69–95). Zurich: Lit Verlag.

Karatasli, S. S., Kumral, S., Scully, B., & Upadhyay, S. (2014). Class, crisis, and the 2011 protest wave: Cyclical and secular trends in global labor unrest. In C. Chase-Dunn, I. Wallerstein, & C. Suter (Eds.), *Overcoming global inequalities* (pp. 184–200). New York, NY: Paradigm.

Karatasli, S. S., Kumral, S., & Silver, B. (2018). *A new global tide of rising social protest? The early twenty-first century in world historical perspective*. Paper presented at the Eastern Sociological Society Annual Meeting. Retrieved from http://content.csbs.utah.edu/~mli/Economics%207004/Silver_Karatasli_Kumral_2018_ESSconference_version.pdf

Marx, K. (1858). Correspondence: Marx to Engels, in Manchester. Retrieved from https://www.marxists.org/archive/marx/works/1858/letters/58_10_08.htm

Marx, K. (1872). La Liberte Speech. Retrieved from https://www.marxists.org/archive/marx/works/1872/09/08.htm

Marx, K. (1867/1992). *Capital Vol. 1: A critique of political economy*. London: Penguin.

Marx, K., & Engels, F. (1848/2002). *The communist manifesto*. London: Penguin.

Mason, P. (2012). *Why it is kicking off everywhere: The new global revolutions*. London: Verso.

McLellan, K. (1995). *Karl Marx: A biography*. London: Papermac.

Milkman, R., Luce, S., & Lewis, P. W. (2013). *Changing the subject: A bottom-up account of occupy Wall Street in New York City*. New York, NY: CUNY, The Murphy Institute.

Polanyi, K. (1944). *The great transformation: Economic and political origins of our time*. New York, NY: Rinehart.

Robinson, A., & Tormey, S. (2009). Is "another world" possible? Laclau, Mouffe and social movements. In A. Little & M. Lloyd (Eds.), *The politics of radical democracy* (pp. 133–157). Edinburgh: Edinburgh University Press.

Schapper, K., Bauer, H., & Moll, J. (1847/2010). Report by the central authority to the league. In *Marx and Engels collected works: Volume 6 Marx and Engels 1845–48* (p. 602). Lawrence & Wishart. Retrieved from http://www.koorosh-modaresi.com/MarxEngels/V6.pdf.

Silver, B. J., & Slater, E. (1999). The social origins of world hegemonies. In G. Arrighi & B. J. Silver (Eds.), *Chaos and governance in the modern world system* (pp. 151–216). Minneapolis: University of Minnesota Press.

Sitrin, M. (2012). Horizontalism and the occupy movements. *Dissent, 59*(2), 74–75.

Sitrin, M. (2014). Goals without demands: The new movements for real democracy. *The South Atlantic Quarterly, 113*(2), 245–258.

Springborg, R. (2011). Whither the Arab spring? 1989 or 1848? *The International Spectator, 46*(3), 5–12.

Therborn, G. (2014). New masses? Social bases of resistance. *New Left Review, 85*, 7–16.

Wallerstein, I. (2012, September). The geopolitics of Arab Turmoil. *Al Jazeera Center for Studies*. Retrieved from https://www.iwallerstein.com/category/articles

Wittke, C. (1950). *The Utopian communist: A biography of Wilhelm Weitling, nineteenth century reformer.* Baton Rouge: Louisiana State University Press.

Žižek, S. (2012). *The year of dreaming dangerously.* London: Verso.

On Samir Amin's call for a Fifth International

Valentine M. Moghadam

ABSTRACT

In his prodigious output, from works on capitalist development to analyses of Islamist movements to involvement in the World Social Forum, Samir Amin's was a consistent voice for struggle against capitalism's domination of the world and its peoples. In this brief essay I address his call for a shift from *movement* to *organization*, indeed, toward a kind of Fifth International and explain why I endorse it.

Samir Amin, a leading scholar and co-founder of the world-systems tradition, died on August 12, 2018. Just before his death, he published, along with close allies, a call for 'workers and the people' to establish a 'fifth international' [https://www.pambazuka.org/global-south/letter-intent-inaugural-meeting-international-workers-and-peoples] *to coordinate support to progressive movements. To honor Samir Amin's invaluable contribution to world-systems scholarship, we are pleased to present readers with a selection of essays responding to Amin's final message for today's anti-systemic movements. This forum is being co-published between* Globalizations [https://www.tandfonline.com/rglo], *the* Journal of World-Systems Research [http://jwsr.pitt.edu/ojs/index.php/jwsr/issue/view/75] *and* Pambazuka News [https://www.pambazuka.org/]. *Additional essays and commentary can be found in these outlets.*

A Marxist, development economist, and internationalist who was born in Cairo to an Egyptian father and French mother and who spent much of his life on the African continent writing, speaking, and strategizing, Samir Amin was truly one of a kind. I came to know his work while in the Iranian student movement in the late 1970s and then as a graduate student in the early 1980s, as his writings on dependency, imperialism, and 'delinking' resonated deeply with students, activists, and scholars from the 'Third World'. I first met him when I attended two of the 'Cavtat Roundtables' in the late 1980s – those unique meetings organized by the Yugoslav Communist Party that brought together socialists, left social democrats, Communists, and independent leftists from across the globe. In 1986, Amin presented a paper at the Cavtat Roundtable entitled 'Culture and Development: Reflections on Arab-Islamic Thought'. He told me at the time that the paper was his contribution to an ongoing debate among Arab intellectuals around epistemological issues related to development and change, and the extent to which 'the West' and its conceptual systems were responsible for the Arab world's cultural and economic stagnation. That paper led to his book, *Eurocentrism*, which inspired a review essay I wrote for the journal *Socialism and Democracy* (Moghadam, 1989).

In his prodigious output, from works on capitalist development to analyses of Islamist movements to involvement in the World Social Forum, Amin's was a consistent voice for struggle against capitalism's domination of the world and its peoples, and in this he was unwavering to the end. In this brief essay I address his call for a shift from *Movement* to *Organization*, indeed, toward a kind of Fifth International (Amin, 2018a) and explain why I endorse it.

The global justice movement and the World Social Forum

The 1990s saw both the consolidation of neoliberal capitalist globalization and its opposite, the making of a global justice movement, which was propelled onto the world stage through the now-famous Battle of Seattle. In the new century the World Social Forum (WSF) was launched, the brainchild of the Brazilian Workers' Party and representatives of social movements and left-wing initiatives from several countries. The first WSF was held in Porto Alegre in 2001 and about every two years since then, convening also in Mumbai, Caracas, Nairobi, Tunis, and Montreal. It is worth noting that the charter of the WSF expressly forbids the formulation of a political program or even working with progressive political parties, and 'a significant group of participants strongly supports maintaining the WSF as an "open space" for debate and organizing' (Chase-Dunn & Nagy, 2018, p. 264). Articles 1 and 5 of the June 2001 WSF Charter of Principles state the following:

> The WSF is an open meeting place for reflective thinking, democratic debate of ideas, formulation of proposals, free exchange of experiences and interlinking for effective action, by groups and movements of civil society … The WSF bring together and interlinks only organizations and movements of civil society from all the countries of the world.

By mid-decade, some participants felt that the time had come for the WSF to shift from a forum for deliberative dialogue to a site for political strategizing. In 2005, Samir Amin was a member of the 'Group of Nineteen', WSF participants who penned the Porto Alegre Manifesto outlining 12 proposals on economic measures, peace and justice, and democracy, 'to give sense and direction to the construction of another, different world'.[1] In summary form, the proposals called for cancellation of debts of developing countries; implementation of the Tobin Tax on speculative capital and similar taxes on international financial transactions; dismantling offshore banking ('fiscal, juridical, and banking paradises'); codifying rights to employment, social security, and the equality of women and men; promoting equitable trade and the protection of cultural heritage; establishing a country's right to agricultural and food sovereignty; banning patents on knowledge pertaining to living beings as well as the privatization of the commons; public policies banning discrimination, sexism, racism, xenophobia, and antisemitism; ending the destruction of the environment; dismantling all foreign military bases; the right of free access to information and support for non-profit media; and the reform and democratization of international institutions.

In 2004, Susan George of the Transnational Institute (and a veteran of the anti-Vietnam war movement) had already penned a call to 'take the movement forward' with a focus on power and a more concerted political agenda.[2] In a 2007 posting, Walden Bello – Filipino sociologist, veteran activist and public figure, executive director of Focus on the Global South, and another manifesto signatory – wondered whether the WSF had run its course and should now 'give way to new modes of global organization and resistance and transformation'.[3] In the face of continued 'horizontalism' of the global justice movement and of the WSF itself, others asked if the movement had the capacity to counter power in its neoliberal, capitalist, or imperialist guises.

A recent two-part book on the global justice movement, *The Movements of Movements* (Sen, 2017, 2018) is composed of essays largely in favor of continued discussion, diversity, direct democracy, and prefigurative action ('horizontalism') but it does include a number of contributions in favor of a more strategic approach. Most of the essays were written in the period 2004–08 and reprinted for the two volumes. In 'The Strategic Implications of Anti-Statism in the Global Justice Movement', Stephanie Ross (2018) criticizes the 'romanticized view of civil society as a realm of freedom and autonomy' and 'rejection of the possibility that state power can be used by progressive forces to create alternatives to capitalism' (p. 201). She concludes: 'While convincing people that "another world is possible" is key, how much more demoralizing is to see that belief unsupported by material changes in relations of power and wealth?' (p. 216). Writing on neoliberalism in Latin America, Emir Sader (2017) is critical of the emphasis on 'the social' at the expense of 'the political', and the way the WSF took up this stance to keep the forum exclusive to 'civil society' and social movements while closed to political parties. He points out that despite the crisis of Mexico's ruling PRI, the Zapatistas chose to remain outside electoral politics and even scorned the left-wing candidate, Andres-Manuel Lopez Obrador (AMLO), in the 2006 elections that were won by the right-wing party (see pp. 504–505). In his call for a return to strategy, the late Daniel Bensaid (2017) argues that 'we need now to be specific about what the other "possible" world is and – above all – to explore how to get there' (p. 518). He mentions two scenarios based on earlier uprisings: an insurrectional general strike and extended popular war.

The contribution by Samir Amin is especially striking. He asks: Who will challenge the new imperialist order, and how? He criticizes those who 'wish to maintain the WSF in a state of maximal impotence' (Amin, 2018b, p. 481). He then takes a look back at the First, Second, and Third Internationals (he mentions in passing the Fourth, or Trotskyist, International), and concludes that it is time to move towards a 'Fifth International'.

Right-wing populism and the New Global Left

The global justice movement was a proactive response to neoliberal capitalist globalization, and the World Social Forum was meant as the progressive answer to the World Economic Forum of businessmen and politicians (see Mertes, 2004). But the movement seemed paralyzed by the 9/11 tragedies and unable to confront the U.S. invasion of Afghanistan soon afterwards. It is worth noting that the United States maintains a military presence there, in what is now its longest war. Nor has Afghanistan regained peace and security, since the United States cast its lot with a tribal-Islamist uprising against a modernizing left-wing government, a move that triggered the government's appeal to the Soviet Union for military assistance and then generated a long and bloody war and ultimately the brutal reign first of the Mujahidin and then the Taliban, prior to the U.S. invasion. Worse, the global justice movement could not prevent the 2003 U.S./U.K. invasion and occupation of Iraq, from which its people still have not recovered. Between 2002 and 2008, the 'Cairo Conferences' brought together an unlikely coalition of Arab leftists, nationalists, and Islamists appalled by the imperialist designs on Iraq, but that coalition failed in the face of state repression as well as its own internal contradictions (Abdelrahman, 2009). As the global economy became ever more neoliberal and reckless, the financial meltdown that occurred in 2007–08 was followed by the Great Recession. The events of 2011 – including the Arab Spring, Occupy Wall Street, and Europe's anti-austerity protests – seemed to augur a new era of challenges to the status quo. Instead, they were followed by more of the same in Europe and the United States, and the disastrous responses by Western powers and their Arab allies to protests in Libya, Syria, and Yemen.

The anarchist anthropologist David Graeber recently wrote that 'we have won' (Graeber, 2018), but I strongly disagree.

Mention should be made of progressive initiatives at the sub-national level, with cities as sites for participatory democracy and human rights application. Benjamin Barber (2014) argued that nation-states had become dysfunctional and that cities were doing a better job of tackling complex problems. Jackie Smith (2017) refers to 'place-based efforts to realize human rights in localized settings' and describes efforts in Pittsburgh, Pennsylvania to realize 'the right to the city' on the part of low-paid workers and racial minorities. The so-called Cleveland model entails green and worker-owned co-operatives that were formed in response to economic distress; in Preston, a northern city in England that was hit by both de-industrialization and austerity, the Centre for Local Economic Strategies identified 12 large institutions anchored to the city – including the city and the county council, the university, the police and the hospital – to redirect the £1.2bn total annual spending power of these anchors to local businesses. In northern Syria, and in the midst of a brutal internationalized civil conflict with the intervention of legions of jihadists from around the world, a Kurdish community has created an experimental autonomous region, Rojava (Knapp, Flach, & Ayboga, 2016). Inspired by the writings of the American anarchist and social ecologist Murray Bookchin, their ideology centers around concepts of democratic confederalism, women's liberation and participation, and the social economy. These are inspiring examples of progressive local initiatives. We know, however, that right-wing populists similarly call for local (as well as national) sovereignty, and the risk of reactionary and exclusionary localism is always present in such experiments. Spain's Andalucia, for example, is now run by a right-wing populist party, Vox. Moreover, the famous Spanish social enterprise, Mondragon, based in the Basque region, remains successful but was hardly able to prevent Spain's economic crisis and austerity policies after 2008. The record of the recent past, as well the rise and spread of right-wing populist movements, parties, and governments in Europe, the United States, and some Global South countries make the call for concerted political action and coordination more urgent. Such movements draw on the support of hardened right-wingers, to be sure, but also citizens who have been left behind by decades of neoliberal economic policy, austerity, and neglect (Hochschild, 2016; Judis, 2016; Rodrik, 2017; Schafer, 2017). Many of those citizens are also fearful of the economic and cultural effects of the massive wave of migrants and refugees – in turn the result of the failures of neoliberal economic policies, state destabilizations, and wars. Such citizens rightly blame the established parties for the migrant and refugee influx as well as the welfare cutbacks, and they trust that the new right-wing parties can turn the tide. Most such parties and governments are decidedly anti-feminist (Moghadam & Kaftan, 2019). Amin correctly notes that the emergence of right-wing populist movements in Europe reflects the failure of the European Union project.

Parallel to the rise of the Global Right are progressive alternatives such as Bernie Sanders's *Our Revolution* in the United States, the British Labor Party under Corbyn, Spain's Podemos, Portugal's Left Bloc, the Front Populaire in Tunisia, and left-wing Green parties in many countries, including the USA. Could their membership and influence grow – as opposed to what happened to Greece's Syriza? Could they build bridges and indeed coalitions with trade unions and feminist organizations to form a powerful alliance of transnational social movement organizations and progressive political parties that could challenge the powers-that-be? Indeed, in recent years, we have seen renewed calls for more concerted political action, coordination, and platforms. Christopher Chase-Dunn and his colleagues (2009, 2014, 2018) have examined prospects for *the World Revolution of 20xx* spearheaded by the *New Global Left* – those groups critical of neoliberal and capitalist globalization and which include popular forces, social movements, and progressive political parties and national regimes. Heikki Patomaki (2018) has called for a World Political Party.[4] The proposals in the 2005 Porto Alegre Manifesto align with the recent call for a *Progressive International*, an initiative of the (Bernie) Sanders Institute in Vermont, USA, and DiEM25, cofounded by the former Syriza finance minister Yannis Varoufakis.[5] Could we be seeing movement toward the making of a united front? Could Samir Amin's call for a kind of Fifth International see the light of day?

There will be resistance, and not just on the part of the transnational capitalist class and its states. In a recent paper (Moghadam, 2018), I have suggested that the World Social Forum, if it changed its Charter of Principles, could become the site for strategic political planning and coordination, inasmuch as it remains the one forum at which such issues are discussed and where the varied progressive groups converge. But many WSF activists remain committed to its original intent. Jai Sen, editor of the huge two-volume book, *The Movements of Movements,* writes in the introduction to the first volume that the WSF has been a space 'where people in movement can gain the possibility of growing through their interactions, learning from their exchanges, and where the possibility also exists of new actors entering and joining the discussions' (Sader, 2017, p. 21). His preference is that 'there are many different movements taking place in our world today, and differing perceptions of justice, and many ways of moving, all of which we can learn from'; these include 'the student-led revolt in France in 1968, the Zapatista movement in Mexico since 1994, the "Battle of Seattle" in 1999, and ... what some call today "political Islam"' (Sader, 2017, p. 16). Sen seems to be offering a very expansive notion of 'justice movements', which may just as well include right-wing populist-nationalist movements. After all, like the political Islam that Sen seems to admire, they too have a sense of grievance and injustice – but one rather different from those who might be defined as the New Global Left.

My response to Sen is: Do we celebrate all struggles, or do we rank them, acknowledging that some may be divisive or violent or ideologically objectionable? Having missed recent opportunities to forge a sustained global movement against the ravages of neoliberal capitalist globalization and its many side effects, when is the time for strategic movement-building? Or do we have to settle for the many disparate and fragmented local struggles, some of them connected from time to time at the WSF, others making demands based on their own identities, and yet others morphing into right-wing populism? Surely such dispersion and division are precisely what reinforce the capitalist world-system. It's worth noting that many of the right-wing populist-nationalist parties and leaderships which have formed or won elections in recent years seem to be in some regular contact with each other, in part through that roving ambassador of the populist-nationalist Right, Steve Bannon. Similarly, the various Islamist parties and movements around the world, especially those of the Muslim Brotherhood variant, have ways of connecting and sharing. (Islamist parties belong squarely on the Right. As Samir Amin noted in his many critiques, Islamist movements are preoccupied with cultural issues rather than the improvement of people's socio-economic conditions and rights.)

Back to the future: toward a new internationalism

In a *Monthly Review* essay, 'Revolution from North to South', Amin (2017) provides a concise but comprehensive survey of political developments since the early 20th century and ends thus:

> In conclusion, I will again point out that the system of neoliberal globalization has entered its last phase; its implosion is clearly visible, as indicated by, among other things, Brexit, Trump's election, and the rise of various forms of neofascism. The rather inglorious end of this system opens up a potentially revolutionary situation in all parts of the world. But this potential will become reality only if radical left forces know how to seize the opportunities offered and design and implement bold offensive strategies based on the reconstruction of the internationalism of workers and peoples in the face of the cosmopolitanism of

the imperialist powers' financial capital. If that does not happen, then the left forces of the West, East, and South will also share responsibility for the ensuing disaster.

For our part, it must be possible to create a coordinating mechanism that connects the disparate struggles around a common goal of creating a world in which the welfare of the people and the planet – not the profits of businesses or elites or self-serving political parties – matter the most. In my view, that would mean something like a very clear, very coherent platform – one that could mobilize the largest number of adherents around core issues, even if some people might not agree on some of the accompanying issues and values. As Samir Amin suggested, the new Global Left needs to look back to the history of socialist movements in order to move forward. In the period after the Bolshevik Revolution, the Third International, also known as the COMINTERN, mobilized the world's socialist and communist parties around specific issues and campaigns. Other large coalitions were the United Front and the Popular Front, both active during World War II. Could one of those models – albeit without the dogmatism and infighting of the past – inspire a more effective WSF?

This could be possible precisely because of the features of the World Social Forum that Walden Bello identified in 'The World Social Forum at the Crossroad':

> Quite a number of 'old movement' groups participate in the WSF, including old-line 'democratic centralist' parties as well as traditional social democratic parties affiliated with the Socialist International. Yet none of these has put much effort into steering the WSF towards more centralized or hierarchical modes of organizing. At the same time, despite their suspicion of political parties, the 'new movements' never sought to exclude the parties and their affiliates from playing a significant role in the Forum. Indeed, the 2004 WSF in Mumbai was organized jointly by an unlikely coalition of social movements and Marxist-Leninist parties, a set of actors that are not known for harmonious relations on the domestic front.

What Bello's observation suggests to me is that any new International would look rather different from the COMINTERN, more inclusive and less dogmatic, and certainly with the participation of many more women than was the case before, but still with a definite structure, a coherent platform, and leadership capable of taking 'the movement' forward in a more strategic manner at national, regional, and global levels. Samir Amin's call for a Fifth International must be taken seriously, as it could be the trigger that sets off what Chase-Dunn and colleagues have referred to as the World Revolution of 20xx. A return to a more formal organizing structure with clear political goals and a unified strategy to achieve those goals through alliances with like-minded political parties and left-wing social movements across the globe could finally pose a more serious challenge to the current global system and prevent its capture by the extreme Right.

Notes

1. Available at https://archive.is/20051112235616/http://www.zmag.org/sustainers/content/2005-02/20group_of_nineteen.cfm.
2. https://focusweb.org/taking-the-movement-forward/.
3. https://www.waldenbello.org/the-world-social-forum-at-the-crossroads/.
4. https://greattransition.org/publication/world-political-party.
5. See https://www.progressive-international.org/open-call/.

Disclosure statement

No potential conflict of interest was reported by the author.

References

Abdelrahman, M. (2009). With the state? Sometimes … with the Islamists? Never! *The British Journal of Middle East Studies, 36*(1), 37–54.

Amin, S. (2017). Revolution from North to South. *Monthly Review, 69*(3).

Amin, S. (2018a). *It is imperative to reconstruct the international of workers and peoples.* International Development Economic Associates (IDEA), 3 July. Retrieved from http://www.networkideas.org/featured-articles/2018/07/it-is-imperative-to-reconstruct-the-internationale-of-workers-and-peoples/

Amin, S. (2018b [2006]). Toward a Fifth International? In J. Sen (Ed.), *The movements of movements: Rethinking our dance* (pp. 465–483). New Delhi: OpenWord and PM Press.

Barber, B. (2014). *If mayors ruled the world: Dysfunctional nations, rising cities.* New Haven, CT: Yale University Press.

Bello, W. (2007). *The forum at the crossroads.* Committee for the Abolition of Illegitimate Debt. Retrieved from http://www.cadtm.org/The-Forum-at-the-Crossroads

Bensaid, D. (2017). The return of strategy. In J. Sen (Ed.), *The movements of movements, part 1* (pp. 517–533). New Delhi: OpenWord and PM Press.

Chase-Dunn, C., & Nagy, S. (2018). The Piketty challenge: Global inequality and world revolutions. In L. Langman & D. A. Smith (Eds.), *Twenty-first century inequality & capitalism: Piketty, Marx and beyond* (pp. 255–278). Leiden: Brill.

Chase-Dunn, C., Neimeyer, R., Saxena, P., Kaneshiro, M., Love, J., & Spears, A. (2009). *The new global left: Movements and regimes.* IROWS Working Paper no. 50. Retrieved from http://irows.ucr.edu/papers/

Chase-Dunn, C., Stabler, A.-S., Breckenridge-Jackson, I., & Herrera, J. (2014). *Articulating the web of transnational social movements.* IROWS Working Paper no. 84. Retrieved from http://irows.ucr.edu/papers/

George, S. (2004). *Taking the movement forward.* Focus on the Global South. Retrieved from https://focusweb.org/taking-the-movement-forward/

Graeber, D. (2018). The shock of victory. In J. Sen (Ed.), *The movement of movements. Part 2: Rethinking our dance* (pp. 393–409). New Delhi: OpenWord and PM Press.

Hochschild, A. R. (2016). *Strangers in their own land: Anger and mourning on the American right.* New York, NY: The New Press.

Judis, J. (2016). *The populist explosion: How the great recession transformed American and European politics.* New York, NY: Columbia Global Reports.

Knapp, M., Flach, A., & Ayboga, E. (2016). *Revolution in Rojava: Democratic autonomy and women's liberation in Syrian Kurdistan.* (Janet Biehl, Trans.). London: Pluto Press.

Mertes, T. (Ed.). (2004). *A movement of movements: Is another world really possible?* London: Verso.

Moghadam, V. M. (1989). Against eurocentrism and nativism: A review essay on Samir Amin's *Eurocentrism* and other texts. *Socialism and Democracy, 9,* 81–104.

Moghadam, V. M. (2018). Feminism and the future of revolution. *Socialism and Democracy, 32*(1), 31–53.

Moghadam, V. M., & Kaftan, G. (2019). *Right-wing populisms North and South: Varieties and gender dynamics.* Women's Studies International Forum, Vol. 75, July–August (originally prepared for the Global Studies

Assoc. conference, Globalization, Race, and the New Nationalism, Howard University, Washington, DC (6–8 June 2018).

Patomaki, H. (2018). *A world political party: The time has come.* Great Transition Initiative (February). Retrieved from https://www.greattransition.org/publication/world-political-party

Rodrik, D. (2017). *Populism and the economics of globalization.* Cambridge: Weatherhead Center for International Affairs. Retrieved from https://drodrik.scholar.harvard.edu/files/danirodrik/files/Populism_and_the_economics_of_globalization.pdf

Ross, J. (2018 [2008]). The strategic implications of anti-statism in the global justice movement. In J. Sen (Ed.), *The movements of movements, part 2: Rethinking our dance* (pp. 201–222). New Delhi: OpenWord and PM Press.

Sader, E. (2017). The weakest link? Neoliberalism in Latin America. In J. Sen (Ed.), *The movements of movements, part 1* (pp. 493–515). New Delhi: OpenWord and PM Press.

Schafer, A. (2017). *Return with a vengeance: Working class anger and the rise of populism* (8 August). Retrieved from www.items.ssrc.org/return-with-a-vengeance-working-class-anger-and-the-rise-of-populism

Sen, J. (2017). *The movements of movements, part 1: What makes us move?* New Delhi: OpenWord and PM Press.

Sen, J. (2018). *The movements of movements, part 2: Rethinking our dance.* New Delhi: OpenWord and PM Press.

Smith, J. (2017). Local responses to right-wing populism: Building human rights cities. *Studies in Social Justice, 11*(2), 347–368.

The rational kernel within Samir Amin's mythological shell: the idea of a democratic and pluralist world political party

Heikki Patomäki

ABSTRACT

Amin's Leninist-Maoist vision is unlikely to be persuasive to twenty-first century citizens. Nonetheless, there is a rational kernel in Amin's call for a new worldwide political organization. Some structures, mechanisms and tendencies of the capitalist world economy are relatively enduring and some patterns recurrent, although the world economy is also fluid, constantly changing and evolving. Although waves of globalization have radically transformed human societies and their economic activities during the past 500 years also in many positive ways, the expansion of the international society and world economy has often been characterized by violence, imperial subjection and colonial expropriation and exclusion. There is a rational kernel also within Amin's analysis of the current world-political situation. Command over space and time by investors and megacorporations is power. Emancipation aims at freedom from domination. The decline of the World Social Forum indicates that progressive politics must move 'beyond the concept of a discussion forum'. My argument is that emancipation from unnecessary, unneeded and unwanted sources of determination requires global transformative agency and planetary visions about alternatives.

Samir Amin, a leading scholar and co-founder of the world-systems tradition, died on August 12, 2018. Just before his death, he published, along with close allies, a call for 'workers and the people' to establish a 'fifth international' [https://www.pambazuka.org/global-south/letter-intent-inaugural-meeting-international-workers-and-peoples] *to coordinate support to progressive movements. To honor Samir Amin's invaluable contribution to world-systems scholarship, we are pleased to present readers with a selection of essays responding to Amin's final message for today's anti-systemic movements. This forum is being co-published between* Globalizations [https://www.tandfonline.com/rglo], *the* Journal of World-Systems Research [http://jwsr.pitt.edu/ojs/index.php/jwsr/issue/view/75] *and* Pambazuka News [https://www.pambazuka.org/]. *Additional essays and commentary can be found in these outlets.*

Samir Amin was an animated spirit throughout his rich life. The essay he published just a month before his death calls for a new beginning of the left, for a new International. Amin's analysis is steadfast and his categories simple and uncompromising. He claims that capitalism always follows the same logic and concentrates power in ever fewer hands. Contemporary capitalism is vehemently upheld by the Triad (United States, Western and Central European countries, Japan). Amin declares that this system is totalitarian in all but name. 'The historical imperialist powers of the Triad have set up a system of collective military control over the planet.' This system amounts to an Orwellian permanent war waged by the West against the rest.

Amin concludes that the only possibility for liberation of 'the workers and the peoples' is to establish a worldwide Organization, a new International. Amin was an active participant in the World Social Forum (WSF) process, so he must have concluded that the WSF is hardly enough for worldwide transformation. He criticizes 'the extreme fragmentation of the struggles', making a tacit reference to various NGOs working locally on single issues such as ecology or women's rights. The new Organization must move 'beyond the concept of a discussion forum'. Moreover, the new Organization cannot be content with a horizontal form, rather it must involve some hierarchy. Adequate statutes can help to avoid the danger of non-democratic leaders.

In the famous afterword to the second German edition of *Capital*, Marx (1873) mentioned the possibility of discovering the rational kernel within the mystical shell of Hegel's philosophy. This is a good metaphor for thinking about Amin's proposal as well, although in this context a better adjective might be 'mythological' rather than 'mystical' (see also Amin, 2007, which is a much longer version of his proposal for a fifth International). Myths are stories that constitute worldviews. Stories are structured and they involve categories in terms of which these stories are told. It looks quite clear that Amin's story and fundamental categories have remained basically the same for several decades. For Amin, the analysis of the current world system is based on Lenin's theory of imperialism; and the main alternative to capitalism is an idealized version of Maoism, premised on delinking from the exploitative relations of the world capitalist system.

Lenin maintained that in capitalism the control over means of production will be ever more concentrated and centralized; banks and finance will play an increasingly important role. Because of the superabundance of capital in the highest stage of capitalism, and especially financial capital, capital turns outwards, resulting in new imperialism. A century later, Amin still concurs with Lenin's analysis. Nothing much has changed. Concentration and centralization continue. Contemporary globalization 'is nothing else but a new form of imperialist globalization'. Amin's view on representative democracy is essentially Leninist as well. Lenin (1917/1999, p. 28) thought that democracy is only a catchword 'with which the capitalists and their press deceive the workers and the peasants'. In a rather similar manner, Amin concludes in 2018 that 'representative democracy, having lost all its meaning, has lost its legitimacy'. Where Amin departs from Lenin is in his depiction of the role of the Triad, which resembles Karl Kautsky's notion of ultra-imperialism. Kautsky (1914/1970) envisaged that capitalist states would begin to co-operate after the Great War and govern the world in a concerted manner, also to prevent anti-imperialist forces from becoming too influential (the ultimate threat was socialism and the end of private property).

After Amin's arrival in Paris in the late 1940s, he joined the French Communist Party (PCF), but later distanced himself from Soviet Marxism and for some time was involved in Maoist circles (see 'Samir Amin', Wikipedia, version revised 22 December 2018). Later he was associated with various circles and organizations (e.g. he worked with the Ministry of Planning of the newly independent Mali 1960–1963 under Modibo Keïta's one-party socialist regime, which turned out rather disturbing to Mali's development); but it seems to me that an idealized version of Mao's China remained Amin's concrete utopia until the end of long career as a public intellectual.

Amin idealized the Maoist model in at least two distinct ways, through one-sided historical description and through normatively tendential counterfactual thinking. For Amin, Maoism was built on a worker-peasant alliance and on that basis, succeeded in realizing national self-sufficiency and egalitarianism. Amin (1981) claims that China's economic development was both impressive and benign in the period of 1950-80. From this standpoint, Amin criticized the 'revisionist' tendencies in China Deng Xiaoping became the *de facto* leader of China in 1978 turning China more openly toward world markets. A quarter of a century later Amin (2006) characterized China's opening in the 1980s as 'indispensable' to some degree, but still continued to praise the successes of Maoism. Amin also ignored, or at least downplayed, the violence of the Cultural Revolution. In the same vein, he did not cease to offer his public support for the Pol Pot regime in Cambodia even when the atrocities of Khmer Rouge were already widely known. As two scholars argued in the early 1980s in their reply to Amin's apparent responses to his critics:

> Pol Pot and his regime were, it is clear, a gang of butchers, whose socialist aspirations and concern for the welfare of the Kampuchean people were demonstrated by genocide and torture. There is clearly no honest way in which Samir Amin can continue to evade this issue, since the 'principles' of 'socialist reconstruction' followed Amin's blueprint so closely. The only conclusion that Amin is not able to draw from the Kampuchean experience is that 'more of the same' is required in the 1980s, that future progress in Kampuchea requires the severing of relationships with Vietnam and the Soviet Union, so that socialism can be constructed on a suitably autarkic base. Such a conclusion can only be sustained by a refusal seriously to examine the consequences of autarkic strategies in the 1970s. (Smith & Sender, 1983, p. 651)

Amin would have preferred a somewhat more democratic regime in Maoist China and in all likelihood also in Cambodia. He (2007, p. 128) stresses the 'democratic deficit' of national populist regimes. On the basis of wishful counterfactual thinking, it is possible to imagine a self-reliant national system that follows the basic tenets of Mao and Pol Pot without their despotic excesses (Amin continued to live in denial of the true extent of the violence in China and Cambodia). Amin's 2018 call for a fifth international does not significantly deviate from this pattern of thought. His last manifesto is an anti-imperialist text – whatever is meant by imperialism – but what is the positive future that it advocates? Amin is not arguing for world democracy, better global governance or world government; his project is not cosmopolitan. What Amin stresses is 'the necessary renewal of national, popular projects'. Therefore, he also criticizes those who use the term 'nationalism' negatively and, by the same token, seizes the opportunity to once again stress the importance of 'delinking':

> The facile accusation of 'nationalism' of those critical of Europe does not hold water. The European project is increasingly visible as being that of the bourgeois nationalism of Germany. There is no alternative in Europe, as elsewhere, to the setting up of national, popular and democratic projects (not bourgeois, indeed anti-bourgeois) that will begin the delinking from imperialist globalization.

It is now time to return to Marx's famous afterword to the second German edition of *Capital*. Marx criticized Hegel for reducing everything to some sort of mystical Idea and for transfiguring and glorifying the existing state of things. This criticism can be applied to Amin. Amin assumes that Lenin can still provide the basic story about the nature of the existing world system ('mystical Analysis'), while he continues to transfigure and glorify the state of things in Mao's China. Marx demanded a thorough scientific, realist and critical analysis of ever-changing social realities. But there were mystical elements also within Marx's own thinking (Bhaskar, 1993, pp. 320–328), which Amin and other Marxists have inherited. For instance, most twentieth century Marxists assumed that social forms develop in stages and that capitalism will be followed by socialism (for half a century, this story survived the endless bifurcations of socialisms). Thus, there is no need to study systematically and critically different alternative possibilities and their likely consequences. Time and again, this has led to transfiguration and glorification of particular socialist and communist regimes, whatever their real effects and however repressive and violent they may have been. Amin (2007, p. 127, p. 132) makes critical comments about the third International and its orthodoxy of national single-party systems, but leaves the meaning of these paragraphs somewhat vague.

Amin's Leninist-Maoist vision – whether qualified in some ways or not – is unlikely to be persuasive to twenty-first century citizens. Nonetheless, there is a rational kernel in Amin's call for a new worldwide political organization. Starting with Amin's descriptive story, it is true that some structures, mechanisms and tendencies of the capitalist world economy are relatively enduring and some patterns recurrent, although the world economy is also fluid, constantly changing and evolving. Think about modern economic growth that started in the 1820s and its consequences; rising but at times also declining inequalities; the growth of megacorporations since the 1860s; processes of financialization; and recurring business cycles and financial crises. In contrast to what Amin indicates, waves of globalization have radically transformed human societies and their economic activities during the past 500 years, also in many positive ways. Yet it is true, as Amin claims, that the expansion of the international society and world economy has repeatedly been characterized by violence, imperial subjection and colonial expropriation and exclusion.

There is a rational kernel also within Amin's analysis of the current world-political situation. Farmers, workers, employees, civil servants, entrepreneurs and citizens are far from being as mobile as goods, financial capital, wealthy individuals or megacorporations. Command over space and time is power and emancipation aims at freedom from domination. A mere discussion forum lacks transformative agency. The decline of the World Social Forum indicates that progressive politics must move 'beyond the concept of a discussion forum'. Amin also correctly criticizes 'the fragmentation of the struggles', as both local and global civil society activities have been dominated by single-issue politics. But it is equally important to highlight the positive aspects of civil society. As Bhaskar (1993, p. 325) argues in criticizing Marx, the social virtues of civil society involve 'a domain of innovation, initiative and enterprise necessary to a dynamic, pluralistic socialist society'. When the concept of *societas civilis* is employed globally it entails that civilizing processes, legality and politics are recognized as global in scope, and that there thus is a planetary civilization in the making. While these considerations are ignored by Amin, he correctly sees structureless anti-authoritarianism as disempowering. And yet Amin's alternative is ambiguous. His scepticism of (especially representative) democracy is not only unfounded but potentially dangerous. The new worldwide organizations must adopt methods of participatory will-formation and democratic procedures of collective decision-making. A sustainable democratic world society can only be created by democratic and peaceful means (see Patomäki, 2019a).

In its general social scientific meaning, globalization refers to the expansion of the field of social relations, and to the decreasing significance of physical and temporal distances. Globalization in this sense is not a thing, an actor, or a mechanism that explains much else apart from the possibility that social relations can be maintained with increasing ease and intensity across time and space. Moreover, globalization in the generic sense is not the same thing as imperialism, colonialism or neoliberalism, although these ideologies have characterized different waves of globalization (the current disintegrative tendencies in global political economy are consequences of the long process of neoliberalization; Patomäki, 2018). Globalization enables and constrains actors, shapes social relations and can be a part of a wide variety of geo-historical dynamics.

Consider for instance the anti-imperialist cosmopolitan imaginary that emerged in the latter half of the eighteenth century and early nineteenth century. It would have been very difficult to translate that imaginary into functional organizations of world governance or government (Patomäki & Steger, 2010). Production remained based on land and agriculture; the speed of communication and transportation across the surface of the planet was limited to the velocity of humans, horses and sailing ships; many people were still willing to sacrifice their lives for the 'divine' rights of the dynastic rulers and aristocracy of particular communities; and the conditions of, say, income tax were only gradually emerging (the British introduced the world's first income tax to fund wars against Napoleon, only to be abolished in 1816). The planetary economy of the nineteenth century relied on the uncoordinated institutions of free trade, the gold standard, transnational finance and power-balancing (Polanyi, 1944/1957). The first functional international organizations proper were established only in the second half of the nineteenth century (for instance, the International Telegraph Union in 1865 to facilitate communications across the world).

The technological dynamism and industrial growth of the world economy have brought about novel global problems, as identified and framed by international organizations and other actors of transnational governance networks, and also novel opportunities. Current global problems include income and wealth disparities affecting access to things, relationships, and practices (Sayer, 2005); ecological problems such as global warming; and weapons of mass destruction. Our fates have become irreversibly intertwined. Awareness of this is part of our collective learning. Emancipation from unnecessary, unneeded and unwanted sources of determination requires both global transformative agency and planetary visions about progressive alternatives. This is the basis of my proposal for a world political party (Patomäki, 2011, 2019b). In a future world democracy, there will be many political parties and a vivid and pluralist civil society.

Disclosure statement

No potential conflict of interest was reported by the author.

References

Amin, S. (2007). Towards the fifth international? In K. Sehm-Patomäki & M. Ulvila (Eds.), *Global political parties* (pp. 123–143). London: Zed Books.

Amin, S. (1981). *The future of Maoism* (N. Finkelstein, Trans.). New York, NY: Monthly Review Press.

Amin, S. (2006, September 21). What Maoism has contributed. *Monthly Review.* Retrieved from https://monthlyreview.org/commentary/what-maoism-has-contributed/

Bhaskar, R. (1993). *Dialectic. The pulse of freedom.* London: Verso.

Kautsky, K. (1914/1970). Ultra-imperialism (Transl. unknown). *New Left Review, 59,* 41–46.

Lenin, V. (1917/1999). *Imperialism: The highest stage of capitalism* (D. Lorimer, Trans.). Sydney: Resistance Books.

Marx, K. (1873). Afterword to the second German edition (H. Kuhls, Trans.). Retrieved from https://www.marxists.org/archive/marx/works/1867-c1/p3.htm

Patomäki, H. (2011). Towards global political parties. *Ethics & Global Politics, 4*(2), 81–102. Retrieved from http://www.ethicsandglobalpolitics.net/index.php/egp/article/view/7334

Patomäki, H. (2018). *Disintegrative tendencies in global political economy: Exits and conflicts.* London: Routledge.

Patomäki, H. (2019a). Emancipation from violence through global law and institutions: A post-Deutschian perspective. In J. Kustermans, T. Sauer, D. Lootens, & B. Segaert (Eds.), *Pacifism's appeal. Ethos, history, politics* (pp. 153–178). London: Palgrave MacMillan.

Patomäki, H. (2019b). A world political party: The time has come. GT (Great Transition) Network Essay, February 2019. Retrieved from https://www.greattransition.org/

Patomäki, H., & Steger, M. (2010). Social imaginaries and Big History: Towards a new planetary consciousness? *Futures, 42*(10), 1056–1063.

Polanyi, K. (1944/1957). *The great transformation. The political and economic origins of our time.* Boston, MA: Beacon Press.

Sayer, A. (2005). *The moral significance of class.* Cambridge: Cambridge University Press.

Smith, S., & Sender, J. (1983). A reply to Samir Amin. *Third World Quarterly, 5*(3), 650–656.

World revolution or socialism, community by community, in the Anthropocene?

Leslie Sklair

ABSTRACT
The idea of a Fifth International has been around for some time and the historical record is not encouraging. We have all been wrestling with the contradictions the Left faces. The transnational capitalist class has taken setbacks in its stride, while the Left flounders almost everywhere. No communist revolution has resulted in the capture of power by the working class. Now we are all confronted by a new, rapidly unfolding ecological crisis, the Anthropocene. I argue that the most effective response is to exit rather than attempt to overthrow capitalism and the hierarchical state by international revolution. Socialists in positions of authority in state institutions and capitalist enterprises can facilitate this process by enacting legislation that helps people to transition to new smaller-scale non-statist social units, such as producer-consumer co-operatives producing their own food and other essential services over time. Mobilizing the ideas of degrowth, anarching, and consumer-producer cooperatives in the digital age, I argue that under Anthropocene conditions democratic socialism is best constructed from the bottom up, community by community, networked in mutually nurturing relationships.

Samir Amin, a leading scholar and co-founder of the world-systems tradition, died on August 12, 2018. Just before his death, he published, along with close allies, a call for 'workers and the people' to establish a 'fifth international' [https://www.pambazuka.org/global-south/letter-intent-inaugural-meeting-international-workers-and-peoples] *to coordinate support to progressive movements. To honor Samir Amin's invaluable contribution to world-systems scholarship, we are pleased to present readers with a selection of essays responding to Amin's final message for today's anti-systemic movements. This forum is being co-published between* Globalizations [https://www.tandfonline.com/rglo], *the* Journal of World-Systems Research [http://jwsr.pitt.edu/ojs/index.php/jwsr/issue/view/75] *and* Pambazuka News [https://www.pambazuka.org/]. *Additional essays and commentary can be found in these outlets.*

The idea of a Fifth International has been around for some time and the historical record is not encouraging. For the past few years I have been wrestling with an apparent contradiction in the work of all of us on the Left. On the one hand, our research demonstrates how powerful and successful consumerist capitalism and its integral system of 'nation-states' has been, never more so than in its current neoliberal/social democratic forms (by which I mean 'New Labour' in the UK and elsewhere). But despite the financial meltdowns in Asia and the EU/USA in the new millennium that were supposed to fatally weaken capitalist hegemony, the system seems chaotically stronger than ever. The transnational capitalist class has taken these setbacks in its stride.

On the other hand, we also argue that workers' movements all over the world can unite to challenge and overthrow the capitalist system. The very term 'International' implies that these revolutions will be organised within the frameworks of those thoroughly discredited 'nation-states' which work well for an increasingly smaller proportion of their populations. So, that's why I have lost faith (this word is deliberately chosen) in the idea of a Socialist International directed towards world revolution. The recent IPCC report on climate change indicates that the capitalist system has lost its way, with even more disastrous potential circumstances (rather fudged in the report). The only way out of this mess, the only chance of having a liveable planet for the generations to come (however utopian and unrealistic it sounds) is to organise small-scale socialist communities to create new forms of less destructive and less hierarchical economic and social relations. However unlikely, this is most likely to succeed community by community in something like producer-consumer cooperatives. My proposals are intended for the long-term and I am only too aware of the 'socialism or barbarism' argument. My critique of the Fifth International idea mainly focusses on the issue of 'what sort of socialism?'

The present dire state of civilization at the global level has been debated *ad nauseum*. Explanations abound – going all the way from flaws in human nature, to misinterpretations of the revealed word of 'God'. What we might call political-economy solutions to these problems are all variations on four main themes. First, capitalist ideologues argue that only free markets and more prosperity will eventually ensure peace and happiness for those who are prepared to work hard; second, caring capitalists and social democrats argue that capitalism can be reformed through welfare states to provide equality of opportunity, again for those who are prepared to work hard; third, progressive anti-capitalists (of various communist or socialist persuasions) argue that the capitalist state must be replaced by a workers' state, again to provide equality of opportunity for those who are prepared to work hard; and fourth, small groups of people argue that it is precisely capitalism (especially in its globalizing forms) and the hierarchical state apparatuses it has created that are at the root of the problem, and that we have to start thinking about what comes after capitalism and the state-form of society if we are to save the planet, eliminate poverty, and find happiness. The difficulty of achieving these worthy goals has gained extra urgency in the new millennium with the identification of the Anthropocene, human-driven (but not by all humans equally in our class-polarised world) potentially catastrophic change in the Earth system. Climate change is only one part of a series of interlocking eco-system problems that are threatening to destroy the conditions that support life on the planet, including human life.

I use the term 'hierarchic state' deliberately in a historically materialist sense to indicate the extent to which capitalism as a mode of production and a totalizing social system has colonised all actually existing states (even self-styled socialist or communist states). The hierarchic tendencies of officialdom and elected office are hard-wired into the state form of society. States cannot be anything but hierarchic and so attempts to reform states fundamentally from within are bound to fail. And this implies that attempts to reform capitalism fundamentally from within are also bound to fail. The best that progressive social movements and elected socialist state actors can do is to help provide spaces for those who wish to live outside the capitalist market and the state – to help and not to hinder them.

Most political-economy solutions for the failures of capitalism cannot deal with the two main fatal flaws of capitalism. The first is the crisis of class polarization – the rich get richer, the poor are always with us, those in the middle (the precariat) are increasingly insecure. The migrant 'crisis' (now being intensified by a looming crisis of 'climate refugees'), is a vivid reminder that the poor cannot necessarily be relied upon to put up with their misery passively forever in the places where they happen to be born. The second fatal flaw of capitalism is ecological unsustainability, now powerfully expressed in terms of the Anthropocene stage of the planet and its destructive fossil fuel driven growth economy. This is starkly exposed by Ian Angus in his book *Facing the Anthropocene* that connects the impetus of capitalist globalization with the very survival of human life on the planet – best theorised as ecocide. Though there are already several different interpretations of the Anthropocene (e.g. geological, materialist, idealist, feminist, postmodernist) most see it as a dire threat to humanity and the future of the planet. In my view the Anthropocene is mainly driven by the tremendous productive capacity of capitalist globalization and the 'culture-ideology of consumerism'. If the predictions of the Anthropocene scientists are correct we must start to think about what comes after capitalism in its various guises and how to achieve something better than capitalist globalization and the international system of hierarchical states that are locked into an endless cycle of growth obsessions and hot and cold wars.[1]

What is to be done?

Marx and then Lenin's answer to this question resulted in some defining moments of the 20th century. But there was always something perverse about the Marxist critique of state power as the executive committee of the capitalist class, and the eagerness with which so-called Communist revolutionaries seized and used state power. What it definitely did not lead to was the capture of power by the working class. The historical record, uneven as it is, strongly suggests that the dictatorship of the proletariat (however defined) cannot produce the withering away of the state. On the contrary, it usually led to a 'new class' of state bureaucrats and Soviet, Chinese and other profoundly undemocratic regimes. When 'communism' collapsed in the1990s as an alternative vision of social and economic progress, it seemed inevitable that what I and others have conceptualized as the transnational capitalist class (TCC) would consolidate power on a global scale. The TCC and its four complementary fractions of corporate, political, technical, and consumerist elites, drive capitalist globalization. The globalizing political fraction of the hierarchic states, working hand-in-glove with the rest of the TCC, are part of the problem, not the solution.

The values on which a socialist global society could be built already exist in principle, but are rarely to be seen in practice, precisely because they conflict with the necessities of capitalist globalization. This can be represented in a series of dichotomies: principles of teamwork and cooperation vs. practices of self-centred individualism and ruthless competition; principles of stewardship of the planet for the common good vs. reckless exploitation of nature for private profit; principles of international friendship and aid vs. practices of cynical diplomacy and imperialist exploitation; principles of genuine corporate social responsibility vs. practices of corporate crime and profiteering and principles of the dignity of labour and the revaluation of labour itself vs. practices of the 'race to the bottom' and class polarization. Reformers and revolutionaries have been trying to shore up socialist principles and practices for over a century, and though millions of people have been dragged out of poverty and hunger in some parts of the world, arguably the global situation today is as bad as it has ever been. That is why we have to abandon the hope of challenging the hegemonic alliance of capital with the state and look for other answers. Putting all our energies into either world socialist revolution or socialism in one country increasingly appear to be self-defeating strategies.

Alternatives to capitalist globalization

Is there a non-capitalist alternative to capitalist globalization? There is and a good place to start is by repeating the aphorism: 'It is easier to imagine the end of the world, than to imagine the end of capitalism'. Whoever actually said this first, it expresses a profound truth about the era of capitalist globalization. Theories of capitalist hegemony, from their origins in Marx, through Gramsci, Althusser (repressive/ideological state apparatuses), Marcuse and the culture industries thesis of the Frankfurt School certainly help to explain why it has been easier to imagine the end of the world than to imagine the end of capitalism. So, we have to begin again to think through what we once conceptualized as democratic socialism and what it might look like in the 21st century.

The power of capitalist hegemony today is so overwhelming (allied as it is with the military and police powers of states) that the only viable strategy for change is a process of negating, avoiding, and eventually consigning capitalism and the state to the dustbin of history. The digital revolution provides simultaneously powerful tools of capitalist exploitation and a means of changing the system. The transnational capitalist class, to put it bluntly, systematically subverts the emancipatory potential of generic globalization, by which I mean the electronic revolution, critical postcolonialisms, and new forms of cosmopolitanism. The electronic revolution could also contribute to dealing with one of the central structural problems of the state in capitalist society, namely the question of size. In 1973 E.F. Schumacher published a not-quite forgotten book, *Small is Beautiful: A Study of Economics as if People Mattered*, challenging many of the orthodoxies of capitalist and socialist economics, notably the obsession with growth. For this he was called a crank. Schumacher's response (on the BBC) to critics was characteristic: 'What's wrong with a crank? It's a small instrument, very simple, it does not involve great capital investment, it is a relatively non-violent technology, and it causes revolutions'.[2]

Huge transnational corporations and huge corporate states, serviced by huge professional and consumer goods and services organizations increasingly dominate the lives of people everywhere with destructive consequences at the individual, community, and planetary levels, so it seems obvious that smaller scale structures might possibly work better to enable people to live happier and more fulfilling lives. My vision of an alternative, radical, progressive, socialist globalization is based on networks of relatively small producer-consumer co-operatives (P-CC) co-operating at a variety of levels to accomplish a variety of societal tasks. Why producer and consumer cooperatives? This, I would argue, is the only way for us to re-connect with nature, to create communities where everyone assumes responsibility to a greater or lesser degree for all the necessities of life and a decent standard of living.

This will necessitate a double strategy: first to slow down capitalism as will inevitably happen if P-CCs succeed in ignoring the capitalist market in one sphere after another, in one place after another; and second to bring into existence a new mode of production based on the different principles and mentalities. We could call ways of thinking, writing and doing that contribute to these ends 'anarching'. P-CCs would begin in the production of food at the local level. Similar proposals in the past have been dismissed with the charge that it would represent a retreat into the new middle ages or new tribal communities, and so on. My answer to this is simple. The middle ages did not have the digital technology that P-CCs could call on, notably networking, ecologically sensitive and highly efficient food technologies, the possibilities of revolutionizing the production of machinery and tools opened up by alternative technologies, already being put into practice all over the world. The problem of barbarism does seem convincing as we look around the world today, but the creation of new mentalities through more empathetic biological and social parenting would help turn the 'tribes' from competitive, violent, and untrustworthy others into cooperating, peaceful, and trustworthy neighbours, near and far.

Prospects for change in the long-term

The creation of new mentalities is a project of many generations, a project that begins with damaged parents and communities gradually acquiring the insights and incentives to nurture children through new forms of upbringing and learning. This would include biological and social parenting, learning from existing communities where all adults accept at least some responsibility for all children. New generations will be less damaged. These children in their turn will nurture their own children to be even less damaged. The design of cooperative communities will play an important part in this process. Transformations in housing, transportation, nutrition, and other necessities of a decent life would free up space for everything that the capitalist market squeezes out or whose pleasures it compromises. The culture-ideology of consumerism has socialized populations all over the world to crave all the material rewards that capitalist consumerism flaunts. Better, more love-based parenting could help people to strive for other, less destructive, life goals and social structures to achieve them. Intrinsic to this change in mentalities is that it does not work only at the level of individuals or isolated family groups but at the level of communities and between communities.

Our present reality is capitalist globalization. How, then, could P-CCs be organized to release the emancipatory potential of generic globalization in a non-capitalist world? The simple and encouraging answer is that they would work, in the early stages of transition at least, much as millions of small-scale co-operative groups work at present in enclaves all over the world. The digital commons (e.g. the open source movement) already makes it possible for millions of like-minded people hungry for change to communicate across the globe for the common good. The viability of global networks of P-CCs rests on many untested assumptions. What would people eat? How would they learn? What would they do for healthcare? Who would provide the power to run the computers? How would they be safe? How would they deal with the anthropogenic degradation of all the eco-systems on which the viability of human survival depends? (This is not simply a question of 'climate change', often used as an ideological metonym for the Anthropocene). All this would depend on a multitude of people who now work in the private or public sectors, directly or indirectly, establishing their own self-managed organizations in their local communities producing food, organizing transport, setting up places of learning and transmission of skills, providing healthcare and running energy systems. Eventually, if these organizations proved successful, something like P-CCs would emerge. Some might be very large, capable of securing their own food and energy supplies. Others would be smaller and would need to be networked with others. It would be both futile and undemocratic to suggest that one size fits all.

States, of course, cannot be abolished overnight, though reconstructed political communities could create more genuinely democratizing forms of economic, social, and political organization to encourage and facilitate networks of P-CCs. The transition from the present capitalist-statist hegemony to a new form of society will be lengthy and problematic, but even the flawed forms of democracy that political systems throw up all over the world should provide openings for socialists to win elections and, at the very least, provide conditions that encourage those wishing to escape the capitalist market and the hierarchic state. Many existing progressive social movements at all levels will have an important part to play in the transition, but only if they seriously come to grips with the dead ends of the market and the hierarchic state. Not all, but most, radical social movements lose their edge the more closely they collaborate with the transnational capitalist class and organs of the hier-archic states, and those that do not usually find themselves isolated and ineffective. The inability of the Left to think through the withering away of the state has had its roots in pointless disputes and antagonisms between Marxists and Anarchists over the last two hundred years. To most people anar-chism is a frightening prospect, associated as it usually has been in the public mind with violence and disorder. The irony is that capitalism and the state have been responsible for far more violence and disorder, at home and abroad. Unless these perceptions change, capitalism and the hierarchic state will persist until they collapse under the stress of their own contradictions and threaten the end of human life on our planet.

While there is general agreement on the Left that we need to move beyond capitalism, the role of the state has always been contentious. In the *Communist Manifesto* Marx and Engels declared: 'In place of the old bourgeois society, with its classes and class antagonisms, we shall have an associ-ation, in which the free development of each is the condition for the free development of all.' The pressing question now is whether the socialist state guarantees the development of all or makes it impossible. My view is that any type of large-scale state makes it impossible because states, by their very nature are hierarchical and repressive to the majority of their populations. Without exception all communist and socialist revolutions either originated or became highly nationalistic in form and content. It is also worth noting that one of the central principles of the Paris Commune was the establishment of a Universal (not a French) Republic, forcing Marx to reconsider his analysis of the state.

People can change. Innovative socio-economic forms outside the capitalist market and the capi-talist state are emerging all over the world on a small scale but such initiatives struggle within the present global system. They struggle because the various modes of cooperation, noble as they are, exist within a sea of competitive capitalism and those who lead them are always faced with hard choices that jeopardise their survival in an inhospitable environment. However, there must be a point at which, in any society, the emancipatory potential of an increasing number of small-scale changes tips the balance, and communities organized along producer-consumer cooperative lines look like realistic alternatives to bourgeois society. Neoliberal ideologues argue that there is no alternative to capitalist globalization and, if we mean by this, the accumulation of material posses-sions for the better-off, they are probably correct. However, if human welfare and happiness are not measured in terms of material possessions, there are clearly better options, particularly if the very survival of human life in the Anthropocene epoch is at risk. If we refuse to believe capitalist (and statist) ideologues and start creating alternative forms of economic, political and cultural organiz-ation and these alternatives prove to be successful in their own terms, then the logic of the market and the hierarchic state can be refuted, undermined, or simply ignored. Capitalism and states will eventually wither away.

Growth, and degrowth

There is a large volume of research that is critical of many facets of capitalist society but not much of it seriously calls capitalism itself into question or tries to envision non-capitalist society. The dogma of ever-increasing growth, the mainstay of capitalist globalization, orthodox Marxism-Leninism, social democracy, and the developmental state must be challenged. A relatively new and revolution-ary idea that suggests such a critique is convivial degrowth, a theory-driven activist movement[3] that aims to decolonize the imaginary of growth (continuous economic growth as the ultimate good) and to establish degrowth (*decroissance* in its original French formulation) as the common-sense conception of a convivial future. This is expressed graphically as follows:[4]

DEGROWTH,
SIMPLY
DIFFERENT

MORE OF   SAME OF   LESS OF
THE SAME   THE SAME   THE SAME

GROWTH   STATIONARY   RECESSION
                 STATE

What would degrowth mean for a socialist P-CC community gradually withdrawing from the hierarchic state. First, the culture-ideology of consumerism would be replaced by a culture-ideology of human rights and responsibilities, prime among which would be a serious commitment to a decent, sustainable standard of living for all. It would certainly mean that the rich would become less wealthy and the poor would become richer in material possessions – and everyone would benefit in non-material riches, eventually. But for this process to start, all the existing critiques of capitalism must abandon the hope that progressive alternatives can thrive by directly challenging the market. For example, in the first instance an emerging P-CC would have the goal of producing its own food with its own resources, providing sustenance to its members free in a non-monetized local economy. This would entail that some members of the community continue to engage in paid employment in the capitalist labour market, supporting the rest in their gradual transition to self-sufficiency in food. It would also entail democratically elected local socialist politicians sympathetic to these goals, making it as easy as possible for them to be achieved, for example by releasing parcels of state-owned land (or legislating for the release of privately-owned unused or under-used land) for the production of food outside the capitalist market.

Revisiting anarchist thinking on the state and hierarchy

In his book on non-violent anarchist thought and practice, *Anarchist Seeds Beneath the Snow*, David Goodway quotes Colin Ward:

> a society which organizes itself without authority, is always in existence, like a seed beneath the snow buried under the weight of the state and its bureaucracy, capitalism and its waste, privilege and its injustices, nationalism and its suicidal loyalties, religious differences and their superstitious separatism … [non-violent anarchism] far from being a speculative vision of a future society … is a description of a mode of human organization, rooted in the experience of everyday life, which operates side by side with, and in spite of, the dominant authoritarian trends of our society.

Goodway continues: 'Acceptance of this central insight is not only extraordinarily liberating intellectually but has strictly realistic and practical consequences'. As Ward says: 'anarchism is already partially in existence … humans are naturally cooperative … current societies and institutions, however capitalist and individualist, would completely fall apart without the integrating powers, even if unvalued, of mutual aid and federation'. If we ever got to a stage in which networks of P-CCs started to emerge and began to work outside the capitalist market and the hierarchic national and local state then we can assume they would be peopled by those who already strive to live lives according to the values of socialist communities. Prime amongst these values would be the belief that we must abolish money and all modes of exchange that sanctify what Marx identified as socially necessary labour time (SNLT) – the root of capitalist exploitation. If the goal is to create communities based on the principle 'from each according to capacity, to each according to need', then it follows that there will be no money, no exchange on the basis of equivalences, and no rationing. People will take what they need. They will give what they can. Adults and children will consider this normal; all will participate in the production of food and the other necessities of life. People will work out for themselves what is the best way to live in communities that are respectful of natural limits and the rest of the world.

Notes

1. For an elaboration of how the mass media report the Anthropocene largely in terms of 'reassurance narratives' consistent with the emerging idea of the 'good' Anthropocene, see Sklair (ed) *The Anthropocene in Global Media: Neutralizing the Risk* (Routledge, forthcoming 2020).
2. http://www.bbc.co.uk/programmes/b079njxm.
3. See https://www.degrowth.info/en/dim/degrowth-in-movements/.
4. Image courtesy of Bàrbara Castro Urío, (http://www.labarbara.net/?page_id=1149).

Disclosure statement

No potential conflict of interest was reported by the author.

Race-class-gender articulation and the Fifth International

Biko Agozino

ABSTRACT

The proposal for a Fifth International to be organized immediately is a call that has been made many times in the past without being fully actualized (League, 2008). The revival of this call by Samir Amin before his death deserves serious consideration in honor of his lifelong dedication to scholar-activism in the interest of revolutionary causes (Amin, 2018). To make a new international successful, the failures of the previous internationals should be studied with a view of avoiding the pitfalls that made them crumble. This reflection will focus on a close reading of the call by Samir Amin to see if it embodies some contradictions that may imperil the cause and course of a new international just like the previous ones.

Samir Amin, a leading scholar and co-founder of the world-systems tradition, died on August 12, 2018. Just before his death, he published, along with close allies, a call for 'workers and the people' to establish a 'fifth international' [https://www.pambazuka.org/global-south/letter-intent-inaugural-meeting-international-workers-and-peoples] *to coordinate support to progressive movements. To honor Samir Amin's invaluable contribution to world-systems scholarship, we are pleased to present readers with a selection of essays responding to Amin's final message for today's anti-systemic movements. This forum is being co-published between* Globalizations [https://www.tandfonline.com/rglo], *the* Journal of World-Systems Research [http://jwsr.pitt.edu/ojs/index.php/jwsr/issue/view/75] *and* Pambazuka News [https://www.pambazuka.org/]. *Additional essays and commentary can be found in these outlets.*

Introduction

The First International Workingmen's Association was formed partly to oppose calls from the cotton capitalists for Britain to enter the American Civil War on the side of the slave-holders (Shraffenberger, 2019). Marx led the opposition from the start of the war by refocusing his opinion editorials that started in 1852 by explaining the European class conflicts to Americans but shifted to the analysis of the war against slavery in the *New York Tribune* in support of the Union Army (Marx, 1852–1862). Marx drafted the constitution of the First International and wrote the congratulatory 'address to the American people' on their re-election of Abraham Lincoln (Marx, 1864). The First International threatened a general strike if Britain joined the pro-slavery rebellion against the United States. They celebrated the victory of the anti-slavery forces in 1865 (Zimmerman, 2013). In *Capital*, there are hundreds of references to the slave, to Africans, the Negro, and to race with clear indication to workers of the world that the abolition of slavery was the precondition for the abolition of 'wage slavery' (Agozino, 2014). C. L. R. James understood this following his study of the errors of the fore-runners of the Third International in his (James, 1937) treatise on *World Revolution*, leading him to declare a year later in *The Black Jacobins*, that the Haitian revolutionaries were 'closer to a modern proletariat than any group of workers in existence at the time' (James, 1938, p. 86). Marx used slavery in two senses, pre-feudal slavery in his earlier writings and industrialized capitalist slavery in *Das Kapital* (Marx, 1867).

For instance, Marx observed that the struggle for the 40-hour week was not won until slavery was ended (Marx, 1867). In other words, the First International was organized against class exploitation of workers in articulation with the struggle against the oppression of nationalities and racial groups and in articulation against gender oppression, despite the male title of Workingmen's Association. The departure from the race-class-gender articulation or intersectionality model that Marx envisaged by the organizers of subsequent internationals may be part of the reasons why the organizational aims were not sustained. That error first appeared in the First International in the sense that the members were all white and all male with the exception of the son-in-law of Marx, Paul Lafargue, who was born in Cuba to a French man and an African woman (Lafargue, 1883), apparently, his wife, Eleanor Marx, was not a member despite being a revolutionary leader in her own rights (Marx, 1891); and the case of a woman, Harriet Law, who wrote to the Association about women's rights and was invited to join the International Workingmen's Association after a debate about the suitability of her membership (Schwarz, 2010).

The call by Samir Amin and articulation theory

By calling for two slots of invitation to be reserved for Africa in the Fifth International, Samir Amin may have been trying to prevent the racist contradictions of Eurocommunism but he still left the gender contradiction unaddressed. Furthermore, by recommending only one slot for Asia and two for 'the United States and the Anglo-Saxon world' as recognized regions, the over-representation of white privilege is likely to prevail contrary to the numerical and communist party track records of China and India which deserve more than one slot each, just like Africa. Given also the internationalist giants that have emerged from the Caribbean, including Cuba, with an impressive record of revolutionary successes, the region should also be recognized as an organizational region of the Fifth International. Moreover, recognizing South America, North America, and Australia as regions does not guarantee that Indigenous Peoples would be adequately represented by white settler colonialists and so Indigenous Peoples deserve to be brought into the International on their own terms.

The split in the First International between the anarcho-syndicalists who wished to focus on economic struggles alone and the Marxists who emphasized the organization of social democratic parties to fight for state power in the interest of all the oppressed is a lesson for those organizing for a Fifth International. Samir Amin alluded to this when he observed in his letter that the Fifth International would also support communities that are struggling against oppressive state power. This implies that the concern of the International would not be class struggles alone in isolation from the struggles against racism and sexism simply because class exploitation is not experienced in isolation from racism or ethnic oppression and sexism. This point needs to be emphasized because it was one of the original concerns of Marx that was relatively lost by Eurocommunism or by those that Derrida called Marx and Sons (Derrida, 2002).

Amilcar Cabral (1972), Walter Rodney (1972), Frantz Fanon (1963), C. L. R. James (1938), and Stuart Hall (1980, 2016) have emphasized that it will be ridiculous for any crude economist to organize the resistance against apartheid, for example, simply and exclusively from the standpoint of class struggles and without the race-class-gender articulation, disarticulation and rearticulation of social relations in societies structured in dominance. As Cabral (1972), who like Fanon, James and Hall, was married to a European, explained to African Americans who asked what they could do to support the struggles in Africa:

> We are not racists. We are fundamentally and deeply against any kind of racism. Even when people are subjected to racism we are against racism from those who have been oppressed by it. In our opinion – not from dreaming but from a deep analysis of the real condition of the existence of mankind and the division of societies – racism is a result of certain circumstances. It is not eternal in any latitude in the world. It is not the result of historical and economic conditions. And we cannot answer racism with racism. It is not possible. In our country, despite some racist manifestations by the Portuguese, we are not fighting against the Portuguese people or whites. We are fighting for the freedom of our people – to free our people and to allow them to be able to love any kind of human being. You cannot love when you are a slave. It is very difficult. In combating racism we don't make progress if we combat the people themselves. We have to combat the causes of racism. If a bandit comes into my house and I have a gun I cannot shoot the shadow of this bandit. I have to shoot the bandit. Many people lose energy and effort, and make sacrifices combating shadows. We have to combat the material reality that produces the shadow. If we cannot change the light that is one cause of the shadow, we can at least change the body. It is important to avoid confusion between the shadow and the body that projects the shadow. We are encouraged by the fact that each day more of our people, here and in Africa, realise this reality. This reinforces our confidence in our final victory. (Cabral, 1972)

It is not enough for the Fifth International to call on Workers of the World to Unite without questioning the extent to which racism, imperialism and patriarchy divide the working class and weaken the struggle to end exploitation as Vladimir Lenin (1917), W. E. B. Du Bois (1935), Kwame Nkrumah (1965), Mao Tse-tung (1963), and Fidel Castro (1966) warned. As Castro put this:

> What the peoples have most in common to unite the people of three continents and of all the world today is the struggle against imperialism (applause); the struggle against colonialism and neocolonialism, the struggle against racism and, in short, all the phenomena which are the contemporary expression we call imperialism, whose center, axis, and principal support of Yankee imperialism. (Castro, 1966)

Harold Wolpe wanted to find out why apartheid imposed cheap wages on exploited mineworkers in South Africa (Wolpe, 1972). He came to the conclusion that the capitalist economy of apartheid was not separate from the pre-capitalist economy or what Cheikh Anta Diop identified as the African Mode of Production (Diop, 1981), similar to what Marx called the Asiatic Mode of Production (Marx, 1843). Thus, the capitalist mode of production is articulated with the pre-capitalist mode of production in such a way that the exploited mineworkers shared their cheap wages with their families in the homelands while the women and children in the homelands shared in having their labor exploited as domestic servants in the homes of white farmers to support the meager earnings of the migrant workers.

It is not only the workers who were exploited since even the peasants cried out that they had been exploited and oppressed a great deal, according to the Arusha Declaration of Julius Nyerere (TANU, 1967). Wolpe applied the theory of articulation by Marx from *Capital* to explain this. Stuart Hall (1980) abstracted the theory and applied it to the racist-sexist-imperialist exploitation of the working class, ethnic minorities and women all over the world, including in the metropole where authoritarian populism thrives by mobilizing the votes of working class people against their own interests, recruiting them to wage war against the working people around the world and empowering them to police the poor at home militarily, by paying them what Du Bois (1935) called the psychological wages of white supremacy. Hall concluded that this calls for a strategy of coalition-building and alliance formation by the international movement against capitalist exploitation, racist oppression and patriarchal domination worldwide.

Critical reflections on the call

With all due respect and support for the call, it appears to me that Samir Amin erred by stating that the first sign of weakness in the previous internationals was due to:

> The extreme fragmentation of the struggles, whether at the local or world level, which are always specific and conducted in particular places and subject-matters (ecology, women's rights, social services, community demands, etc.) The rare campaigns conducted at the national or even world level have not had any significant success in that they have not forced any changes of the policies being carried out by those in power. Many of these struggles have been absorbed by the system and foster the illusion that it is possible to reform it. (Amin, 2018)

The above formulation is deeply flawed because there is evidence that the ecological movement, women's movement, civil rights movement, and community demands for the legalization of marijuana, for instance, have won significant policy changes from the lumpen bourgeoisie worldwide. Instead of seeing these as separate struggles that are doomed to failure, the Fifth International should aim to exercise hegemony over them by offering intellectual and moral leadership through alliance and coalition building the way that the South African Communist Party did in the anti-apartheid struggle (SACP, 2012).

Samir Amin's letter rightly warned against the dangers of fracturing the Fifth International the way that the previous ones were fractured by internal contradictions. However, when he included the struggle against patriarchy or for women's rights among the possible fracture points in the International, he made a serious mistake that should be guarded against. The struggle against the oppression of women is indeed a core part of the struggle against all forms of oppression given that the oppressed women are our mothers and grandmothers, our wives and co-workers, our daughters and our girl-friends, our comrades.

There is no right that would be guaranteed to women that would be a threat to the working class and that was why Marx and Engels were keen to organize against the oppression of women at a time that the structural conditions did not allow women to participate in large numbers in the First International (Brown, 2014). Today, no serious international organization against oppression can afford to marginalize the struggles of women and Indigenous Peoples for fear of fragmentation. The Fifth International must strategically embrace the struggles against patriarchy and racism and structurally aim for gender parity and racial diversity among the officers of the International to make it more sustainable.

While warning the Fifth International against the dangers of fragmentation, Samir Amin appeared quite ready to fragment Africa by carving North Africa or the Mediterranean world out of Africa as one of the regions to be given a quota representation at the initial meeting of the international. He also appeared to be clannish by nominating Tunisia as a possible host of the initial meeting whereas South Africa has one of the oldest communist parties in the world (SACP, 2012) that happens to remain in a ruling coalition with the African National Congress, deserving more of the honor to host such a meeting on African soil in spite of the inevitable contradictions arising from the involvement in what Joe Slovo called the national democratic revolution against apartheid (Slovo, 1988). Given that the African states are organized as the African Union Commission without dichotomizing North Africa from what is pejoratively called Sub-Saharan Africa, according to Herbert Ekwe-Ekwe (2012), the Fifth International should be supportive of the Pan African movement (Agozino, 2017) that has been going on for almost as long as the International itself. In this direction, the sixth region of the African Union Commission, the African Diaspora also deserves a seat at the table of the Fifth International.

The call by Samir Amin for the invitation to the initial meeting of the International to be limited to a few leaders of about ten or twelve flies in the face of the fact that the First International was reputed to have had as many as 8 million members. Twelve leaders in a room somewhere are engaged in a seminar and not necessarily organizing an International Movement. While endorsing the strategic call by Amin for leaders to be recognized, it may be better to allow a million leaders to emerge from local to the global levels, organically as Gramsci would have preferred (Gramsci, 2000).

Conclusion

The strategy for a successful International should learn from the First International that organizing locally to oppose oppression globally is the way to go. Let the Fifth International start by simultaneously organizing a social democratic party in every locality in the world and let those parties elect their delegates to attend future conventions of the Fifth International. The clarion call of Samir Amin should be extended beyond his 'Dear comrades, Dear activists, Dear workers' to include students, the unemployed, farmers, women, and Dear despised Africans and Indigenous Peoples.

Finally, we may need to update the Internationale song (Pottier, 1871). It is dated with the Paris Commune and it is culturally specific to the extent that the rendition does not capture the mood of the Hip Hop generations around the world. Let the Fifth International commission composers and artists to come up with a new song for the current era. The new song will be sensitive to critical race-class-gender articulation theory and praxis instead of simply rallying the working class that has been bribed with psychological wages of whiteness and weakened by anti-union policies. We may need to jazz up the lyrics by adding opposition to white supremacy (which is a threat to all) and imperialist patriarchy so that we may sound more convincing when the chorus reiterates the refrain,

The International working class

Shall be the human race!

Disclosure statement

No potential conflict of interest was reported by the author.

References

Agozino, B. (2014). The Africana paradigm in *Capital*: The debts of Karl Marx to people of African descent. *Review of African Political Economy, 41*(140), 172–184.

Agozino, B. (2017, May 11). Draft platform of Africana mass party. *Pambazuka News*. Retrieved from https://www.pambazuka.org/democracy-governance/draft-platform-africana-mass-party

Amin, S. (2018, July 3). Letter of intent for an inaugural meeting of the international of workers and peoples. *IDEAs network*.

Brown, H. (2014, June 1). Marx on gender and the family: A summary. *The Monthly Review*. Retrieved from https://monthlyreview.org/2014/06/01/marx-on-gender-and-the-family-a-summary/

Cabral, A. (1972). Connecting the struggles: An informal chat with Black Americans. Reproduced in *Pambazuka News*, September 26, 2010. Retrieved from https://www.pambazuka.org/governance/connecting-struggles-informal-chat-black-americans

Castro, F. (1966, January 15). *At the closing session of the rricontinental conference*. Havana. Retrieved from https://www.marxists.org/history/cuba/archive/castro/1966/01/15.htm

Derrida, J. (2002). *Marx and sons*. Paris: Presses Universitaires de France.

Diop, C. A. (1981). *Civilization or barbarism? An authentic anthropology*. Paris: Presence Africaine.

Du Bois, W. E. B. (1935). *Black reconstruction in America: An essay on the role which black folk played in the attempt to reconstruct of democracy in America, 1860–1880*. New York, NY: Harcourt, Bruce. Retrieved from http://ouleft.org/wp-content/uploads/2012/blackreconstruction.pdf

Ekwe-Ekwe, H. (2012, January, 18). What exactly does 'sub-Sahara Africa mean? *Pambazuka News*.

Fanon, W. (1963). *The wretched of the earth*. New York, NY: Grove Books.

Gramsci, A. (2000). *The gramsci reader: Selected writings 1916–1935*. (D. Fiorgacs, Ed.). New York, NY: New York University. Retrieved from http://people.duke.edu/~dainotto/Texts/GramsciReader.pdf

Hall, S. (1980). Race, articulation and societies structured in dominance. In UNESCO (Ed.), *Sociological theories: Race and colonialism* (pp. 305–345). Paris: UNESCO.

Hall, S. (2016). *Cultural studies 1983: A theoretical history*. Durham, NC: Duke University Press.

James, C. L. R. (1937). *World revolution 1917–1936: The rise and fall of the communist international*. London: Furnell and Sons. Retrieved from https://www.marxists.org/archive/james-clr/works/world/index.htm

James, C. L. R. (1938). *The Black Jacobins: Tussaint L'ouverture and the San Domingo revolution*. London: Secker & Warburg.

Lafargue, P. (1883). *The right to be lazy and other studies*. Saint Pelagie Prison, Charles Ker, Co-Operative. Retrieved from https://www.marxists.org/archive/lafargue/1883/lazy/

League of the Fifth Internationalists. (2008). *Who are the fifth internationalists?* Retrieved from http://www.fifthinternational.org/about-us

Lenin, V. (1917). *Imperialism: The highest stage of capitalism*. Moscow: Progress Press, 1963. Retrieved from https://www.marxists.org/archive/lenin/works/1916/imp-hsc/

Marx, E. (1891) *The working class movement in America*. With Edward Aveling. London: Swan Sonnenschein & Co.

Marx, K. (1843). *Critique of Hegel's philosophy of right*. Cambridge: Cambridge University Press, 1970.

Marx, K. (1852–1862). *Articles in New York Daily Tribune*. Retrieved from https://www.marxists.org/archive/marx/works/subject/newspapers/new-york-tribune.htm

Marx, K. (1864). *Address of the international working men's association to Abraham Lincoln, president of the United States of America*. Presented to U.S. Ambassador Charles Francis Adams January 28, 1865. Retrieved from https://www.marxists.org/archive/marx/iwma/documents/1864/lincoln-letter.htm

Marx, K. (1867). *Das Kapital*. Berlin: Variag von Otto Meisener.

Nkrumah, K. (1965). *Neocolonialism: The last stage of imperialism*. London: Thomas Nelson & Sons. Retrieved from https://www.marxists.org/subject/africa/nkrumah/neo-colonialism/

Pottier, E. (1871). *The international*. Paris. Retrieved from https://www.marxists.org/history/ussr/sounds/lyrics/international.htm

Rodney, W. (1972). *How Europe underdeveloped Africa*. London: Bogle L'Ouverture.

SACP. (2012). *The South African road to socialism: The 13th congress political programme of the SACP, 2012–2017*. Pretoria: SACP. Retrieved from https://www.sacp.org.za/docs/docs/2012/draftpol2012.pdf

Schwarz, L. (2010, July 20). Remembering Harriet Law. *Workers' Liberty*. Retrieved from https://www.webarchive.org.uk/wayback/archive/20100720113437/http:/www.workersliberty.org/node/8793

Shraffenberger, D. (2019). Marx and the American Civil War. *International Socialist Review*, Issue 80: Features. Retrieved from https://isreview.org/issue/80/karl-marx-and-american-civil-war

Slovo, J. (1988). *The South African working class and the national democratic revolution*. Pretoria: SACP. Retrieved from https://www.marxists.org/subject/africa/slovo/1988/national-democratic-revolution.htm

TANU. (1967). *The Arusha declaration and TANU's policy on socialism and self reliance*. Dar es Salaam: Tanzania. Published by the Publicity Section, TANU, Dar es Salaam.

Tse-tung, M. (1963, August 12). Statement in support of the American Negroes in their just struggles against racial discrimination by U.S. Imperialism. *Peking Review*, 9(33). Retrieved from https://www.marxists.org/subject/china/peking-review/1966/PR1966-33h.htm

Wolpe, H. (1972). Capitalism and cheap labour-power in South Africa: From segregation to apartheid. *Economy & Society*, 1(4), 425–456.

Zimmerman, A. (2013, July 2). The Civil War was a victory for Marx and working-class radicals. *The New York Times*. Retrieved from https://www.nytimes.com/roomfordebate/2013/07/02/who-won-the-civil-war/the-civil-war-was-a-victory-for-marx-and-working-class-radicals?module=ArrowsNav&contentCollection=undefined&action=keypress&region=FixedLeft&pgtype=undefined

Forging a diagonal instrument for the global left: the vessel

Rebecca Álvarez and Christopher Chase-Dunn

ABSTRACT
This article takes up Samir Amin's challenge to rethink the issue of global political organization by proposing the building of a diagonal political organization for the Global Left that would link local, national and world regional and global networks and prefigurational communities to coordinate contention for power in the world-system during the next few decades of the 21st century. The World Social Forum (WSF) process needs to be reinvented for the current period of rising neo-fascist and populist reactionary nationalism and to foster the emergence of a capable instrument that can confront and contend with the global power structure of world capitalism and aid local and national struggles. This will involve overcoming the fragmentation of progressive movements that have been an outcome of the rise of possessive individualism, the precariat, and social media. We propose a holistic approach to organizing a vessel for the global left based on struggles for climate justice, human rights, anti-racism, queer rights, feminism, sharing networks, peace alliances, taking back the city, progressive nationalism and confronting and defeating neo-fascism and new forms of conservative populism.

Samir Amin, a leading scholar and co-founder of the world-systems tradition, died on August 12, 2018. Just before his death, he published, along with close allies, a call for 'workers and the people' to establish a 'fifth international' [https://www.pambazuka.org/global-south/letter-intent-inaugural-meeting-international-workers-and-peoples] to coordinate support to progressive movements. To honor Samir Amin's invaluable contribution to world-systems scholarship, we are pleased to present readers with a selection of essays responding to Amin's final message for today's anti-systemic movements. This forum is being co-published between Globalizations [https://www.tandfonline.com/rglo], the Journal of World-Systems Research [http://jwsr.pitt.edu/ojs/index.php/jwsr/issue/view/75] and Pambazuka News [https://www.pambazuka.org/]. Additional essays and commentary can be found in these outlets.

Social movements have been important drivers of social change since the Stone Age. They both reproduce and alter social structures and institutions. In this essay, we use the world-systems perspective to examine the possibilities for increasing the cohesiveness and capability of progressive global social movements. The comparative evolutionary world-systems perspective studies the ways that waves of social movements have driven the rise of more complex and more hierarchical human societies over the past millennia. A long-run historical and global perspective is helpful for comprehending the current moment and for devising political strategies that can help mitigate the problems that must be addressed in the 21st century so that humanity can move toward a more just, peaceful and sustainable global future. The contemporary world-system is entering another era that is similar in many ways to the 'age of extremes' that occurred in the first half of the 20th century (Hobsbawm, 1994). Devising a helpful political strategy for the Global Left requires that we understand the similarities and differences between the current period and the first half of the 20th century. It also requires that we understand the cultures of the movements and counter-movements that have emerged in the last few decades, as well as their structural organizations, which are critical for movement success. The current period is daunting and dangerous, but it is also a period of great opportunity for moving humanity toward a qualitatively different and improved world society.[1]

The global social justice movement and the World Social Forum process

The global social justice movement that emerged beginning in the 1990s with the regional successes of the Zapatistas in Southern Mexico formed in response to the neoliberal globalization project. The Pink Tide that followed was the advent of leftist-populist political regimes in most Latin American countries based on movements against the neoliberal structural adjustment programs promoted by the International Monetary Fund (Chase-Dunn, Morosin, & Álvarez, 2015). In 2001 the World Social Forum (WSF) was founded as a reaction to the exclusivity of the neoliberal World Economic Forum. Its purpose was to provide a global venue for popular progressive movements that were opposed to the neoliberal globalization project. The founding conferences were held in Porto Alegre, Brazil with the support of the Brazilian Workers Party who had just won the presidency under the leadership of Ignacio de Lula Silva, a former auto worker. The WSF adopted the slogan 'Another World Is Possible' to counter Margaret Thatcher's claim that there was no alternative to neoliberal globalization. The WSF held most of its global meetings in the Global South[2] but also sponsored important local and national meetings in all the world regions. This was an important venue for the emerging New Global Left and the global justice movement, but it did not include all of the movements of the Left (see below). It was intended to be a venue for activists from grass roots social movements to collaborate with one another.

The social forum process eventually spread to most regions of the world. Just a few months after the first annual event in 2001, the World Social Forum's International Council approved a 14-item Charter of Principles. It identified the intended use of the forum space by 'groups and movements of civil society that are opposed to neo-liberalism and to domination of the world by capital and any form of imperialism' (World Social Forum Charter of Principles, 2001). The Charter did not permit participation by those who wanted to attend as representatives of organizations that were engaged in, or that advocated, armed struggle. Nor were governments, political parties or churches supposed to send representatives to the meetings. There was a great emphasis on diversity and on horizontal, as opposed to hierarchical, forms of organization. The use of the Internet for communication and mobilization made it possible for broad coalitions and loosely knit networks of grass roots movement activists to engage in collective action projects.

The participants in the social forum process engaged in a manifesto/charter-writing frenzy as those who sought a more organized approach to confronting global capitalism and neoliberalism attempted to formulate consensual goals and to put workable coalitions together (Wallerstein, 2007).

One issue that was debated was whether the World Social Forum should itself formulate a political program and take formal stances on issues. A survey of 625 attendees at the World Social Forum meeting in Porto Alegre, Brazil in 2005 asked whether the WSF should remain an open space or should take political stances. Almost exactly half of the respondents favored the open space idea (Chase-Dunn et al., 2008). Thus, trying to change the WSF Charter to allow for a formal political program would have been very divisive.

But this was deemed not to be necessary. The WSF Charter also encouraged the formation of new political organizations. Those participants who wanted to form new coalitions and organizations were free to act, as long as they did not do so in the name of the WSF as a whole. The Assembly of Social Movements and other groups issued calls for global action and political manifestoes in Social Forum meetings at the both the global and national levels. Meeting in Bamako, Mali in 2006 a group of participants issued a manifesto entitled 'the Bamako Appeal' at the beginning of the meeting. The Bamako Appeal was a call for a global united front against neoliberalism and United States neo-imperialism (see Sen, Kumar, Bond, & Waterman, 2007). Samir Amin, the famous Marxist economist and co-founder of the world-system perspective (along with Immanuel Wallerstein, Andre Gunder Frank and Giovanni Arrighi), wrote a short essay entitled 'Toward a fifth international?' in which he briefly outlined the history of the first four internationals (Amin, 2008).[3] Peter Waterman (2006) proposed a 'global labor charter' and a coalition of women's groups meeting at the World Social Forum produced a feminist global manifesto that tried to overcome divisive North/South issues (Moghadam, 2005; Moghadam & Kaftan, 2019).[4]

There has always been a tension within the global left regarding antiglobalization versus the idea of an alternative progressive form of globalization. Samir Amin (1990) and Waldon Bello (2002) are important socialist advocates of deglobalization and delinking of the Global South from the Global North in order to protect against neo-imperialism and to make possible self-reliant and egalitarian development. Alter-globalization advocates an egalitarian world society that is integrated but without exploitation and domination. The alter-globalization project has been studied and articulated by Geoffrey Pleyers (2011) as an 'uneasy convergence' of largely horizontalist autonomous and independent activist groups and more institutionalist actors like intellectuals and NGOs. In our proposal for a way forward for the Global Left we advocate combining horizontalism and capable coordination in an instrument that can support and defend egalitarian projects and communities and struggle effectively against the power of reactionary states, firms and populist movements.

The culture of the world revolution of 20xx

There was an impasse in the global justice movement between those who wanted to move toward a global united front that could mobilize a strong coalition against the powers that be, and those who preferred local prefigurative horizontalist actions and horizontalist network forms of organization that renounce organizational hierarchy and refuse to participate in 'normal' political activities such as elections and lobbying. Prefigurationism is the idea that small groups can intentionally organize social relations in ways that can provide the seeds of transformation to a more desirable form of future human society. Horizontalism abjures hierarchy in organizations. It was inspired by Robert Michels's (1968 [1915]) observation that all organizations eventually become conservative because the leadership ends up mainly trying to defend their own interests and the survival of the organization. The natural history of parties and social movement organizations is to adapt to the existing exigencies of the world-system by giving up on revolutionary aspirations.

These horizontalist political stances had been inherited from the anti-authoritarian and anti-bureaucratic New Left movements of the world revolution of 1968. The New Left of 1968 embraced direct democracy, attacked bureaucratic organizations and was resistant to the building of new formal organizations that could act as instruments of revolution (Arrighi, Hopkins, & Wallerstein, 1989

[2012]). Institutions that had been instruments of revolutionary change and challengers to existing power structures were thought to have become sclerotic defenders of the status quo when they got old.

This resistance to institutionalized politics and contention for state power has also been a salient feature of the world revolution taking place today. It is based on a critique of the practices of earlier world revolutions in which labor unions and political parties became bogged down in short-term and self-interested struggles that were seen to have reinforced and reproduced the global capitalism and the interstate system. This rejection of formal organization is reflected in the charter of the World Social Forum as discussed above. And the same elements were strongly present in the Occupy movement as well as in most of the popular revolts of the Arab Spring (Mason, 2013).

Paul Mason's (2013)[5] analysis contends that the social structural basis for horizontalism and anti-formal organization, beyond the disappointment with the outcomes of the struggles carried out by the Old Left, was due to the presence of a large number of middle-class students as activists in the movements. The world revolution of 1968[6] was led mainly by college students who had emerged on the world stage with the global expansion of higher education since World War II. John W. Meyer (2009) explained the student revolt and the subsequent lowering of the voting age as another extension of citizenship to new and politically unincorporated groups demanding to be included, analogous to the earlier revolts and incorporations of men of no property and women.

Mason points out the similarities (and differences) with the world revolution of 1848, in which many of the activists were educated but underemployed students. He also argues that the composition of participation in the current world revolution has been heavily composed of highly educated young people who are facing the strong likelihood that they will not be able to find jobs commensurate with their skills and certification levels. Many of these 'graduates with no future' have gone into debt to finance their educations, and they are alienated from politics as usual and enraged by the failure of global capitalism to continue the expansion of middle-class jobs. These graduates can be considered part of Guy Standing's (2014) 'precariat', as they are increasingly forced to participate in the gig economy with little hope of future stable employment. Highly educated young people share an uncertain economic future with poor workers across the globe which could produce a transnational alliance of globalized precariats. Mason also points out that the urban poor, especially in the Global South, and workers in the Global North whose livelihoods have been attacked by globalization were important elements in the revolts that occurred in the Middle East, Spain, Greece and Turkey. Mason also stresses the importance of the Internet and social media for allowing disaffected young people to organize and coordinate large protests. He sees the 'freedom to tweet' as an important element in a new level of individual freedom that has been an important driver of these middle-class graduates who enjoy confronting the powers-that-be in mass demonstrations. This new individual freedom is cited as another reason why the activists in the global justice movement have been reticent to develop their own organizations and to participate in legitimate forms of political activity such as electoral politics.

But Mason and other participant/observers in the global justice movement somewhat overemphasize the extent to which the movement has been incoherent regarding goals and shared perspectives. Surveys of attendees at both world-level and national-level Social Forums have found a relatively stable multicentric network of movement themes in which a set of more central movements serve as links to all the other movements based on the reported identification of activists with movements (Chase-Dunn & Kaneshiro, 2009). All the twenty-seven movement themes used in the surveys were connected to the larger network by means of co-activism, so there was a single linked network without subcliques (Chase-Dunn & Kaneshiro, 2009, Figures 1–3). This multicentric network was quite stable across venues.[7] This suggests that there has been a fairly similar structure of network connections among movements that is global in scope and that the global-level network of movements is also very similar to the network that exists among Social Forum activists from grassroots movements within the U.S. (Chase-Dunn, Fenelon, Hall, Breckenridge-Jackson, & Herrera, 2019). The central cluster of movement themes to which all the other movements were linked included human rights; anti-racism; environmentalism, feminism, peace/anti-war, anti-corporate and alternative globalization.

Whereas the Global Left contained both anti-globalizationists who advocated greater local autonomy (Amin, 1990; Bello, 2002) as well as those who favored an alternative and more egalitarian form of globalization (Pleyers, 2011); the whole issue of anti-globalization has taken a turn with the rise of right wing populism and hypernationalism supported to a great extent by some who were losers in the neoliberal globalization project.

Justice globalism as a discourse

An organizational structure that can gain the allegiance of large numbers of activists, especially young ones, will need to consider the culture of the Global Left that has emerged since the World Revolution of 1968 by reviewing the findings of two careful studies.

Manfred Steger, James Goodman, and Erin K. Wilson (2013) presented the results of a systematic study of the political ideas employed by forty-five NGOs and social movement organizations associated with the International Council of the World Social Forum. Using a modified form of morphological discourse analysis developed by Michael Freeden (2003) for studying political ideologies, Steger, Goodman and Wilson analyzed texts (web sites, press releases and declarations) and conducted interviews to examine the key concepts, secondary concepts and overall coherence of the political ideas expressed by these organizations as proponents of 'justice globalism'.

The key concepts of justice globalism extracted by Steger et al. (2013: Table 2.1 pp. 28–29) are:

- participatory democracy,
- transformative rather than incremental change,
- equality of access to resources and opportunities,
- social justice,
- universal human rights,
- global solidarity among workers, farmers and marginalized peoples, and
- ecological sustainability

More detailed meanings of each of these concepts have emerged in an on-going dialectical struggle with market globalism (neoliberalism). Steger et al. discuss each of these and evaluate how much consensus exists across the forty-five movement organizations they studied. They find a large degree of consensus, but their results also reveal a lot of on-going contestation among the activists in these organizations regarding the definitions and applications of these concepts.

For example, though most of the organizations seem to favor one or another form of participatory democracy, there was awareness of some of the problems produced by an overemphasis on horizontalist processes of participation and on-going debates about forms of representation and delegation.

Some of the organizations studied by Steger et al. eschew participation in established electoral processes, while others do not. Steger et al. highlight the importance of 'multiplicity' as an approach that values diversity rather than trying to find 'one size fits all' solutions. They note that the Charter of the World Social Forum values inclusivity and the welcoming and empowerment of marginalized groups. Prefiguration has found wide support from most global justice activists social movement organizations. The Zapatistas, the occupy activists and many in the environmental movement have engaged in efforts to construct more egalitarian and sustainable local institutions and communities rather than mounting organized challenges to the global and national structures of power. The discussion of global solidarity in Steger et al. emphasizes the centrality of what Ruth Reitan (2007) has called 'altruistic solidarity' – identification with poor and marginalized peoples – without much consideration of solidarity based on common circumstances or identities. Steger et al. do, however, mention the important efforts to link groups that are operating at both local and global levels of contention.[8]

The Steger et al. study is a useful example of how to do research on political ideology and it provides valuable evidence about ideational stances and culture of the New Global Left. It and the movement network results summarized above imply that the New Global Left has a degree of coherence that can be the basis of greater articulation.

Transnational alternative policy think-tanks

William Carroll's (2016) thorough study of global justice transnational alternative policy groups examined the problem of how to build a transnational counter-hegemonic bloc of progressive social forces (Carroll, 2016, p. 23). Carroll's study examined sixteen progressive transnational think-tanks from both the Global North and the Global South.[9] Carroll's results agree with the findings of the Steger et al. study summarized above regarding the discursive content of the global justice movement. Carroll also notes that the progressive counter-hegemonic think tanks that he has studied have been trying to produce knowledge that is useful for prefigurative social change and a democratic and egalitarian forms of globalization in contrast to the neoliberal globalization project. Carroll critiques localist and anti-organizational approaches and proposes:

> counter-hegemonic globalization: a globally organized project of transformation aimed at replacing the dominant global regime with one that maximizes democratic political control and makes the equitable development of human capabilities and environmental stewardship its priorities. (Carroll, 2016, p. 30)

Arab Spring, Pink Tide, neo-fascism and structural deglobalization

The global political, economic, and demographic situation has evolved in ways that challenge some of the assumptions that were made during the rise of the global justice movement and that require adjustments in the analyses, strategies, and tactics of progressive social movements. The Arab Spring, the Latin American Pink Tide, the Indignados in Spain, and the rise of New Leftist social media-based parties in Spain (Podemos) Italy and in Greece and the spike in mass protests in 2011 and 2012 were interpreted as the heating up of a world revolution against neoliberal globalization that had started in the late 20th century with the rise of the Zapatistas (Chase-Dunn, Stäbler, Breckenridge-Jackson, & Herrera, 2014). But the outcomes of some of these movements have brought the tactics of the global justice movement into question. The left-wing Syriza Party, elected in Greece in 2015, was a debacle that was crushed by the European banks and the EU. They doubled down on austerity, threatening to bankrupt the pensioners of Greece unless the Syriza regime agreed to new structural adjustment policies, which it did. This was a case in which another world was possible but did not happen. This disappointment was felt by the other new leftist social media parties in Italy and Spain as well as the global justice movement and the Social Forum process.

The huge spike in global protests in 2011–2012 was followed by a lull and then a renewed intensification of citizen revolts from 2015–2016 (Youngs, 2017). The Black Lives Matter movement, the Dakota Access Pipeline protest, the #MeToo movement, the global Women's Marches and the Antifa rising against neo-fascism showed that the World Revolution of 20xx was still happening. However, the mainly tragic outcomes of the Arab Spring and the decline of the Pink Tide progressive populist regimes in Latin America were bad blows for the global left.

The Social Forum process was late in coming to the Middle East and North Africa, but it eventually did arrive. The Arab Spring movements in the Middle East and North Africa were mainly rebellions of progressive students and young people using social media to mobilize mass protests against aging authoritarian regimes. The outcome in Tunisia, where the sequence of protests started, has been fairly good thus far. But the outcomes in Egypt, Syria and Bahrein were disasters (Moghadam, 2018).[10] Turkey and Iran should also be added to this list. The mass popular movements calling for democracy were defeated by Islamist movements that were better organized and by military coups and/or outside intervention. In Syria, parts of the movement were able to organize an armed struggle, but this was defeated by the old regime with Russian help. Extremist Muslim fundamentalists took over the fight from progressivists, and the Syrian civil war produced a huge wave of refugees that combined with economic migrants from Africa to cross the Mediterranean Sea to Europe. This added fuel to the already existing populist nationalist movements and political parties in Europe, propelling electoral victories inspired by xenophobic and racist anti-immigrant sentiment. In Iran, the green movement was repressed. In Turkey, Erdogan has prevailed, repressing the popular movement as well as the Kurds. All these developments, except Tunisia, have been major setbacks for the global left.

Right-wing populist politicians have exploited cleavages along cultural lines, rallying individuals against foreigners and minorities. Left-wing populist movements, on the other hand tended to garner support based on economic cleavages. They pointed to the wealthy 1% and large corporations as responsible for the economic crises and austerity policies of the 21st century (Rodrik, 2018). Thus, the neoliberal globalization project and the crises of late global capitalism have produced increasing political polarization as the context in which the New Global Left needs to reconsider its culture and attitudes toward organizational issues.

The unhappy outcome of the Arab Spring, the demise of the Pink Tide, the rise of populist right-wing and neo-fascist movements and parties and the possible arrival of another period of deglobalization are developments that suggest that the global left needs to devise strategies that can be more effective in confronting the crises of global capitalism and building a more egalitarian, democratic and sustainable world society. But this project also needs to be cognizant of the contemporary culture of the global left.

The vessel[11]: forging a diagonal instrument for the global left

A new discourse has emerged in the past few years regarding possibilities for greater articulation among the movements of the global left and around the ideas of united fronts and popular fronts and new forms of organization. The tendency of progressive social movements to form around single issues and identity politics is increasingly seen as a problem that stands in the way of mobilizing more effectively to both allow people to construct more egalitarian and sustainable projects and communities and to become a significant and consequential player in world politics. This has been recognized and addressed in different ways by both activists and political theorists for the last twenty years. John Sanbonmatsu's (2004) defense of a global counter-hegemonic project of the Left locates the roots of horizontalism and the celebration of diversity in the rise of the new social movements and postmodern philosophy in the years following the world revolution of 1968. He contends that the post-modern emphasis on differences and diversity undercuts the ability of progressive forces to join together to struggle for social change. Post-modern critical sociology was a somewhat understandable reaction against Stalinism and the primary focus on workers' parties taking state power that was the *modis operandi* of the Old Left. But neo-Leninists such as Jodi Dean (2012, 2016) have pointed out the limitations of leaderless mass protests as a method for producing political change. Zeinab Tufeki's (2017) study of movements that have been enabled by social networking notes their fragility and susceptibility to disruption. Greg Sharzer (2012, 2017) recounts the fate of utopian communities over the past two centuries that are usually either die out for become reincorporated back in to capitalist business as usual.

Samir Amin (2008, 2018) proposed a new progressive international to serve as an instrument for the global justice movement in world politics. His proposed fifth international invokes the memory of the earlier socialist and communist internationals, raising fears of vanguardism among the horizontalists. But the organizational and issue foci of Amin's proposal have elements that are different from earlier internationals. The fifth international is an alliance of national entities but it would permit participation from more than one legitimate group per country. Amin's differs from many other global justice activists in seeing national progressive projects as the most important arena of struggle, raising the issue of the content of progressive nationalism.

The World Social Forum held in Salvador, Brazil in 2018 focused on how the Social Forum process could be reinvented to more effectively confront the rise of right-wing forces (Mestrum, 2017, 2018). The demise of the U.S. and European Social Forums may mean that the Social Forum process is winding down. If that is the case the question is: What can replace and improve upon the Social Forum? Given the numerous competing interest groups, all with legitimate claims, the puzzle is how to unite them in a global social justice movement that is inclusive but that also focusses on the main problems confronting humanity in the 21st century.

An integrated political movement would need to 'name the enemy' (Starr, 2000). The global right has been effective in large part because it has constructed its own enemies as 'the globalists', 'the establishment' and 'immigrants'. A capacious global social justice movement will need to name the predations of the transnational corporate class and the neo-fascist and populist Global Right as enemies and to make evident the connections between these enemies and the oppression and exploitation of the majority of the human population of both the Global South and the Global North.

The Amin and Dean versions of neo-Leninism differ in some respects regarding their notions of agency. Amin was a Third Worldist who saw the workers and peasants of the Global South as the main agents of progressive social change. Dean is more of a workerist who thinks that organized workers led by dedicated communists from the Global North and the Global South can unite to transform global capitalism. While Dean is enthused by the affective spirit shown by crowds in 2011, she contends that an organized party will be necessary to mobilize a progressive transformation of global capitalism. She says 'That perspective which gives body to the political subject is the party' (Dean, 2016, p. 19). Neither Dean nor Amin directly address the issue of vanguardism that was one of Lenin's most important contributions to the methodology and strategy of the communist movement.[12] Amin is sensitive to the charge of vanguardism, but contends that there are statutory structures that can be used ensure democratic control of a global political party. Amin (2018) says

The aim should be to establish an *Organization* (the new Internationale) and not just a 'movement'. This involves moving beyond the concept of a discussion forum. It also involves analysing the inadequacies of the notion, still prevalent, that the 'movements' claim to be horizontal and are hostile to so-called vertical organizations on the pretext that the latter are by their very nature anti-democratic: that the organization is, in fact, the result of action which by itself generates 'leaders'. The latter can aspire to dominate, even manipulate the movements. But it is also possible to avoid this danger through appropriate statutes. This should be discussed.

We agree with Amin and Dean that the anti-organizational ideologies that have been a salient part of the culture of progressive movements since 1968 have been a major fetter restricting the capability of these movements to effectively realize their own goals. But these ideas and sentiments run deep and so any effort to construct organizational forms that can facilitate progressive collective action must be cognizant of this embedded culture. The Internet and social media, allowing cheap and effective mass communications, have been blamed for producing specialized single-issue movements. We suggest that virtual communications and democratic decision-making technologies can be harnessed to produce more sustained and integrated organizations and effective tools that can be used to contend for power in the streets and institutional halls of the world-system. We also think that the old reformist/revolutionary debate about whether to engage in electoral politics is a fetter on the ability of the global left to effectively contend.[13] We agree that changing the policies of states or taking power in them should not be the only goals of progressive social movements. States are not, and have never been, whole systems. They are organizations that exist in a larger world economy and interstate system. And while they should not be the sole target of progressive movements, their organizational resources can be used to facilitate the building of a postcapitalist global society. The autonomists correctly perceive that dependence on state resources and support, as well as on funding from mainstream foundations, often compromise the integrity and flexibility of social movement organizations in their ability to challenge existing power structures. But progressive transnational social movements should be prepared to work with progressive state governments in order to try to change the rules of the global economic order (Evans, 2009, 2010).[14] If social movement organizations become part of the problem rather than part of the solution new less dependent and compromised social movement organizations can take up the struggle. A multilevel movement of movements is needed that promotes within-country regions, national, world regions, global North, global South and whole global (Earth-wide) levels of organization and empowers all of them without unduly empowering the national level.

Progressive transnational social movements should also be willing to work at the local level with city governments to implement progressive goals such as a universal basic income, as these cities can then serve as progressive examples (Harvey, 2012; Lowrey, 2018; Van Parijs & Vanderborght, 2017; Wright, 2010). This includes learning from cities in the Global South and applying lessons learned in the Global North. For instance, a universal basic income has been piloted in the twenty-first century in Kenya and Brazil and is now being introduced in Stockton (California) and Chicago. While there is a legitimate critique that a nonlivable universal basic income that is used to supplement work is subject to control and thus potentially exploitative, a livable basic income which comes in addition to the social safety net instead of replacing it can be a radical tool for the redistribution and sharing of wealth. We agree with Paul Mason (2015) that the anti-utopianism of the Old Left and some in the New Left was somewhat misplaced.[15] Prefiguration is a good idea. Sharing networks, coops, community banks, zero emissions homes, farms and industries are worthwhile endeavours for activists of the global left (Wallerstein, 1998). But these local projects need to be linked and coordinated so that they can effectively contend in national and world politics. Explaining how to structure such a progressive international effectively requires an understanding of horizontalism, verticalism, and our proposed synthesis, found in diagonalism. Only then can a party network (partnet) be strong and yet flexible enough to withstand the challenges of global organizing be constructed.

Diagonal organizational structure

The idea of leaderless movements and organizations is an anarchist trope that has been critiqued by both Marxists (Epstein, 2001) and feminists (Freeman, 1972–73). Political organizations need to have institutionalized procedures for making decisions and ways to hold leadership accountable so that mistakes can be rectified. These requisites are not so important when the world-system is humming along with business as usual, but when systemic crises erupt, and powerful popular right-wing social movements and regimes emerge, leaderlessness becomes an unacceptable luxury. An alternative to Leninist 'march-in-line' must be found. While the culture of the contemporary global left usually equates the idea of a political party with vanguard parties or electoral machines, there is a recent literature that argues that new forms of party organization are possible in the age of internet communication (Carroll, 2015; Dean, 2012, 2016).

Wiki farms[16] facilitate the formation of virtual organizations that combine the merits of open networks with leadership structures (data stewards) that allow groups to collectively author documents and to make group decisions. Horizontalism valorizes leaderlessness and informality, usually paired with consensual decision-making. Horizontalist organizations, also called 'self-organization' (Prehofer & Bettstetter, 2005) have several advantages: resilience (you can kill some of them but there is redundancy), flexibility and adaptability, individual entities interact directly with one another, and there is no larger hierarchy that can be disrupted. These desirable characteristics are those that are stressed by advocates of horizontalist networks. But critics of horizontality point out that structurelessness does not prevent the emergence of informal structures among groups of friends, and participants that are not linked to these friendship nets have no mechanisms for regulating the power of the informal networks (Freeman, 1972–73).

Diagonalism combines horizontalism with a semi-centralized formal organizational structure that is itself democratic and flexible.[17] A diagonal organization is a complex of horizontally connected individuals, small groups and larger regional organizations with a decision-making structure by which groups can discuss and adopt policies and implement them. Hierarchies are as flat as is possible consistent with organizational capacity and composite groups may report to more than one leadership group.[18] Leadership is rotational and maximizes opportunities for participatory democracy. Organizational bureaucracy is kept to a minimum, but legitimate representatives or delegates from horizontal groups make collective decisions and help to formulate policies and plan actions for the whole organization. Degrees of hierarchy can be flexible depending upon the nature of the task. High stakes, high risk tasks usually require more hierarchy. Local groups can adjust their organizational structures to the context and the nature of the task. The Vessel itself should maintain democratic and flexible decision-making and implementation structures.

The Vessel is a **diagonal network formed of project affinity groups and local communities that share the results of their experiments and constructions and coordinate with one another for political actions, including mass demonstrations, electoral campaigns and mobilizations of support and contention.** Diagonalism links horizontal networks of individuals and groups with a legitimate leadership structure composed of designated **delegates** who are empowered to carry out the decisions of the organization that appoint them. Delegates make group decisions by means of both consensus and voting. Multiple organizations can represent communities and nations. The

Council of the Vessel will be a compromise between horizontal leaderless and hierarchical command structures in which leadership is held by delegated individuals or groups. The Vessel will focus on the articulation of central issues and will formulate visions, strategies and tactics for the global left. It will promote communication and collaboration among transnational, national and local projects.[19] The Vessel should not be a political party in the old sense, but it should be allowed, unlike the World Social Forum, to adopt resolutions and to support candidates and campaigns. It should have a designated structure composed of a chosen facilitating delegate council to coordinate collective decision-making and to deal with problems of security and communications.[20] Existing progressive global organizations should be encouraged to join. Functions of the vessel and member organizations will vary depending upon circumstances, but the vessel level should specialize in the politics of international organizations and global issues, whereas the local, national and world regional organizations can focus on those issues which are salient in their contexts.

Issues

The main issues that we think should constitute the focus of the Vessel are:

- Climate justice,
- Human rights,
- Anti-racism, decolonization, and indigenous rights,
- Feminism and queer rights,
- Sharing networks,
- Peace/anti-war alliances,
- Local and city-based progressive grassroots activism,
- Anticorporate transnationalism (tax justice, etc.), and
- Democratic global governance.

The Vessel should also coordinate efforts to combat 21st century fascism and right-wing populism and should encouraged participation with and make alliances (united fronts; popular fronts) with NGOs and political parties that are willing to collaborate with these efforts.[21]

Human rights and anti-racism have been central in the network of movements participating in the social forum process. Global Indigenism (Chase-Dunn, Grimes, & Anderson, 2019; Hall & Fenelon, 2009) has been an increasingly important issue for the global left. The rights of colonized peoples, racial and ethnic minorities, indigenous peoples, and queer people are central to the inclusive concerns of the global left. The climate justice movement is already a collaborative project combining environmentalists with those who focus on the most vulnerable communities (Bond, 2012; Foran, 2018; Foran, Gray, & Grosse, 2017). Feminism has been one of the central movements in the social forum network of movements (Moghadam, 2018). Sharing networks are a potentially potent tool for organizing postcapitalist institutions that can transform the logic of global capitalism (Danaher & Gravitz, 2017; Mason, 2013). The peace/antiwar movements need local and national mobilization against militarism (Benjamin, 2013) as well as engagement with international governmental organizations in order to prevent the emergence of wars among core states in the coming multipolar world. The existing international political organizations are under attack from right-wing forces. The Vessel needs to advocate the strengthening and democratization of global governance institutions that can help keep the peace as humanity passes through the coming multipolar phase of interimperial rivalry and to move in the direction of an eventual democratic and collectively rational form of global governance. Progressive nationalism is an important defensive tactic against the appropriation of nationalism by the right-wing populists and neo-fascists. The deglobalizing world is reinventing nationalism as a response to the crises produced by the neoliberal globalization process. In many cases, this nationalism has verged into neo-fascism. The global left has been resolutely cosmopolitan and internationalist, but how could it engage the rising wave of nationalism to propose more cooperative relations with peoples abroad and with the Global South? The Vessel also needs to provide support help to formulate analyses and strategies for movements at the local and national levels who are fighting against the rise of right-wing authoritarianism and the suppression of progressive popular movements.

Conclusion

Rather than giving way to cynicism and resignation, the global left needs to face up to the setbacks that have occurred and devise a new strategy for moving humanity in a better direction. One possible solution lies in the approach taken by the organizers of DiEM25, a movement organization that is already agitating for a progressive international. While at the moment it is limited to European nations and North America (including Mexico), its diagonalist approach is well-suited for a flexible organization that can take on the global right-wing movement and the transnational capitalist class. The next few decades will be chaotic, but the movements and institutions we build can make things better. Whether or not the big calamities all come at once or sequentially, we need to pursue a strategy of 'disaster postcapitalism'[22] that plants the seeds of the future during the chaos. It is not the end, just another dark age, and an opportunity for transition to a much better world-system. The vessel can take us there.

Notes

1. This is an update of an earlier essay that reviewed the sociological literature on coalition formation, the history of united and popular fronts in the 20th century, and considered which of the central tendencies of the new global left might be in contention for providing leadership and integration of the network of anti-systemic movements that have been participating in the World Social Forum process (Chase-Dunn et al., 2014).
2. The terminology of the world-system perspective divides the Global South into the periphery and the semiperiphery. This turns out to be an important distinction for comprehending political developments in the Global South. Activists from the semiperiphery have been far more likely to participate in the Social Forum process, and activists from the periphery have been much more critical of international political organizations than those from either the Global North or the semiperiphery (Chase-Dunn et al., 2008).
3. This was an early version of the call that this forum is addressing.
4. Waterman (2010) also criticized the vanguardism of the Bamako Appeal and other proposals for a new internationalism and championed the movement of movements structure of the global justice forces.
5. Paul Mason is a 59-year-old British journalist who is well-known to scholars of transnational social movements for his perceptive ethnographic coverage of the global justice movement (Mason, 2013). Mason is a former Trotskyist who is active in the British Labor Party. Mason is an intrepid protagonist of the precariat with a solid grounding in the history of progressive movements and ideas and political economy.
6. World revolutions are named after a symbolic year in which important events occurred that characterize the nature of the constellation of the rebellions designated: 1789, 1917, 1968 and now 20xx because it is still too soon to name the current world revolution.

7. The surveys were conducted at Social Forum meetings in Porto Alegre, Brazil in 2005, Nairobi, Kenya and Atlanta, Georgia in 2007 and Detroit, Michigan in 2010.
8. While human rights is a very central movement theme in the network of movement of global justice movements, the indigenist rights movement contests the version of human rights that is enshrined in the United Nations Universal Declaration of Human Rights of 1948. The indigenistas stress the importance of community rights over the rights of individuals and the idea that 'Mother Earth' has rights.[8] These contentions have been shared by the many activists who sympathize with, and identify with, indigenous peoples (Chase-Dunn, Fenelon, et al., 2019).
9. Some well-known examples are the Rosa Luxemburg Foundation, the Third World Forum, the Centre for Civil Society, Development Alternatives with Women for a New Era and Focus on the Global South.
10. Val Moghadam (2018) shows how gender relations and women's mobilizations prior to the protest outbreaks, along with differences in political institutions, civil society and international influences, explain most of the variance in the different outcomes of the Arab Spring.
11. The instrument should be named by those who do the work to create it. Our suggestion of 'Vessel' is meant to be inclusive and diagonal. Others have suggested the Fifth International (Amin, 2008), an International of Workers and Peoples (Amin, 2018); the Postmodern Prince (Gill, 2000; Sanbonmatsu, 2004) and the World Party (Wagar, 1999).
12. In 'What Is to Be Done' (Lenin, 1902) Lenin proposed that a dedicated cadre of professional revolutionaries was needed to lead the workers beyond trade unionism.
13. In November of 2018 Bernie Sanders and Yanis Varoufakis issued a call for a Progressive International to unite against the rise of neo-fascist and right-wing populist parties (Progressive International, 2018).
14. Paul Mason rightly contends that state organizations will be needed for dealing with the daunting global problems of the 21st century. The traditional and neo-anarchist rejection of all states as necessarily instruments of oppression obscures the extent to which states sometimes be democratic and can be instruments of the oppressed rather than of the oppressors. Marc Fleurbaey's (2018) concept of the possibility of an 'emancipatory state' is a helpful move in the right direction.
15. We doubt that Mason's (2015) transitional program to postcapitalism, a global society in which wage labor has been replaced by the provision of free goods produced by networked machines, is a possibility for the next few decades, but we agree that this is a desirable goal for humanity.
16. A wiki farm is a collection of wikis running on the same web server and sharing one parent wiki engine.
17. Keith Hayson (2014, pp. 48–520) outlines an agenda for building an organizational diagonalism that is intended to produce a useful compromise between anarchistic horizontalism and organizational hierarchy that makes leadership and accountability possible.
18. In management theory control structures with multiple reporting lines are called matrix organizations (Gottleib 2007).
19. Digital organizations and the discourse on net governance make new forms of network organizations possible. Organizations need to be able to make decisions. This can be done hierarchically or by means of group voting or discussions, or various combinations of these. The Vessel will recognize both horizontal authority structures and allow subgroups to adopt the structures that they need. Organizations also need to specify their boundaries and protect themselves against those who would like to disrupt them, or worse. These jobs are best done by all active members, but it may be found necessary to delegate security jobs to individuals or subgroups. The best practices can be developed as things progress.
20. Forging the Vessel should be started at a meeting held under the auspices of the World Social Forum in 2019 or 2020.
21. This is list is a proposal for discussion. The development of a set of central issues should be among the first matters of discussion at the forging meetings.
22. This is a play on Naomi Klein's (2007) idea of disaster capitalism.

Disclosure statement

No potential conflict of interest was reported by the authors.

References

Amin, S. (1990). *Delinking: Towards a polycentric world.* London: Zed Books.

Amin, S. (2008). Towards the fifth international? In K. Sehm-Patomaki & M. Ulvila (Eds.), *Global political parties* (pp. 123–143). London: Zed Books.

Amin, S. (2018, July 3). Letter of intent for an inaugural meeting of the international of workers and peoples. *IDEAs Network.* Retrieved from http://www.networkideas.org/featured-articles/2018/07/it-is-imperative-to-reconstruct-the-internationale-of-workers-and-peoples/

Arrighi, G., Hopkins, T. K., & Wallerstein, I. (1989 [2012]). *Antisystemic movements.* London: Verso.

Bello, W. (2002). *Deglobalization.* London: Zed Books.

Benjamin, M. (2013). *Drone warfare.* London: Verso.

Bond, P. (2012). *The politics of climate justice: Paralysis above, movement below.* Durban, SA: University of Kwa-zulu Natal Press.

Carroll, W. K. (2015). Modes of cognitive praxis in transnational alternative policy groups. *Globalizations, 12* (5), 710–727. doi:10.1080/14747731.2014.1001231

Carroll, W. K. (2016). *Expose, oppose, propose: Alternative policy groups and the struggle for global justice.* New York, NY: Zed.

Chase-Dunn, C., Fenelon, J., Hall, T. D., Breckenridge-Jackson, I., & Herrera, J. (2019). Global indigenism and the web of transnational social movements. In I. Rossi (Ed.), *New frontiers of globalization research: Theories, globalization processes, and perspectives from the global south.* Springer Verlag.

Chase-Dunn, C., Grimes, P., & Anderson, E. N. (2019). Cyclical evolution of the global right. *Canadian Sociological Review.*

Chase-Dunn, C., & Kaneshiro, M. (2009). Stability and change in the contours of alliances among movements in the social forum process. In D. Fasenfest (Ed.), *Engaging social justice* (pp. 119–133). Leiden: Brill.

Chase-Dunn, C., Morosin, A., & Álvarez, A. (2015). Social movements and progressive regimes in Latin America: World revolutions and semiperipheral development. In P. Almeida & A. Cordero Ulate (Eds.), *Handbook of social movements across Latin America* (pp. 13–24). Dordrecht, NL: Springer.

Chase-Dunn, C., Reese, E., Herkenrath, M., Giem, R., Gutierrez, E., Kim, L., & Petit, C. (2008). North-South contradictions and bridges at the world social forum. In R. Reuveny & W. R. Thompson (Eds.), *North and South in the world political economy* (pp. 341–366). Malden, MA: Blackwell.

Chase-Dunn, C., Stäbler, A., Breckenridge-Jackson, I., & Herrera, J. (2014, July 17). Articulating the web of transnational social movements. Presented at the world congress of sociology in Yokohama. Retrieved from http://irows.ucr.edu/papers/irows84/irows84.htm

Danaher, K., & Gravitz, A. (Eds.). (2017). *The green festival reader.* London: Routledge.

Dean, J. (2012). *The communist horizon.* London: Verso.

Dean, J. (2016). *Crowds and party.* London: Verso.

Epstein, B. (2001). Anarchism and the anti-globalization movement. *Monthly Review, 53*(4), 1–14.

Evans, P. B. (2009). From situations of dependency to globalized social democracy. *Studies in Comparative International Development, 44*, 318–336.

Evans, P. B. (2010). Is it labor's turn to globalize? Twenty-first century opportunities and strategic responses. *Global Labour Journal, 1*(3), 352–379. doi:10.15173/glj.v1i3.1082

Fleurbaey, M. (with Olivier Bouin, Marie-Laure Djelic, Ravi Kanbur, Helga Nowotny and Elisa Reis). (2018). *A manifesto for social progress. Ideas for a better society.* Cambridge: Cambridge University Press.

Foran, J. (2018). *Taking or (re) making power?: The new movements for radical social change and global justice.* London: Zed Books.

Foran, J., Gray, S., & Grosse, C. (2017). 'Not yet the end of the world': Political cultures of opposition and creation in the global youth climate justice movement. *Interface: A Journal for and about Social Movements, 9* (2), 353–379.

Freeden, M. (2003). *Ideology: A very short introduction.* Oxford: Oxford University Press.

Freeman, J. (1972–73). The tyranny of structuralessness. *Berkeley Journal of Sociology, 17*, 151–165.

Gill, S. (2000). Toward a post-modern prince?: The battle of Seattle as a moment in the new politics of globalization. *Millennium: Journal of International Studies, 29*(1), 131–140.

Gottlieb, M. R. (2007). *The matrix organization reloaded.* Westport, CT: Praeger.

Hall, T. D., & Fenelon, J. V. (2009). *Indigenous peoples and globalization: Resistance and revitalization.* Boulder, CO: Paradigm Press.

Harvey, D. (2012). *Rebel cities: From the right to the city to the urban revolution.* London: Verso.

Hayson, K. (2014). A brief for diagonalism – a dialectical take on David Graeber's the democracy project. Retrieved from https://www.academia.edu/7289524/A_Brief_for_Diagonalism_-_A_Dialectical_Take_on_David_Graebers_The_Democracy_Project

Hobsbawm, E. J. (1994). *The age of extremes: A history of the world, 1914–1991.* New York, NY: Pantheon.

Klein, N. (2007). *The shock doctrine: The rise of disaster capitalism.* New York, NY: Henry Holt.

Lenin, V. (1902). What is to be done? Retrieved from https://www.marxists.org/archive/lenin/works/1901/witbd/

Lowrey, A. (2018). *Give people money: How a universal basic income would end poverty, revolutionize work, and remake the world.* New York, NY: Crown.

Mason, P. (2013). *Why its still kicking off everywhere: The new global revolutions.* London: Verso.

Mason, P. (2015). *Postcapitalism.* New York, NY: Farrer, Straus and Giroux.

Mestrum, F. (2017). Reinventing the World Social Forum: How powerful an idea can be. *Open Democracy.* Retrieved from https://opendemocracy.net/francine-mestrum/reinventing-world-social-forum-how-powerful-idea-can-be

Mestrum, F. (2018). The World Social Forum is dead! Long live the World Social Forum? *Alternatives International.* Retrieved from http://www.alterinter.org/spip.php?article4654

Meyer, J. W. (2009). *World society: The writings of John W. Meyer.* New York, NY: Oxford University Press.

Michels, R. (1968 [1915]). *Political parties.* New York, NY: Simon and Schuster.

Moghadam, V. M. (2005). *Globalizing women: Transnational feminist networks.* Baltimore, MD: Johns Hopkins University Press.

Moghadam, V. M. (2018). Feminism and the future of revolutions. *Socialism and Democracy, 32*(1), 31–53. doi:10.1080/08854300.2018.1461749

Moghadam, V. M., & Kaftan, G. (2019). Right-wing populisms north and north: Varieties and gender dynamics. *Women's Studies International Forum, 75.* doi:10.1016/j.wsif.2019.102244

Pleyers, G. (2011). *Alter-globalization.* Malden, MA: Polity Press.

Prehofer, C., & Bettstetter, C. (2005). Self-organization in communication networks: Principles and design paradigms. *IEEE Communications Magazine, 43*(7), 78–85.

Progressive International. (2018). An open call to all progressive forces. Retrieved from https://www.progressive-international.org/open-call/

Reitan, R. (2007). *Global activism.* London: Routledge.

Rodrik, D. (2018). Populism and the economics of globalization. *Journal of International Business Policy.* doi:10.1057/s42214-018-001-4

Sanbonmatsu, J. (2004). *The postmodern prince.* New York, NY: Monthly Review Press.

Sen, J., Kumar, M., Bond, P., & Waterman, P. (2007). *A political programme for the world social forum?: Democracy, substance and debate in the Bamako appeal and the global justice movements*. Indian Institute for Critical Action: Centre in Movement (CACIM), New Delhi, India & the University of KwaZulu-Natal Centre for Civil Society (CCS), Durban, South Africa.

Sharzer, G. (2012). *Nolocal: Why small-scale alternatives will not change the world*. Aireford: Zero Books.

Sharzer, G. (2017). Cooperatives as transitional economics. *Review of Radical Political Economics*, 49(3), 456–476. doi:10.1177/0486613415627154

Standing, G. (2014). *A precariat charter: From denizens to citizens*. London: Bloomsbury.

Starr, A. (2000). *Naming the enemy: Anti-corporate movements confront globalization*. London: Zed Books.

Steger, M., Goodman, J., & Wilson, E. K. (2013). *Justice globalism: Ideology, crises, policy*. Thousand Oaks, CA: Sage.

Tufekci, Z. (2017). *Twitter and tear gas: The power and fragility of networked protest*. New Haven, CT: Yale University Press.

Van Parijs, P., & Vanderborght, Y. (2017). *Basic income: A radical proposal for a free society and a sane economy*. Cambridge, MA: Harvard University Press.

Wagar, W. W. (1999). *A short history of the future*. Chicago, IL: University of Chicago Press.

Wallerstein, I. (1998). *Utopistics: Or historical choices of the twenty-first century*. New York, NY: New Press.

Wallerstein, I. (2007). The World Social Forum: From defense to offense. Retrieved from http://www.sociologistswithoutborders.org/documents/WallersteinCommentary.pdf

Waterman, P. (2006). Toward a global labour charter for the 21st century. Retrieved from https://laborstrategies.blogs.com/global_labor_strategies/global_unionism/page/4/

Waterman, P. (2010). Five, six, many new internationalisms! (Nine reflections on a fifth international). Retrieved from http://www.europe-solidaire.org/spip.php?article16650

World Social Forum Charter of Principles. (2001). Retrieved from http://www.universidadepopular.org/site/media/documentos/WSF_-_charter_of_Principles.pdf

Wright, E. O. (2010). *Envisioning real Utopias*. London: Verso.

Youngs, R. (2017, October). What are the meanings behind the worldwide rise in protest? *Open Democracy*. Retrieved from https://www.opendemocracy.net/protest/multiple-meanings-global-protest

Truncated 21st-century trajectories of progressive international solidarity

Patrick Bond

ABSTRACT

What potentials exist for realizing a new internationalism consistent with the visions of Samir Amin, Africa's greatest political economist and one of the leading Marxists of his generation? To answer requires tracing back several decades, to interpret Amin's own strategy for establishing first, continental and then, global networks mixing radical scholars and activists. Many missteps were taken, among which were gaps between top-down intellectual formulations (and manifestos) and bottom-up strategic narratives (often lacking a coherent ideology). Because of these limitations, even Amin's most opportune political networking faltered, proving unsustainable. On most such occasions, it was Amin's own auto-critique that assisted his allies in developing more profound formulations. It is in these various initiatives to which Amin generously gave his time, energy, resources and political commitment that we can learn some of the most powerful lessons for future internationalism.

Samir Amin, a leading scholar and co-founder of the world-systems tradition, died on August 12, 2018. Just before his death, he published, along with close allies, a call for 'workers and the people' to establish a 'fifth international' [https://www.pambazuka.org/global-south/letter-intent-inaugural-meeting-international-workers-and-peoples] *to coordinate support to progressive movements. To honor Samir Amin's invaluable contribution to world-systems scholarship, we are pleased to present readers with a selection of essays responding to Amin's final message for today's anti-systemic movements. This forum is being co-published between Globalizations* [https://www.tandfonline.com/rglo], *the* Journal of World-Systems Research [http://jwsr.pitt.edu/ojs/index.php/jwsr/issue/view/75] *and Pambazuka News* [https://www.pambazuka.org/]. *Additional essays and commentary can be found in these outlets.*

1. Introduction: from high theory to African development to global geopolitical economy

The possibilities of progressive internationalism are exemplified by Samir Amin's extraordinary networking, which was in many respects the world's cutting edge in personal and institutional terms over the last half-century.[1] Amin was born into a petit-bourgeois Cairo family in 1931 and educated in Paris during the 1950s. There, increasingly radicalized, he elaborated a unique, neo-Marxist theory of unequal exchange and super-exploitation to explain Third World underdevelopment. Amin's career was mainly based in Dakar, Senegal, where he first lectured in economic planning and then built Africa-wide organizations during the 1960s–70s, with a focus on non-capitalist, patriotic-developmental politics. Among his successes were the Council for the Development of Social Science Research in Africa, still the continent's leading intellectual institution with 4000 members. He worked within the sometimes-heterodox offices of the United Nations, based initially at the African Institute for Economic Planning and Development (IDEP) in Dakar from 1963–79. He was fired by UN Economic Commission for Africa leader Adebayo Adedeji due to explicit pressure from the United States government, for pushing the institution too far leftwards (Amin 2006, p. 181).

Never flatfooted nor discouraged, though, Amin from the early 1970s built a preferred organizational vehicle: a network of likeminded institutes, the Third World Forum (TWF). His objective was

> to bring together intellectuals who were critical of conventional concepts of development … In April 1973, the Allende government in Chile invited us to organize a meeting in Santiago. I remember this as the date when the Forum really saw the light of day.[2]

The origins of a South-centric organic intelligentsia with global visions are to be found here, and through the 1980s, Amin's TWF generated scores of books and other major publications. By the early 1990s, as neoliberal corporate globalization penetrated every part of the world, Amin recommitted to jumping scale to the global. In 1997 he established the World Forum for Alternatives (WFA) in Cairo. As Amin (2006, p. 195) put it, the WFA most opposed the pro-corporate, Northern-centric logic of the World Economic Forum and indeed

> first appeared on the international stage when it organized the 'anti-Davos' in January 1999, on the occasion of the annual elite conference at Davos. We were, of course, denied access to the holy precinct itself, but we took up position fifty meters away, on the other side of the snow-covered street in this beautiful winter resort. Our small group included a number of committed intellectuals and figures from mass movements in the five continents, chosen for their high degree of representativeness: the farmers' organizations of Burkina Faso, Brazil and India; the labor unions of South Africa, Korea and Brazil; the neo-Zapatistas of Chiapas in Mexico; the activists of the World March of Women; the 'Sans' in France and the ATTAC group. Helped into Davos by *Le Monde Diplomatique*, we were there to say that it was we, not the club of billionaires, who represented the real world.[3]

The following February, the activist-oriented Peoples Global Action summit in Geneva cemented Amin's role in linking theoretical, analytical, strategic and activist perspectives. There, his praxis approach to challenging world power combined with hopes for revived Third World nationalism in the Latin American Pink Tide that began at roughly the same time. The first major wave of coordinated protests against corporate globalization began in Geneva in mid-1998 (when the Multilateral Agreement on Investment was the target), Seattle in late 1999 (World Trade Organization), Washington and Prague in 2000 (World Bank and IMF), Gothenburg (European Union summit) and Genoa in 2001 (G8), and Durban and Johannesburg in 2001–02 (United Nations global conferences on racism and environment), to provide a few examples. In these sites, a strategic orientation emerged: the 'globalization of people' against the 'globalization of capital' (Bond 2003).

But just as global-scale economy and ecology became intertwined in social movements' sensibilities and alliances, the George W. Bush era interrupted this process, as Washington declared war on Islam in 2001. The 9/11 terrorist attacks frightened organized labor's leadership away from the global justice movements, in the process derailing the emerging alternative economic, social and environmental agendas. The Northern left prioritized mobilization against U.S. and European militarism, especially the Iraq War (albeit with ever-weaker anti-war rallies after 15 million rallied unsuccessfully in March 2003). The subsequent mass movements of the 2000s – however disconnected and limited by their national bases – defended civil liberties in the internet era, advocated for climate policies, offered intense critiques of national financial elites in scores of 'Occupy' cities in 2011, and overthrew several local tyrants during that year's global protest wave.

As for social movements that retained much of their strength in the Global South, the main potential site to regularly unify their politics was the World Social Forum (WSF), established in 2001 by Brazilian and French social democrats as a direct competition to Davos. But after starting with great potential, the biannual WSF became less relevant during the 2010s given its organizers' reluctance to generate a tough ideology and organization fit for the times, in part because of the excessive influence of mild-mannered international NGOs and the general sense of 'horizontality' and over-valorization of micro-based struggles. There were, still, thousands of global-justice advocates adopting anti-war, anti-surveillance, anti-emissions and anti-finance targets, but the major multilateral institutions slipped out of the public eye, even though they were amongst the parties most responsible for implementing neoliberalism, austerity for the *Global* South and hedonistic capital accumulation for the *Global* North.

The 2008–09 world crisis was perhaps the best chance since the 1960s to reintroduce anti-capitalist internationalism, a politics sometimes misinterpreted as 'anti-globalization'; after all, so much of it was based on globalizing people's movements, against global capital. The 2000s called for a more sophisticated version of internationalism than had existed up until then, one suffused with a forceful decarbonization agenda, with feminism, with anti-racism/xenophobia, and with leadership from the South, and especially from workers, peasants and indigenous peoples (i.e. not from the typical middle-class intelligentsia who had become ambassadors and interpreters of anti-corporate globalization). But the movements were far too fragile to make the links that were anticipated by Amin (2018).

Moreover, elites still promoted 'growth', whether in the form of neoliberal-parasitic accumulation (especially in the financial, commercial and IT sectors) or global-credit-Keynesianism (fueled by Quantitative Easing monetary laxity, low interest rates and bailouts, such as advocated by the IMF's managing director Dominique Strauss-Kahn from 2008–11). When top-down strategies failed to solve global capitalism's overaccumulation and environmental crises, and when the far right mobilized working-class Northern workers more effectively in 'populist' ways, Amin grew increasingly restless. In discussions in Dakar over the course of a week in January 2018, he told me of the ways he hoped future organizing of what he called a 'new international front of the workers and the peoples' might proceed (Amin 2018). But to do so meant coming to grips, he acknowledged, with three disappointing initiatives during the prior 15 years: the 2005–10 efforts to build a Fifth International at the World Social Forum – in Porto Alegre and Bamako, Mali – and through Venezuela's political-party sponsorship at Hugo Chavez's peak strength.

2. The world left's early 21st-century false dawns

Although global managers were losing confidence and legitimacy, the various nationally-bound left progressive opposition parties and social movements were not strong enough to provide genuine alternatives. The WSF proclaimed, 'Another World is Possible!' – a nebulous phrase indicative of the global left's low confidence levels – but aside from a few sector-specific sector attacks on global corporate power and neoliberal multilateralism (of which three are described below), international civil society achieved little in this period. The Brazilian turn leftwards in 2003 under Workers Party leadership, and the more radical Latin American Pink Tide countries of Venezuela, Bolivia and Ecuador, also ebbed within a decade. The Brazilian Petrobras-financed WSF meetings and various

Caracas conferences sponsored by Chavez (where Amin played a leadership role) were ultimately of little use to the global justice movement. And the Latin American leftists' carbon addictions and export orientation soon proved fatal once the commodity super-cycle peaked in 2011 and crashed in 2015 (e.g. oil's fall from $120/barrel in 2011 to a low of $26/barrel five years later). Brazil witnessed especially intense social protest, initially from the left in 2014 after the Workers Party adopted more explicitly neoliberal policies such as increased public transport fares. And clampdowns on indigenous, environmental and community activists – generally of the left – were increasingly common there as well as in the Andes and Amazon. Ecuadoran activists, especially, fought a neo-caudillismo that often appeared anti-imperialist (e.g. in opposing Bretton Woods Institution dictates and giving safe harbor to WikiLeaks founder Julian Assange) but that then substituted Chinese extractive corporates for their Western predecessors in sacred sites like the Yasuni Park.

Taking another false step, Amin often held out hope that social-democratic allies in Europe would join an anti-U.S. front, especially after 2003s fracturing of the imperial core over the Iraq War. The continent's increasingly extreme uneven geographical development, dysfunctional currency, and subsequent immigration crisis offered other areas in which activists engaged in vital (if ultimately fruitless) campaigning. They soon found the balance of forces – whether in continental sites like the European Social Forum or in national settings – was becoming more skewed towards capital. Their efforts were inadequate to defeat the fascist tendencies that flowed from these two processes. Hopes that the frustrated working classes of Southern Europe might generate a more radical left were dashed, once in power, by the Greek Syriza and Italian Five-Star parties, and in Spain where Podemos appeared to hit its support ceiling at just over 20 percent in 2015–16. One potential exception, perhaps, is Great Britain: the Labour Party's remarkable 2017 electoral comeback campaign behind Jeremy Corbyn and his Momentum movement attracted many pro-Brexit and former-UK Independence Party voters, although there, residual Blairite apparatchiks within Labour remain powerful. As divided as the Tories were over Brexit, they still held power during the crucial break from Europe in 2019.

As for the 'emerging markets' and semi-periphery, during the 2010s there was occasional rhetorical opposition to Western dominance over multilateralism from leaders of the Brazil, Russia, India, China and South Africa (BRICS) bloc. But these also proved illusory when it came to BRICS practices, which were not ultimately anti-imperial but instead better described as subimperial, insofar as they relegitimized the global corporate-dominated systems of financial, trade and climate governance (Garcia and Bond 2018). The BRICS would be considered skeptically by the world left, given ongoing totalitarian control of society in China (under Xi Jinping) and Russia (Vladimir Putin), and the rise of far-right regimes in India in 2014 (Narendra Modi) and Brazil in 2018 (Jair Bolsonaro), not to mention corporate power's resurgence in South Africa in 2018 (Cyril Ramaphosa).

Through the anti-apartheid sanctions movement from the 1960s–80s, the latter country was one of the greatest cases of internationalist anti-corporate power. But from 1994, the pressure on Nelson Mandela's African National Congress to achieve a democratic transition by adopting neoliberal economic policies soon generated far worse inequality, poverty and unemployment than during apartheid. Several generations' worth of international solidarity were destroyed. Amin was as critical of post-apartheid South Africa (Bond 2018) as he was of the anti-systemic movements' 1990s–2010s failures.

As he put it, three weeks before his death, in a call to reconstruct a new international, the world left would have to transcend the extreme fragmentation of the struggles, whether at the local or world level, which are always specific and conducted in particular places and subject-matters (ecology, women's rights, social services, community demands, etc.) The rare campaigns conducted at the national or even world level have not had any significant success in that they have not forced any changes of the policies being carried out by those in power. (Amin 2018)

However, there were exceptions to this unusually pessimistic assessment, and at least three community-rooted, globally-oriented campaigns from the early 2000s should be commended. First, healthcare advocacy movements – led by South Africa's Treatment Action Campaign and followed by the International People's Health Movement – protested and lobbied successfully to end multinational corporate pharmaceutical monopolization of patents on life-saving drugs, especially AIDS medicines. Life expectancy in countries with high HIV+ rates soared, e.g. South Africa from 52 in 2005 to 64 a dozen years later. Second, 'water warriors' – led by citizens' movements in Cochabamba, Bolivia and Ottawa, Canada – were opposed to commodification of household water (as well as mega-dams, bottled water, water trading and similar causes), and they linked up internationally to oppose water privatizers (e.g. Suez, Biwater, Veolia, Thames) and to promote public water commons. Third, landless people worked through the global network Via Campesina – and especially the Brazilian Movement of Landless Workers – to give solidarity during land occupations and defense against corporate land grabbing.

In contrast, the North's left certainly witnessed regression. Amin (2018) was especially annoyed that, what in the 1960s–90s appeared as excellent sources of international solidarity, had faded by the 2000s:

> The peoples of the Triad (USA, Western and Central Europe, Japan) have renounced international anti-imperialist solidarity, which has been replaced at best by 'humanitarian' campaigns and 'aid' programmes that are controlled by the capital of the monopolies. The European political forces that inherited left-wing traditions thus now support the imperialist vision of existing globalization. A new right-wing ideology has gained support among the people. In the North, the central theme of anti-capitalist class struggle has been abandoned, or reduced to a greatly incomplete expression – for the benefit of a so-called new definition of the left-wing 'partner culture' or communitarianism, separating the defence of specific rights from the general fight against capitalism.

Amin's (2018) proposal for a New International is therefore grounded much more in struggles from the Third World:

> The history of the last century was in fact that of the revolt of the peoples of the peripheries of the world system who were engaged in a socialist de-linking or in attenuated forms of national liberation, whose page has, for the moment, been turned. The re-colonization now under way, which has no legitimacy, is therefore fragile.

That fragility comes in part because of social resistance when confronted with South governments' capitulations to global capital. In 2001, the WSF was the vehicle for this resistance but by 2005, frustrations caused by the WSF's failure to address *ideology* had risen to the point 19 international left leaders signed a Porto Alegre manifesto, an exercise repeated in 2006 under Amin's leadership in Bamako. Neither were successful, nor was the 2007–09 'Fifth International' call by Chavez, and the reasons are worth recalling.

3. Amin's international manifesto authorship

The Porto Alegre milieu was, at peak in the early 2000s, an enervating biannual gathering of tens of thousands of local and international radicals (Conway 2012; Santos 2006; Smith et al 2014).

However, and in the new global movement's greatest disappointment, just before the onset of the Iraq War, in February 2003 the WSF-catalysed protest of 15 million activists failed to change power relations. Two years later, Amin and 18 other leading left intellectuals felt it was necessary to offer more ideological coherence within the WSF process. In January 2005, they generated 'twelve proposals for another possible world',[4] which in abridged form represented demands to:

(1) Cancel the external debt of southern countries;
(2) Implement international taxes on financial transactions, foreign direct investments, consolidated profit from multinationals, weapons trade, and activities causing large greenhouse effect gas emissions;
(3) Progressively dismantle all forms of fiscal, juridical and banking paradises;
(4) All inhabitants of this planet must have the right to be employed, to social protection and retirement/pension, respecting equal rights between men and women;
(5) Promote all forms of equitable trade, reject all free-trade agreements and laws proposed by the World Trade Organization, and putting in motion mechanisms allowing a progressive upward equalization of social and environmental norms;
(6) Guarantee the right to for all countries to alimentary sovereignty and security by promoting peasant, rural agriculture;
(7) Forbid all type of patenting of knowledge on living beings (human, animal or vegetal) as well as any privatization of common goods for humanity, particularly water;
(8) Fight by means of public policies against all kinds of discrimination, sexism, xenophobia, anti-semitism and racism and fully recognize the political, cultural and economic rights (including the access to natural resources) of indigenous populations;
(9) Take urgent steps to end the destruction of the environment and the threat of severe climate changes due to the greenhouse effect, resulting from the proliferation of individual transportation and the excessive use of non-renewable energy sources;
(10) Demand the dismantling of all foreign military bases and the removal of troops on all countries, except when operating under explicit mandate of the United Nations, especially for Iraq and Palestine;
(11) Guarantee the right to access information and the right to inform, for/by all citizens;
(12) Reform and deeply democratize international institutions by making sure human, economic, social and cultural rights prevail. This implies incorporating the World Bank, the International Monetary Fund and the World Trade Organisation into the decision-making mechanism and systems of the United Nations.

Nearly all of these ideas correlated to actual struggles underway, but nowhere in the manifesto were such campaigns recognized (even with lip service), much less offered statements of solidarity or much-needed linkages to parallel campaigns. Grassroots activist parallels were found in ideas such as decommodification, commoning, international solidarity, 'deglobalization' of capital, activist empowerment and the like. If such conceptual threads tying together concrete activism had indeed been referenced, for example, the final sentence above would have been omitted: there was a general sense in the radical movements that these U.S./EU-controlled multilaterals could not be reformed and acted far too readily as tools of imperial capital. Instead of 'fix it', the call against imperialism's global economic governance was to 'nix it'.[5]

Could Amin and the 18 other authors have drawn on the ongoing activism to reflect that militancy, instead of parachuting down a dozen manifesto statements? Fragmentation of the radical movements was certainly a barrier to finding a coherent fusion. Yet one WSF document drafted two years earlier – the January 2003 Call of Social Movements (endorsed by 153 organizations from all corners of the earth) – and the periodic gatherings of these movements (whether at the WSF or within their particular sectors) would have been the basis for a universalizing manifesto, but one better grounded in campaigning at personal- and household-levels, on shopfloors, in communities and at national, regional and global scales.

The following year, in January 2006, the 9000-word Bamako Appeal followed, at a gathering just prior to the decentralized WSF (which took place in Mali's capital).[6] Amin guided a group of intellectuals and strategists who generated much deeper principles, long-term objectives and immediate action plans.[7] The unifying language included a call for 'internationalism joining the peoples of the South and the North who suffer the ravages engendered by the dictatorship of financial markets and by the uncontrolled global deployment of the transnational firms'.

But the peoples of the world were not simply suffering ravages, they were fighting back.[8] To be sure, in its nearly 9000 words, the Bamako Appeal did make (very occasional) reference to such campaigning. But drawing on these struggles occurred in an overly general way (by the 'anti-globalization movement') or in technicist form, in which massive movements like Via Campesina (mentioned just once) were directed to play institutional roles ill-suited to their militancy.[9]

If the main problems with the Porto Alegre and Bamako manifestos were lack of connectivity to active struggles and a failure to comprehend – much less specifically link, including ideologically – the dots between these, then the opposite problem hampered Chavez' 5th Socialist International. At 2009–10 gatherings Fuentes (2009) expressed a desire for 'a space for socialist-oriented parties, movements and currents in which we can harmonize a common strategy for the struggle against imperialism, the overthrow of capitalism by socialism'. The core group included left parties in power: the Movement for Socialism from Bolivia, the Farabundo Martí National Liberation Front from El Salvador, the Sandinista National Liberation Front from Nicaragua and the PAIS Alliance from Ecuador, along with the Proposal for an Alternative Society from Chile, the New Nation Alliance from Guatemala, and the Socialist Alliance from Australia.

This project was not only based in parties; in the Anglophone world it was promoted actively by Michael Albert of the Z Communications network, an entrepreneurial activist who was expert at linking networks both through the formidable U.S.-based platform of radical writers he had assembled – at one point using TeleSUR in Caracas as their base – and, from 2003, the 'Life After Capitalism' project within the WSF. But after an April 2010 gathering hosted by Chavez, the International's momentum was quickly lost, particularly because the larger European parties and those from the old Soviet Third International tradition were ultimately uninterested – or in some cases were specifically hostile to the competition. Chavez's death in 2013 and the end of the commodity super-cycle also terminated that project.

4. Conclusion: the value of manifesto demands as movement stepping stones

One lesson we might draw from the lacunae in Amin's earlier internationalisms was not necessarily one he agreed with in 2018, when formulating the call for further networking under the banner of a new international. At least one convincing theory of social change, propounded by Vicente Navarro (1993), takes as a premise Amin's analysis of capitalism's limits, and also suggests making the sorts of demands Amin and his allies have done for decades – most of which are entirely reasonable (not loony-left fantasies), in terms of logistics, technology, administration, and fiscal and financial resources. At that stage, the differential character of reformism – 'reformist' or 'non-reformist', to

use Andre Gorz's (1967) framing – are immediately evident. At the stage where the social movements push harder for transformative (non-reformist) demands, the capitalist system refuses to concede these (in Navarro's case, single-payer national health insurance) for a simple reason: it seeks to
retain prevailing class power relations intact. And it is then that a more durable radical politics presents itself, as social struggles waged below hit the ceiling of what is possible under capitalism.

What the 19 Porto Alegre signatories, the Bamako Appeal authors and the Chavez 5th International strategists failed to do, was ground their analysis in that era's leading social movements'
politics, including concrete struggles which then – and today – desperately needed international solidarity, networking and institution-building (Sen and Kumar 2007). Those politics sometimes generate parallel demands to those of the left intelligencia, but not always. Indeed often the
geographically-localistic, sectorally-narrow and urgent character of local social struggles cuts against
the grain of the universal, longer-term approach that Amin advocated. It's a long-standing problem,
as Frantz Fanon (1967, p. 186) remarked: 'For my part the deeper I enter into the cultures and the
political circles, the surer I am that the great danger that threatens Africa is the absence of ideology.'

And there, finally, is where Amin's project should be celebrated, and joined: in comparing notes
about the diverse ideas, experiences and most importantly, *concrete struggles* that are in play across
the world. From there, the principles, analyses, strategies, tactics and alliances of the global left
become clearer. It is only in this process that an ideology suitable for the century is capable of
being forged.

Notes

1. In prior years, models for this internationalist anti-capitalist networking included Berlin-based communist Willi Münzenberg, or subsequently – albeit in military-charismatic mode – Che Guevara. For a
   review of forty years of efforts by Amin's networks and similar institutions, see the survey by William
   Carroll (2016) of what he termed Transnational Alternative Policy Groups, under a rubric Amin exemplified: 'expose, oppose, propose'.
2. Allies whom Amin brought to the TWF were a mix of revolutionaries, independent leftists, communists
   and socialists, dependencia-nationalists and social democrats, including Latin Americans Celso Furtado,
   Fernando Henrique Cardoso, Enrique Iglesias, Juan Somavia, Enrique Oteiza and Pablo Gonzalez Casa-
   nova; numerous Africans including Claude Ake, Justinian Rweyemamu, Ismail Abdallah, Lamine
   Gakou, and from Algiers the Applied Economics Research Centre; and from Asia, Paresh Chattopadhay,
   Amiya Bagchi, Lau Kin Chi, Ramkrishna Mukerjee, Kien Theeravit, Suthy Prasartset, Ponna Wignaraja,
   Paul Lin, Gamani Corea and George Asniero. His closest comrades in Dakar included Lily Bayoumy,
   Bernard Founou and Cheickh Gueye, and in Cairo, Mamdouh Habashi and Helmy Shawary. Among
   Northern sponsors was Swedish prime minister Olaf Palme, a fact which assisted fundraising from 'var-
   ious institutions in Norway, Finland, the Netherlands, Canada and Italy, as well as the EU and the UN
   University' (Amin 2006, p. 182). His main english-language publisher was Monthly Review Press but he
   also published recent books in a Fahamu (*Pambazuka*) series headquartered in Kenya, as well as French
   and Arabic publishing houses.
3. Amin (2006, p. 195) continued:

   > The Davos organizers, like the narrow-minded Swiss authorities, were so furious that it was
   > impossible to produce the surprise a second time round. Hence the idea of a World Social
   > Forum, on a different scale, for which Porto Alegre seemed a natural choice because of the con-
   > siderable resources that the Brazilian Workers Party could mobilize for it there. The success of
   > Porto Alegre I, in January 2001, did not feature on the front pages of the major Western news-
   > papers. The enemy's chosen strategy was to boycott the whole initiative.

4. The signatories were Aminata Traore and, revealing a formidable gender bias, 18 men: Adolfo Perez
   Esquivel, Eduardo Galeano, Jose Saramago, Francois Houtart, Boaventura de Sousa Santos, Armand

Mattelart, Roberto Savio, Riccardo Petrella, Ignacio Ramonet, Bernard Cassen, Samir Amin, Atilio Boron, Samuel Ruiz Garcia, Tariq Ali, Frei Betto, Emir Sader, Walden Bello and Immanuel Wallerstein.

5. To that end, a push for a Third World debtors' cartel – as had been proposed by Fidel Castro, Julius Nyerere and others two decades earlier – came from leading Southern Hemisphere Jubilee movement activists, at the same time a World Bank Bonds Boycott was gathering pace, what with city councils in major U.S. cities (even San Francisco, unanimously) withdrawing their municipal funds from Bank securities. Their effort, truncated in the mid-2000s (due largely to funder fatigue), was to start a 'run on the Bank' (Bond 2003).

6. Indeed from 2004, the WSF moved between Porto Alegre and Mumbai, Caracas, Karachi, Bamako, Nairobi, Belem, Dakar and Tunis (twice), before even trying Montreal in 2016, but the novelty and energy wore off over time.

7. To illustrate, the ten points entailed strategies:

   (1) for a multipolar world system founded on peace, law and negotiation
   (2) for an economic reorganization of the global system
   (3) for regionalizations in the service of the people and which reinforce the south in global negotiations
   (4) for the democratic management of the planet's natural resources
   (5) for a better future for peasant farmers
   (6) to build a workers' united front
   (7) for a democratization of societies as a necessary step to full human development
   (8) for the eradication of all forms of oppression, exploitation and alienation of women
   (9) for the democratic management of the media and cultural diversity
   (10) for the democratization of international organizations and the institutionalization of a multipolar international order

8. In South Africa, as noted, the Treatment Action Campaign had just months earlier turned the corner on AIDS by compelling governments to acquire generic drugs and provide them through public health system. Activists also successfully demanded that a UN Global Fund be set up to supply such medicines and strengthen public health systems in the cases of AIDS, TB and malaria.

9. The Appeal remarks on the need to get agriculture away from WTO control by entrusting the international regulation of agricultural trade to an institution of the United Nations, possibly the Food and Agricultural Organization. In particular, by reforming its organization on the tripartite model of International Labor Organization, which would associate to this regulation the representatives of agricultural trade unions (International Federation of Agricultural Producers and Via Campesina) beside representatives of the agro-alimentary firms (which act already in the shadows on the governments negotiating with the WTO) and of the national states.

Disclosure statement

No potential conflict of interest was reported by the author.

References

Amin, S. (2006). *A life looking forward*. London: Zed Books.

Amin, S. (2018, August 23). Letter of intent for an inaugural meeting of the International of Workers and Peoples. *Pambazuka*. Retrieved from https://www.pambazuka.org/global-south/letter-intent-inaugural-meeting-international-workers-and-peoples

Bond, P. (2003). *Against global apartheid*. London: Zed Books.

Bond, P. (2018, December). Africa's pioneering Marxist political economist, seen from South Africa: Samir Amin, 1931-2018. *Codesria Bulletin*, *42*(4), 55–58. Retrieved from https://www.codesria.org/IMG/pdf/-153.pdf?9642/db253746558848af24808dba19e58f800c070af0

Carroll, W. (2016). *Expose, oppose, propose*. London: Zed Books.

Conway, J. (2012). *Edges of global justice*. New York, NY: Routledge.

Fanon, F. (1967). *Toward the African revolution*. New York, NY: Monthly Review Press.

Fuentes, F. (2009, November 27). Venezuela: Hugo Chavez calls for international socialist unity. *Links*. Retrieved from http://links.org.au/node/1378

Garcia, A., & Bond, P. (2018). *Amplifying the contradictions. The socialist Register 2019*. London: Merlin Press. Retrieved from https://socialistregister.com/index.php/srv/article/view/30948

Gorz, A. (1967). *Strategy for labor*. Boston: Beacon Press.

Navarro, V. (1993). *Dangerous to your health*. New York, NY: Monthly Review Press.

Santos, B. (2006). *The rise of the global left*. London: Zed Books.

Sen, J., & Khumar, M. (Eds.). (2007). *A political Programme for the world social Forum?* New Delhi: India Institute for Critical Action: Centre in Movement and Durban: Centre for Civil Society. Retrieved from http://ccs.ukzn.ac.za/files/CACIM%20CCS%20WSF%20Politics.pdf

Smith, J., Karides, M., Becker, M., Brunelle, D., Chase-Dunn, C., Della Porta, D., … Vazquez, R. (2014). *Global democracy and the world social Forum*. Boulder: Paradigm Publishers.

What is to be done? The importance of Samir Amin's answer

Radhika Desai

ABSTRACT
We consider Samir Amin's last political will and testament as a commission to the international left. From the perspective of geopolitical economy, which has much in common with what Samir called the world-wide law of value and delinking, accepting this commission requires the left to correct course from that on which much of the western left, at least, has been set over the past many decades, losing its way on questions of imperialism and productive organization. We discuss the questions of imperialism and anti-imperialist resistance, contradiction, reform and revolution and political organization as they arise from Samir's text.

Samir Amin, a leading scholar and co-founder of the world-systems tradition, died on August 12, 2018. Just before his death, he published, along with close allies, a call for 'workers and the people' to establish a 'fifth international' [https://www.pambazuka.org/global-south/letter-intent-inaugural-meeting-international-workers-and-peoples] *to coordinate support to progressive movements. To honor Samir Amin's invaluable contribution to world-systems scholarship, we are pleased to present readers with a selection of essays responding to Amin's final message for today's anti-systemic movements. This forum is being co-published between* Globalizations [https://www.tandfonline.com/rglo], *the* Journal of World-Systems Research [http://jwsr.pitt.edu/ojs/index.php/jwsr/issue/view/75] *and* Pambazuka News [https://www.pambazuka.org/]. *Additional essays and commentary can be found in these outlets.*

Samir Amin has left us his answer to the eternal political question, 'What is to be done?', as his last political will and testament. In doing so, he has charged us with continuing his unceasing political engagement with events and developments world-wide, his sober exploration of the possibilities for human emancipation, his dogged development of Marxism in the face of the new demands of history, and of ruthless criticism of established orthodoxies. I want to argue here that if we are to take up this commission, we need to recognise that what he has left us with constitutes a long overdue indictment of the broad direction of the left, particularly the dominant Western left and Western Marxism, over recent decades.

Something is clearly wrong when the surfeit of opportunities for left mobilization offered by four decades of neoliberalism, successive financial crises, mounting inequality, widespread overburdening and hopelessness are foregone in country after country, and grasped instead by fearsome far right formations which cut figures more closely resembling the fascist right of the interwar years than any right political formation since. Something is also clearly wrong when the large swaths of the

Western left and Western Marxism cannot countenance the further advance of multipolarity, the shift in the world economy's centre of gravity away from the west for the first time in the history of the capitalist world, without political confusion or even hostility instead of considering its anti-imperialist potential.

A left reconstruction is urgent and that is what Samir's text seeks. It is a short text, one to be read against the background of his oeuvre and life. And inevitably, of course, against that of our own ideas.

Geopolitical economy or the worldwide law of value

Those against which I offer the present reading fall under the rubric of what I have recently dubbed geopolitical economy (Desai, 2013), a new approach to understanding relations between nations in a capitalist world, one that draws on Samir's work. Geopolitical economy insists on the materiality of nations, on the essential economic role states must play in the capitalist world. Capitalist states must manage capitalism's contradictions through domestic and international actions, the latter including imperialism, formal and informal. Socialist ones of course have a clear economic role, not only in organising a planned economy but also, at the interface of its interaction with the wider world economy dominated by capitalist and imperialist states, limiting their ability to externalise their contradictions.

As such, geopolitical economy challenges the prevailing cosmopolitan ideas about the world economy such as free trade, globalization, US hegemony or empire. In these, either no state matters or only one does. They are not theories but ideologies. Just as dominant ideologies within societies reflect the interests of the dominant classes, so internationally, the dominant ideologies reflect those of the dominant countries. Their function is to inform and justify a world economy opened to dominant capitalist countries' goods and capital and to serve its labour and raw material needs, an openness necessitated precisely by capitalism's contradictions and imposed by imperialism.

However, wishes not being horses even for the most powerful countries, this is not the end of the story. Imperialism is resisted, making capitalist international relations dialectical. In the dialectic of uneven and combined development that drives them, dominant capitalist nations seek to create and maintain the unevenness of world capitalist development that favours them. While colonies cannot resist and are forced open, there are many countries with the power and will to do so in the only way possible: state directed or 'combined' development using protection, industrial policy etc. This was true of the industrialization of the first countries to challenge Britain's original industrial and imperial dominance back in the 1870s, which had already made the world multipolar. It was also true of the actually existing communisms beginning with Russia and the attempts at national development in the early post-war decades. And it is true of the rise of China and other emerging economies today. Productive capacity has spread only in this fashion, not through markets let alone, as some Western Marxists suggested, via imperialism (Warren, 1980). Such 'combined development' has also ensured the further advance of multipolarity.

Each phase of this necessarily national spread of productive capacity has constrained the imperial core of capitalism, narrowing its options, forcing it into national containers and making it more susceptible to working people's demands at home. After 1917, 'communist' combined development became an option as well as the earlier capitalist forms, and this new form was at once more popular and more relevant to development without imperial power and therefore to the Third World.

Geopolitical economy as briefly outlined here was not only influenced by Samir's extensive oeuvre, including his view of imperialism and anti-imperialism and the critical idea of 'de-linking', but also entered into our intellectual engagement over the years.

In September 2008, while major financial institutions were crashing in the Anglosphere, I was about to begin my presentation at the social forum in Malmö, Sweden, when a thin white-haired man, at once unassuming and arresting, entered the room and sat down. I spoke on 'When was Globalization? Origin and End of a US Strategy'. Sceptics had already refuted the main claims of globalization discourse, I explained, undermining the notion it was some new phenomenon sweeping all before it. My own argument built on this refutation, asking why, then, did we begin talking about globalization in the 1990s. My answer was that it was a particular strategy of US dominance aimed, in particular, at lifting capital controls so dollar-denominated financial bubbles could shore up the dollar. As I delivered my talk, I could see the white-haired man listening attentively, nodding agreement at key points. After it was over, we began talking, first in meeting room and then walking out. He expressed complete agreement with my argument, adding points to bolster it here and there, particularly on matters relating to the financialized US economy. With so much to agree about, at some point I had to say: 'You know, I don't know your name'. His answer, Samir Amin, was, as you can imagine, one of the most wonderful surprises of my life. His agreement and approval had already been very gratifying then and mean more as time goes on and I realise certain critical truths more keenly.

Many years later, we had the chance to interact more deeply and broadly at one of the regular workshops of the *Historiches Kritisches Wörterbuch des Marxismus* in Berlin, this time on the 'Widerspruche des Nationalen' (Contradictions of the National). In long conversations over several days of formal sessions, lunches, dinners and coffees in the halls and gardens of the sprawling conference complex, we explored our extensive common ground, tossing our ideas, critiques of more and less politically distant thinkers and pivotal facts on which we built our arguments back and forth, each toss refining them a little more. Our agreements became particularly important in the sessions because Samir and I, along with Michael Löwy, inevitably ended up resisting and rolling back the general disdain for matters national. I still cherish the memory of Samir's interjection after a long response I made to a question: 'I completely agree with Radhika!'

In our correspondence thereafter, when I sent him a particularly critical intervention of mine (Desai, 2016), Samir said, *inter alia*, 'I loved your insisting on what you call "the geopolitical economy". I call it: "the law of value operating at the global level of the capitalist/imperialist system"' (personal correspondence 10 June 2016). Samir was right. We used differing terminology. We approached matters differently given our different backgrounds, personal and intellectual, and we explored different things beyond the core of our agreement. However, the broad thrust of our thinking, trying to give a historical materialist account of the workings of the capitalist world, understanding imperialism but also giving anti-imperialism its due, putting class as well as nation in the frame of historical materialist analysis, was the same. So were our purposes: to identify political and policy imperatives and recommendations for advances towards socialism.

Revolution and anti-imperialism or why combined development is revolutionary

The most valuable thing about Samir's proposal for a new international is his insistence that it be one of workers *and peoples*. In this insistence lies his challenge to the Western left's and Western Marxism's critical political about-turn, away from the abiding concern with imperialism that characterized twentieth century Marxism and towards an analysis of 'capitalism' shorn of imperialism.

This about turn has cost these currents their purchase on politics over recent decades. In the early post-war decades, analysis of imperialism dominated left discussion. After all, contrary to Second International expectations, amid the crisis of imperialist capitalism that issued in the 'Thirty Years' Crisis' of 1914–45, the Russian and Chinese Revolutions inaugurated the cycle of revolutions, socialist and national, that rolled back imperialism in the 'backward' parts of Europe and in Asia. The fate of the Second and Third Worlds dominated discussion amid a general 'revolt against the West' (as one historian characterized the twentieth century, Barraclough, 1964).

Soon after, however, the Western left distanced itself from the concept of imperialism, not because anyone had demonstrated that it was unnecessary but perhaps as a manifestation of the ebbing of anti-imperialism (Patnaik, 1995). It was not just that Western Marxism now asserted that 'Capitalism does not need a subordinated hinterland or periphery, though it will use and profit from it if it exists' (Brewer, 1990, p. 57) or even that some rather notoriously, took to considering it a 'pioneer of capitalism' (Warren, 1980). Far more on the left considered it a non-issue, a distraction from class and socialism, or worse, an affliction they termed 'Third Worldism': the weak-mindedness of those so easily impressed by 'the image of guerrillas with coloured skins amid tropical vegetation' (Hobsbawm, 1994, p. 443) as to privilege the revolutionary potential of Third World peasants over that of First World workers. Dreams of Third World Revolution, national or social, were futile or perverse or even dangerous (the views ran the gamut of Hirschman's list of arguments against change: futility, perversity, jeopardy). By seeking to defy the 'global' logic of capital, Third World countries only increased 'pressures to external political compromise and internal political degeneration' that emanate from a world capitalist market dominated by the advanced industrial world (Brenner, 1977, p. 92). With no option but to obey western capitalism, the anti-imperialist Third World, having once been the Prince of Denmark in Marxism's and the left's *Hamlet*, was now written out of the script. Without it, no wonder the Western left and Western Marxism appear to have been running a production of the absurdist *Rosencrantz and Guildenstern are Dead* instead.

This political about turn had at least two major effects on the western left. Internationally, as western aggression intensified in the wake of the disintegration of the Soviet Union, beginning with the dismemberment of Yugoslavia, large parts of the western left aligned with western powers against an array of Third World governments. This was done in the name of 'humanitarian intervention' against 'brutal dictators' (Johnstone, 2002 is a still relevant critique) or, as lately in the case of Venezuela, by failing to choose between western aggression and an allegedly incompetent, corrupt, and authoritarian government (e.g. Hetland, 2019, for a critique see Martin, 2019). No wonder Western Marxists marked Russian Revolution's centenary remarkably ambiguously, seeking, as one representative volume had it, to understand but also 'transcend' its legacy and 'look forward more than back' (Panitch & Albo, 2017, ix). This amounted to depriving the record of national and social revolutions since 1917 and anti-imperialism itself, of any role in socialism. This stance leaves so much of the left, in the west and elsewhere, standing ineffectually on the sidelines, unable to get a handle on a world being transformed by the further ebbing of imperialism. Its most prominent signs include the rise of China and other emerging economies, the fissures in the western alliance and the ability of so many countries, whether Russia or China or even Italy, to defy western designs.

On the other hand, having written the actual history of revolutions out of the script, such a Marxism is also inevitably trapped in a magical conception of revolution at home despite the most propitious conditions created by four decades of neoliberalism. During these decades, neoliberalism failed to restore the dynamism of western capital and end the growth slowdown it entered in the 1970s. It was, moreover, able to impose the costs of its prescriptions on working people and so many Third World countries. Despite this, and though Western Marxism hardly lacks erudition and intellectual fire-power, it is unable to light the way for the left. This failure has left working people more susceptible to appeals of the right than the left and Third World peoples without solidarity.

The left's economic agenda remains confined to questions of redistribution, void of any plan for a socialist reconstruction of the *productive economy*. In its place there reigns a vague opposition to planning and state direction and an equally vague commitment to small scale enterprises, whether worker owned or cooperative, stances which can only be labelled Proudhonist (Desai, 2011). Any proper socialist organization of the economy would require a sober assessment of the actual sources of such productive dynamism that capitalist economies have demonstrated, sources that are less likely to be located in the market than in the state. It would require an assessment of the achievements, mistakes and failures of the varieties of actually existing communisms in the face of imperialism. And, last but not least, it would require appreciating how imperial relationships underpin western productive capacities and material living standards and what it would take to replace them with an egalitarian, domestically and internationally just and, of course, sustainable economy (Desai, 2017). So far all this lies beyond the Western left and Western Marxist pale.

Today, however, with the West trapped in secular stagnation and China and other emerging economies growing faster, the frontiers of imperialism as being pushed father back and, perhaps because of that, interest in imperialism is growing once again (Cope, 2012; Desai, 2013; Ness & Cope, 2015; Patnaik & Patnaik, 2016; Smith, 2016). To be sure, there are many problems with the pattern of this growth China and the emerging economies, problems that arise at least as much from imperialist attempt to undermine it as from domestic power structures. Rectifying them will, however, increase the progressive potential of this development which, even in this distorted form, is narrowing the options of western imperialist capitalism and making economies more national and therefore more susceptible to democratic pressures.

Samir's warning against the degeneration of anti-imperial struggles into 'reactionary backward-looking illusions expressed by religious or pseudo ethics' is critical here. On the one hand, there is no doubt that in many Third World countries lacking the political capacity to challenge imperialism through socialist forms national capitalisms have taken root. There, these reactionary ideologies have typically been the hand-maidens of an intensification of capitalist power and control. However, they remain, for reasons indicated by Samir, volatile and unstable, not least because they cannot fulfil the aspirations they must arouse to get to and/or remain in power. On the other, while these Third World capitalist classes certainly expect to 'construct a "developed" national capitalism capable of actively shaping the international environment in their favour', popular pressures demand a more and more reformed capitalism and a far broader based prosperity than these capitalisms can provide. This is certainly my analysis of the political dynamics of capitalist India over recent decades (Desai, 2004, 2010b, 2014).

By insisting on placing peoples and nations, alongside workers, as protagonists of socialism, Samir signalled the critical need to re-integrate capitalism and imperialism, class struggle and international struggle in a single perspective. Unless this is done, the progressive potential of emerging multipolarity cannot be realized and internationalism can only be perverted into an endorsement of inevitably imperialist cosmopolitan ideas and practices.

Contradiction

Samir never flinched from facing up to the immensity of capitalist power today. He outlines it in the text before us, referring *inter alia* to the extreme centralization of power in the hands of financial oligarchies, the 'domestication of the main right-wing and left-wing parties, the unions and the organization of so-called civil society', the hollowing out of democracy, totalitarian control over society, and the intensification of the exploitation of the Third World amounting to a practical 'reco-lonization' of the world. However, he also never lost the sense of contradiction so central to Marxism and so lost on so many contemporary Marxists in the west. He concluded the account of the main dimensions of capitalist power with the observations that this immense power was also 'fragile' and that we are living in the 'autumn' of capitalism. Samir also considered some, at least, of these dimensions of (apparent) power symptoms of this fragility and senility such as the military control the west seeks over the world. It was more swagger than power.

This insistence on contradiction in a voice as authoritative as Samir's is critically important today. The same neoliberal decades over which the left gave up its concern for imperialism also witnessed a rejection of the very notion of contradiction. This move was ultimately rooted in the incursion of neoclassical economics into Marxism in the late nineteenth century. As is well-known, neoclassical economics emerged in the 1870s as a response to working class organization as well as the intellectual threat of Marxism and other radical currents. It was theoretically and methodologically antithetical to Marxism. Despite this, already in the late 19th century, intellectuals trained in neoclassical econ-omics first, arriving at Marxism later, sought to fit the latter into the former. The result was to replace Marx's critique of political economy with a 'Marxist economics' which owed more to neoclassical economics than Marx. No wonder its practitioners found Marx had a problem with 'transforming' values into prices, no wonder they think there is no demand problem or that the rate of profit does not fall (Desai, 2010a, 2016, 2017). This trend remained contested for decades. By the 1970s, how-ever, Western Marxism had, in any case, vacated the ground of the materialist analysis of society for the academically greener pastures of the 'social' and 'cultural' (as if Marxism could permit them to be examined in isolation from the material). It now took Marxist economics' word when it came to understanding matters 'economic' (also not separated by Marx from the rest of the historical social formation).

With the erasure of Marx's more esoteric but essential conception of the contradictions of capital accumulation, the western left also abandoned the wider idea of contradiction: that the ruling class may try to achieve many objectives – increase profits, intensify Third World exploitation, control dissent – but it may not succeed. In place of a volatile and contradiction-ridden capitalist order that Marx portrayed, the Western left first created an idol of a capitalism with the productive powers of Prometheus and the staying power of Methuselah and then worshipped at its altar. It is bereft of the wider sense that, to an important extent, capitalists are in the position of the half-trained sor-cerer's apprentice, not in control of the spirits they have conjured up and that understanding this, identifying the precise points at which capitalist control is failing, is critical. It is needed to identify the most effective lines of working class and anti-imperialist advance and so the left is prepared to defend humanity from the often devastating consequences of these contradictions.

Instead, the western left chastises those who speak of contradictions for 'predicting nine of the past five recessions'. It is unmindful or uncaring (one does not know which is worse) that it is para-phrasing Paul Samuelson, who defanged Keynes's radical critique of neoclassical economies (Desai, 2009; Desai & Freeman, 2009) to turn it into 'bastard Keynesianism', on the predictions of the stock market. Settled in these questionable convictions, the western left produces tome after tome attesting to the 'global' power of capital and the 'hegemonic' power of the US or the West.

What could be more critical, at a time when the West's entanglement in the tendencies prolonging the 'Long Downturn' seems more intractable than ever, when it cannot grow even at anaemic rates without the aid of continuously inflated financial bubbles, when many Third World countries are growing faster than ever, when western purchase on international events is slipping, when cracks in the European Union are lengthening and widening, to speak of the contradictions, fragility and senility of imperialist capitalism?

Reform and revolution

Which brings me the matter of the stark opposition between revolution and reform that prevails on the left and which Samir also rejected. Such an opposition could not have been farther from the minds of Marx or Engels or any serious revolutionary. The ten demands listed in *The Communist Manifesto* or the Bolshevik call for 'Peace, Bread and Land' or Chinese communist land reform could hardly appear more 'reformist'. However, demands *per se* are neither reformist or revolutionary but situations make them so. The most modest demand, if the ruling class is unable or unwilling to fulfil it and provided the people are sufficiently organized to say, well, in that case, we'll fulfil it ourselves, can become revolutionary.

Revolutionaries like Samir remembered on the one hand that reforms can strengthen the ability of working people to fight for more (Patnaik, 2009) and on the other that each reform – whether the welfare state in the west or the seemingly paltry provision of providing 150 days of employment to one member of every poor family in India, in so far as it reduces the commodification of labour and constitutes even a small constraint on the power and prerogatives of capital, is an advance. On the other hand, Samir never discounted what popular pressures could achieve even in bourgeois nationalist Third World countries: as a recent obituary has it, he went to work for the governments of Egypt and Mali in the 1960s because he believed that 'given an appropriately enlightened government and adequate social sanction, trajectories of development that advanced social good could be engineered even within non-socialist economies' (Chandrashekhar, 2018).

Of course, such gains in capitalist countries are fragile and, as is well known, were set back during the neoliberal decades. However, their significance, notwithstanding these setbacks, was part of the reason Samir took a very long-term view of revolution. It was something that occurred in chapters and episodes in different parts of the world at different times, that ebbed and flowed, advanced and retreated, would take centuries to complete but is *ongoing*.

Organization

For some time, I've seen the western left's problems as being its captivity in what I've called Proudhonist economics and network politics. The first, already addressed above, rejects any conception of a general organization of society and economy, otherwise known as planning, to replace their market organization. This amounts to accepting society's capitalist and imperialist organization by default. I've already dealt with this problem above. Suffice it to add here that, obviously, in a socialist society such general organization has to be democratic and decentralised.

Network politics, for its part, rejects the only way this can be achieved – through the general organization of people in a party or something matching its organizational capacities. Instead, 'movements', 'horizontal' rather than vertical structures considered inherently anti-democratic are favoured. Samir is absolutely right to insist on establishing an organization, not just a movement, not just internationally but within countries.

We live in times that recall Yeats's ominous forebodings in 'The Second Coming': the 'falcon' of the capitalist world can no longer hear the capitalist falconer, the 'best lack all conviction' while 'the worst are full of passionate intensity'. From the US and Britain to Europe, from Brazil and Argentina to Egypt and the Philippines, the harvest of discontent sown by over four decades of neoliberalism is being reaped by the worst the right can produce. The left is rudderless and needs re-invention. That is what Samir is calling for. And that requires retracing our steps back to the tradition of revolutionary communism which stretches in a single line from the popular currents of the seventeenth and eighteenth century revolutions, including the Haitian, through the 19th century upheavals whether the European 1988, Taiping Rebellion or the Paris Commune to the revolutionary situation created worldwide by the first and second world wars in Europe and the revolutions against imperialism that rolled out after 1917. That is why Samir thought we should study them.

Disclosure statement

No potential conflict of interest was reported by the author.

References

Barraclough, G. (1964). *An introduction to contemporary history*. London: Penguin.
Brenner, R. (1977). The origins of capitalist development: A critique of neo-Smithian Marxism. *New Left Review*, I/104, July–August, 25–92.
Brewer, A. (1990). *Marxist theories of imperialism: A critical survey* (2nd ed.). London: Routledge.
Chandrashekhar, C. P. (2018). In memoriam: Samir Amin: A Marxist from the third world. *Frontline*, 1, September. Retrieved from https://www.networkideas.org/news-analysis/2018/09/obituary-samir-amin-1931-2018/
Cope, Z. (2012). *Divided world, divided class*. Montreal: Kersplebedeb.
Desai, R. (2004). Forward march of Hindutva halted? *New Left Review*, 30, 49–67. Second series, November–December.
Desai, R. (2009). Keynes Redux: World money after the 2008 crisis. In W. Anthony & J. Guard (Eds.), *Bailouts and bankruptcies* (pp. 123–144). Winnipeg: Fernwood Press.
Desai, R. (2010a). Consumption demand in Marx and in the current crisis. *Research in Political Economy, 26*, 101–141.
Desai, R. (2010b). Hindutva's ebbing Tide? In S. Ruparelia, S. Corbridge, J. Harriss, & S. Reddy (Eds.), *Great transformations* (pp. 172–185). New York, NY: Routledge.
Desai, R. (2011). The new communists of the commons: 21st century proudhonists. *International Critical Thought, 1*(2), 204–223.
Desai, R. (2013). *Geopolitical economy: After US hegemony, globalization and empire*. London: Pluto Press.
Desai, R. (2014). A latter-day fascism? *Economic and Political Weekly, XLIX*(35), 48–58.
Desai, R. (2016). The value of history and the history of value. In T. Subasat (Ed.), *The great meltdown of 2008: Systemic, conjunctural or policy-created?* (pp. 136–158). Cheltenham: Edward Elgar.
Desai, R. (2017). Capital at 150. *Red Pepper*, September 2017, pp. 48–49.
Desai, R., & Freeman, A. (2009). Keynes and the crisis: A case of mistaken identity. *Canadian Dimension*, July.
Hetland, G. (2019). Venezuela's deadly blackout highlights the need for a negotiated resolution to the crisis. *The Nation*. 13 March. Retrieved from https://www.thenation.com/article/venezuela-blackout-us-sanctions-maduro/
Hobsbawm, E. (1994). *Age of extremes: The short twentieth century*. London: Michael Joseph.
Johnstone, D. (2002). *Fool's crusade: Yugoslavia, NATO and western delusions*. New York, NY: Monthly Review Press.
Martin, J. (2019). Who's to blame for the crisis in Venezuela? *Venezuelanalysis*, 17 March. Retrieved from https://venezuelanalysis.com/analysis/14392

Ness, I., & Cope, Z. (2015). *The Palgrave encyclopedia of imperialism and anti-imperialism*. London: Palgrave.

Panitch, L., & Albo, G. (2017). *Rethinking revolution: Socialist register 2017*. London: Merlin.

Patnaik, P. (1995). Whatever happened to imperialism. In *Whatever happened to imperialism and other essays?* (pp. 102–106). New Delhi: Tulika.

Patnaik, P. (2009). Socialism and welfarism. International development economics associates. Retrieved from http://www.networkideas.org/news/aug2009/print/prnt250809_Socialism.htm

Patnaik, P., & Patnaik, U. (2016). *A theory of imperialism*. New York, NY: Columbia University Press.

Smith, J. (2016). *Imperialism in the twenty-first century: Globalization, super-exploitation, and capitalism's final crisis*. New York, NY: Monthly Review Press.

Warren, B. (1980). *Imperialism, pioneer of capitalism*. (J. Sender, Ed.). London: New Left Books.

The fifth *International*: international or global?

Owen Worth

ABSTRACT

This short piece questions Samir Amin's interpretation of what he meant by the *International*. In envisaging a fifth International, Amin tends to rely on a collection of inter-connected self-determined sovereign entities that resembles more of a traditional understanding of internationalism and less of the transnational global expression developed at the World Social Forums. This suggests that such an approach falls into the same problems that Rosa Luxemburg illustrated during the Second International where she outlined the dangers of what we might refer to today as 'left nationalism'.

Samir Amin, a leading scholar and co-founder of the world-systems tradition, died on August 12, 2018. Just before his death, he published, along with close allies, a call for 'workers and the people' to establish a 'fifth international' [https://www.pambazuka.org/global-south/letter-intent-inaugural-meeting-international-workers-and-peoples] *to coordinate support to progressive movements. To honor Samir Amin's invaluable contribution to world-systems scholarship, we are pleased to present readers with a selection of essays responding to Amin's final message for today's anti-systemic movements. This forum is being co-published between* Globalizations [https://www.tandfonline.com/rglo], *the* Journal of World-Systems Research [http://jwsr.pitt.edu/ojs/index.php/jwsr/issue/view/75] *and* Pambazuka News [https://www.pambazuka.org/]. *Additional essays and commentary can be found in these outlets.*

The deaths of Samir Amin and Bob Cox in 2018 saw two giants from the left depart the stage at a time when the world order; which they did so much to provide a basis for which to study, is in a state of flux. Heavily involved with the workings of the World Social Forum, it is no surprise then that some of Samir Amin's last contributions were to call for a new or 'fifth' *International* (Amin, 2018, 2019). In light of what Amin saw as the abandonment of anti-capitalist struggles in the north in favour of communitarianism and of anti-imperialist struggle in the south in favour of capitalist development, an *International* was required for the left to tackle the global capitalist system in a manner that is both strategic and coherent. Whilst I firmly agree with the premise of a new *International*, I question the form that Amin seems to suggest it should take in regards to confronting the world order. Rather than returning to the logistics of national components, such a body should be geared towards global goals which move beyond the aspirations of 20th century socialism. In doing so, it is apt to remind ourselves of the contribution that Rosa Luxemburg made during the second *International*, particular as it this year witnesses the century anniversary of her tragic death.

Amin's understanding of the neoliberal world order was such that 'globalisation' was seen as a form of imperialism and should be understood in the same manner that traditional 19th century forms of Imperialism had been. The United States, the European Union and East Asia thus represent a 'triad' of Imperialist entities that have managed a world capitalist system reliant upon the exploitation and commodification of resources (Amin, 2018). The expanding global market that has epitomised the nature of globalisation is one that has been upheld by the ruling classes within this triad, led, but not necessarily dominated by the US. As such, a co-ordinated form of internationalism is needed to confront the structures of the contemporary order in a manner that goes far beyond the 'open-confines' inherent within the World Social Forum (WSF, 2007). This form of internationalism would need to commit towards a set of strategic actions that can formally bring together the constellation of socialist and labour organisations across the world in the manner that bonded the international organisations of the 19th and 20th century. In light of the lack of practical strategic thinking from the left in terms of confronting the neoliberal order, this 'call for arms' should be commended. By providing an institutional space where transformative politics can be nurtured, the problems of coherence and fragmentation that have dodged the building of any alternative hegemonic opposition in the neoliberal age can potentially be addressed (Worth, 2013). We are still left to wonder what form such a body would take, and, going forward, how such an idea of 'internationalism' would be understood and realised in terms of its role in confronting capitalism. It is here where Amin's own understanding of the term runs into problems.

Which internationalism?

The notion of internationalism is one that contains several meanings and has different connotations depending on how it is applied and understood. Amin's own use of the term appeared to be one which resembled a traditional form of the *inter*-national. That is that the nation-state remains the prime location for socialism to be built, through the premise of popular democracy and sovereignty. Rather than an attempt to construct a global polity or alternatively a form of world government per se, this suggests that the nation-state itself provides the space where a collection of nationally-specific projects can be forged. The role of any international system here would thus be to facilitate solidarity and partnerships between these respective parts. This was indeed very much the form taken through the building of 20th Century Socialism (Glaser & Walker, 2007).

Amin's attacks on the European Union and indeed his defence of the nation-state in terms of facilitating certain forms of popular sovereignty (2016) would suggest that he favoured this traditional approach. Yet, at the same time, Amin's understanding of internationalism is one whereby the respective sovereign parts of the world system require different roles in order to contest its character. Whilst Amin does stress the need for 'sovereign projects' he also suggests that these entail different meanings, dependent upon where they are developed. Within the triad, he believes that the nation-state should re-assert their sovereignty so they can embark upon forms of nationalisation programmes common within 20th century social democracy as a means of reducing the influence of global capital. He also adds that in the South, regional organisations such as ASEAN, ALBA[1] or more substantially the BRICS are better placed to challenge the system (Amin, 2014). In this way, Amin is consistent with his notable earlier work, seen in classics such as *Unequal Exchange*, where he suggested that any means of disrupting the imperialist workings of the world system as a whole would lead to its potential collapse (Amin, 1976).

As a result, Amin welcomed the Brexit result as he believed this was a symptom of the implosion of a European project, which had emerged as a key lynch-pin of the Euro-American Imperialist system (Amin, 2016). More prominently here, he also attacked accusations that those who criticised the EU from the position of national sovereignty were 'nationalist' in nature and furthermore suggested that the only left-wing response to the EU from groups within Europe currently available was indeed to retreat back to the level of the nation-state (Amin, 2016). It is here where Amin's *inter*-nationalism perhaps becomes more prominent and his overall vision of an international movement becomes quite limited in its outlook. For whilst, on one level, it is understandable – particularly when viewed from the position of the South – that the EU is understood entirely through the lens of an imperialist construct, it provides an analysis which is reductionist to a point which underplays the transformative potential that might emerge from it. This point is not meant to re-play the familiar arguments over whether or not the EU has the potential to provide a vehicle for transformative social change or that as a neoliberal construction it cannot be reformed (see for example the recent debates between Streeck, 2014 and Habermas, 2014), which is not for debate here. Instead, it is to stress that by going back to the model of the nation-state as the main component for internationalism, a departure from the ontological confines inherent within dialectical materialism is evident. Yet Amin appears quite adamant in his belief that as the globalisation of the contemporary era is reminiscent of the globalisation of classical Imperialism, then a response needs to emerge from within similar national processes at it did in the late nineteenth and twentieth century (Amin, 2013). In this sense, rather than looking beyond twentieth century national sovereignty in order to transcend capitalism, a reversion back to such existing national frameworks are preferable.

Amin's understanding of internationalism is thus one which follows the premise of 'left nationalism' that became the hallmark of the different forms of post-war European Socialist and Social Democratic Parties of the 20th century. Likewise, whilst his own work both academically and practically within the WSF did much to stress the importance of non-state groups, from peasant revolts to International NGO campaigning, he still stressed that in the core triad, national strategies still remained the best chance to rupture the workings of the international capitalist system. This appears in contrast to the aspirations of the global justice movements and to the spirit of radical global civil society It also seems less receptive of ideas such as cosmopolitan democracy and the idea of transformation at the global level, which have made up much understanding of how internationalism in the 21st century is perceived (Held, 2004; Kalder, 2001; Patomäki & Teivainen, 2004). At the same time, the substantial body of work associated with autonomous and 'open' Marxist has been quick to point to how struggles can be won within civil society through disrupting forms of production in different ways (Bailey, Clua-Losada, Huke, & Ribera-Almandoz, 2017). The most significant demonstration of this was from Holloway's account of the Zapatistas uprisings in Mexico in 1994 in light of the NAFTA regime coming into effect. The premise here being that the contestation of the neoliberal system can be successfully made without the need of a formal political victory at the centre of power (Holloway, 2002). Indeed, if the last few decades have shown us anything, it has been that national strategies have been undermined both by transformations to global society from above the state and by radical forms of localism from below.

Perhaps the most significant shortcoming of understanding an internationalist strategy around a traditional collection of national struggles – or as an *inter*national one- is in terms of wider ambition. This can certainly be seen within the European context. Whilst a critique of Euro-centrism remains central to any international project geared towards resisting the confines of the present system, the idea that European nation-states need to retreat back into their national shells in order to re-group remains highly problematic from both a practical and a historical sense. It also represents a dangerous precedent. For whilst the rise of the far right is discussed and taken seriously by many urging for the return of national strategies, the very move towards national self-determination itself adds to the environment that allows it to flourish. This becomes especially the case within states across Europe. For, whilst post-colonial nationalist struggles looked to forge forms of nationalism which seek to reject international exploitation, its form in Europe has been so intrinsically linked to Imperialism that it becomes unwise to engage in its structure content, no matter how it might be ideologically constructed (Anderson, 1991).

There have of course been several accounts that seek to demonstrate how nationalism and Marxism are not as incompatible as sometimes portrayed (Munck, 1986; Nimni, 1991) and several more that are quick to remind us that the very nature of internationalism is based on the construction of national variations of socialism (Lewis, 2000). Yet, the problem with all forms of nationalism, no matter how 'progressive' they appear, is that by their very nature they promote divisions which lead to tensions between respective nation-states. These divisions inevitably lead to the potential for clashes between states that have historically been marked by conflicts (Ryan & Worth, 2010). More substantially, they reduce the potential of wider international solidarity as strategies retreat back to the confines of the national, neglecting wider struggles in favour of those drawn out at a national level (Radice, 2000). Thus, whilst it might appear feasible to suggest that national strategies placed within a wider international framework can confront and oppose international capitalism, the mechanism of popular sovereignty to achieve this remains highly problematic and limits any potential to move beyond the confines of the Westphalian state-system.

Luxemburg and internationalism

The form of how internationalism should be expressed within the socialist movement was discussed in earnest in the first decades of the 20th century. In the Second *International*, Rosa Luxemburg provided one of the most devastating and powerful criticisms of national self-determination that there has ever been. Arguing against Lenin, she insisted that any form of sovereign right to self-rule would lead to fragmentation that would weakness the struggle against international capitalism. She also condemned any form of nationalism as a tool used by the bourgeoisie in order to divide the proletariat (Luxemburg, 1976). From a wider ontological perspective, Luxemburg saw the nation-state as the distinct product of capitalism and believed that by limiting strategy around one of its key institutional components, it restricts the potential to move beyond it (Luxemburg, 1986). Thus, for Luxemburg, the whole notion of dialectical materialism should be understood not through the development of existing structures but as a process where new structures emerge and develop over time. Likewise, Internationalism should not be something restricted by structures of the present, nor by pre-existing norms such as national sovereignty, but instead be understood as a mechanism that could move beyond the confines of the present towards the realms of the 'possible' (Worth, 2012).

One hundred years after her death, Luxemburg's understanding of dialectical materialism is far more relevant in the contemporary era of globalisation than it was in the first decades of the twentieth century when nationalism was so significant within every realm of European politics. Even during the debates between Lenin and Luxemburg at the time, Lenin did concede that many of Luxemburg's fears were relevant. Lenin favoured large national multi-cultural units in order to address ethnic divisions and prevent fragmentation from occurring (Davis & Luxemburg, 1976).

The move in world politics in the 21st century towards regionalism sees a greater opportunity for such spatial developments to grow. Therefore, any move that seems to support a retreat back to smaller units based upon sovereign self-determination would appear regressive, even to those at the time that rejected Luxemburg's critiques of nationalism. In addition, the events that followed the Second

International – the failures of the Soviet forms of 'real' or 'state' socialism, the self-destructive pursuit of post-colonial nationalism and the stagnation of European social democratic forms of left nationalism – have all showed us that Luxemburg was correct in many of her assertions. In particular, the belief that national self-determination, by its very nature, creates divisions which are unable to contain would appear to have been proved correct in many respects. This is not to say that self-determination was central to the overriding failure of 20th century socialism, but that by insisting upon the principles of national sovereignty and self-autonomy, the flames of nationalism become stoked to a level that division takes precedence over unity.

In light of recent phenomena such as the sovereign debt crisis and the Brexit vote, it is understandable that any form of internationalism would look to locate itself back within a national-first understanding of *internationalism*. Yet, Rosa Luxemburg's criticisms within the Second *International* show just how such a move both negates an awareness of dialectics in terms of emancipatory potential. and allows for the re-creation of division (Luxemburg, 1971, 1976). In the current era, geo-political developments such as transnational civil movements, regionalism and socio-cultural globalisation might have been shaped and forged by a transnational capitalist class, overwhelmingly located in the 'triad', intent upon building and consolidating a neoliberal capitalism (van der Pijl, 1998). Yet, the struggles against them have moved far beyond the realm of the nation-state to a degree that any potential fifth *International* would require the need to create a framework that moves beyond the configuration of 20th century national units and towards global confrontation.

In the light of Brexit, many others have also stressed the need to return to the mechanism of national sovereignty as the main instrument for confronting neoliberalism (Lapavitsas, 2018; Mitchell & Fazi, 2017; Whyman, 2018). Using the logic of Luxemburg, we see the same potential problems related to division and potential fragmentation emerge that has daunted the socialist movement before. For example, if Germany, France or indeed in this instance, the UK were to revert to national specific bodies as a means of countering, opposing and in due course replacing the EU, then why shouldn't their respective parts fragment further? This has particular relevance to the UK, which like the EU, was built upon Imperial ambition and where both Scotland and Wales, and well as perhaps the City of London might look to assert their own right of self-determination and popular sovereignty. Likewise, on the same basis, as Germany was unified on an Imperialist ambition, would it have to fragment into smaller units as it was prior to its independence in order to move forward? As I stressed earlier, back in the Second *International*, Lenin and his allies conceded these concerns were real urging against any fragmentation through the formation of larger units (Davis & Luxemburg, 1976). Yet, here we see the opposite. Ultimately we have a suggestion for an *International* where its parts look toward disintegrating from larger units to re-asset their sovereign right as nation-states in order to combine towards a greater unified goal. These are obstacles that are evident before we even look at the institutional requirements that would underpin such an *International*.

Conclusion

I sincerely believe that some form of a new *International* is required in order to confront the dynamics of the neoliberal order, one that is particularly geared towards its ideological contestation. In this respect Amin's call for a renewal of Internationalism should be welcomed. I also believe that Amin's critiques of the north from the perspective of the south are vital to any understanding of the workings of global capitalism. In addition and of far more importance here, he is correct in in his assessment that socialism in the north was very quick to disregard internationalism when it suited them in the second half of the Twentieth Century (Amin, 2013, pp. 121–122). The idea that international alliances are formed and that strategies are devised whereby representatives are geared towards different objectives depending on their positioning within global productivity is also an important one.

It is the form that such an *International* should take that concerns me however. Alongside his argument that the best means to attack the system is through disintegration, Amin is keen to stress the importance of popular struggles and sovereignty as a means of achieving this. Whilst in the south, there are several ways in which this can be achieved, he suggests that in the north, this means the return to the confines of the nation-state and ultimately to the premise of 'left nationalism'. If this results in an international where individual states reside behind the protection of sovereignty and self-determination, then any wider unity will be undermined. Rather than detract from transnational developments that have emerged from the social reproduction of globalisation, any future international needs to be ordered at the global level and upon global innovations. Retreating back to the sanitary of the nation-state will merely weaken any potential to build an alternative world order. 100 years on from her brutal murder by the side of a Berlin canal, Rosa Luxemburg's testament on the follies of nationalism remain as important as ever.

Note

1. It should be pointed out that this was written prior to ALBA's (The Bolivarian Alliance for the Americas) disintegrating due to the economic collapse in Venezuela and the withdrawal from the group of Ecuador.

Disclosure statement

No potential conflict of interest was reported by the author.

References

Amin, S. (1976). *Unequal development: An essay on the social formation of peripheral capitalism.* New York, NY: Monthly Review.

Amin, S. (2013). *The implosion of contemporary capitalism.* New York, NY: Monthly Review.

Amin, S. (2014). Popular movements toward socialism: Their unity and diversity. *Monthly Review.* Retrieved from https://monthlyreview.org/2014/06/01/popular-movements-toward-socialism/

Amin, S. (2016). Brexit and the EU implosion: National sovereignty for what purpose? *Pambazuka News.* Retrieved from https://www.pambazuka.org/global-south/brexit-and-eu-implosion-national-sovereignty-what-purpose

Amin, S. (2018). It is imperative to reconstruct the internationale of workers and peoples. *IDEAs* Retrieved from http://www.networkideas.org/featured-articles/2018/07/it-is-imperative-to-reconstruct-the-internationale-of-workers-and-peoples/

Amin, S. (2019). *Only people make their own history: Writings of capitalism, imperialism and revolution.* New York, NY: Monthly Review.

Anderson, B. (1991). *Imagined Communities*. London: Verso.

Bailey, D., Clua-Losada, M., Huke, N., & Ribera-Almandoz, O. (2017). *Beyond defeat and austerity*. London: Routledge.

Davis, H., & Luxemburg, R. (1976). The right of self-determinism in Marxist theory- Luxemburg Vs Lenin. In *The national question* (pp. 1–36). New York, NY: Monthly Review.

Glaser, D., & Walker, D. (2007). *Twentieth century Marxism: A global introduction*. London: Routledge.

Habermas, J. (2014). Merkel's European failure: Germany dozes on a Volcano. *Constellations (Oxford, England), 21*(2), 159–310.

Held, D. (2004). *Global covenant: The social democratic alternative to the Washington consensus*. Cambridge: Polity Press.

Holloway, J. (2002). *Change the world without taking power*. London: Verso.

Kalder, M. (2001). *Global civil society*. Cambridge: Polity Press.

Lapavitsas, C. (2018). *The left case against the EU*. Cambridge: Polity Press.

Lewis, T. (2000). Marxism and nationalism. *International Socialist Review*. Retrieved from https://isreview.org/issues/13/marxism_nationalism_part1.shtml

Luxemburg, R. (1971). *Selected writing*. New York, NY: Monthly Review.

Luxemburg, R. (1976). *The national question*. New York, NY: Monthly Review.

Luxemburg, R. (1986). *Reform or revolution*. London: Militant Press.

Mitchell, W., & Fazi, T. (2017). *Reclaiming the state*. London: Pluto Press.

Munck, R. (1986). *The difficult dialogue: Marxism and nationalism*. London: Zed Books.

Nimni, E. (1991). *Marxism and nationalism*. London: Pluto Press.

Patomäki, H., & Teivainen, T. (2004). The world social forum: An open space or the movement or movements. *Theory, Culture and Society, 21*(6), 145–154.

Radice, H. (2000). Responses to globalisation: A critique of progressive nationalism. *New Political Economy, 5* (1), 5–21.

Ryan, B., & Worth, O. (2010). On the contemporary relevance of left nationalism. *Capital & Class, 34*(1), 54–59.

Streeck, W. (2014). Small-state nostalgia? The current union, Germany, and Europe: A reply to Jurgen Habermas'. *Constellations, 21*(2), 213–221.

van der Pijl, K. (1998). *Transnational classes and international relations*. London: Routledge.

Whyman, P. (2018). *The left case for Brexit*. London: Civitas.

World Social Forum. (2007). *Constitution*. Nairobi: WSF.

Worth, O. (2012). Accumulating the critical spirt: Rosa Luxemburg and critical IPE. *International Politics, 49*(1), 136–153.

Worth, O. (2013). *Resistance in the age of Austerity*. London: Zed Books.

Carrying on Samir Amin's legacy

Boris Kagarlitsky

ABSTRACT
The academic Marxism of the 20th century has shied away from this responsibility, preferring relatively comfortable staying within the walls of universities. Unlike these academic thinkers Samir Amin was one of the few who did not accept this situation. He never considered himself merely a theorist: connection to praxis was vital for him. From this perspective he advocated a project of Fifth International to address sharp and systemic crisis afflicting leftist movements. Each new stage of the evolution of capitalism requires a corresponding transformation of the anti-capitalist forces. Nevertheless, a new political alternative can't be constructed artificially. It can only gradually emerge out of collective experience of different struggles.

Samir Amin, a leading scholar and co-founder of the world-systems tradition, died on August 12, 2018. Just before his death, he published, along with close allies, a call for 'workers and the people' to establish a 'fifth international' [https://www.pambazuka.org/global-south/letter-intent-inaugural-meeting-international-workers-and-peoples] *to coordinate support to progressive movements. To honor Samir Amin's invaluable contribution to world-systems scholarship, we are pleased to present readers with a selection of essays responding to Amin's final message for today's anti-systemic movements. This forum is being co-published between* Globalizations [https://www.tandfonline.com/rglo], *the* Journal of World-Systems Research [http://jwsr.pitt.edu/ojs/index.php/jwsr/issue/view/75] *and* Pambazuka News [https://www.pambazuka.org/]. *Additional essays and commentary can be found in these outlets.*

When Karl Marx wrote his famous Eleventh Thesis on Feuerbach, demanding that philosophers not only explain the world, but also change it, he set before his followers a major problem, not only theoretical or even political one, but also moral. This is because one can only change the world through practical action – praxis. This means that no matter how good and adequate the theory is, it is never sufficient. Praxis involves passion, an uncertainty of the result, a possibility of an error and a responsibility for it.

The academic Marxism of the 20th century has shied away from this responsibility, preferring relatively comfortable staying within the walls of universities, engaging in a fascinating immersion into the depths of an intellectual quest. In fairness, one must admit that this choice was not entirely voluntary. Neither communist parties, which consolidated their ideological canons as an unshakable and formal symbol of faith, nor social democratic organizations, which preferred empirical search for specific short-term solutions to local problems of capitalism, required any new theoretical discoveries. Moreover, they were mortally afraid of them, systematically banishing, and often repressing those thinkers who defiantly tried to find new theoretical paths. History severely punished left-wing organizations for such disregard for the theory. Although it would be wrong to reduce the reasons for the collapse of the communist parties and the crisis of social democracy only to this one factor, the gap between theory and practice undoubtedly aggravated the catastrophe. In turn, academic Marxism, locked in a cozy academic ghetto, became toothless, safe for the ruling classes, and increasingly boring.

Samir Amin was one of the few Marxist thinkers who did not accept this situation. He never considered himself merely a theorist: connection to praxis was vital for him. As a political activist, he was forced to leave his native Egypt. On many occasions, he was subjected to sharp criticism when he did not shy away from an unpopular position that he considered to be politically justified. Even when speaking of theoretical analysis, he was full of passion. Not simply aiming to discuss ongoing processes, Samir Amin also constantly sought ways to influence them. He did not always turn out to be right, but ultimately this is the essence of praxis. Only one who does nothing at all makes no mistakes; only an idea that does not affect any practical matters causes no controversy. At the very end of his life, Samir Amin called for the creation of a new Fifth International in order to respond to the crisis of neo-liberal globalization. This was the outstanding thinker and activist's sort of last will and testament, appealing to those who must seize the banner and carry it further. But what can and should be done practically?

The idea of the need for a new international was brought forth not only by the obvious crisis into which the world capitalist system has plunged at the end of the second decade of the 21st century, but also by a sharp and systemic crisis afflicting leftist movements. All political forms that the conflict between labor and capital took over the course of the 20th century exhausted themselves in the new millennium. The 20th century, which indeed also began with an acute crisis of the world capitalist order, spawned a whole series of global structures and movements that offered themselves as alternatives. Along with the appearance of communist and social democratic parties, which developed primarily in Europe, class struggle on the periphery of the world system gave rise to various versions of national liberation and populist movements, which also challenged the bourgeois order. The end of the 20th century, however, was marked by a deep crisis or even a collapse of all these organizations. The picture that we are presented with at the moment looks very sad. The world communist movement is no more. The state parties that headed the states of the Eastern bloc underwent profound bureaucratic degeneration and ceased to exist. The industrial bourgeois economy had not overcome its inherent contradictions: on the contrary, these contradictions transpired with greater clarity. At the beginning of the 21st century, China became not just a part of the capitalist world-system, but its most important stabilizer. It played a crucial role in the global bourgeois counter-reformation process. Transferring production to the Middle Kingdom has become an important factor in attacking workers' rights in old industrial countries, while the new Chinese bourgeoisie, which has become a player on the global market, actively demands from its former Western teachers even more aggressive elimination of social guarantees. Of course, today we are witnessing how the crisis begins to engulf the Chinese model itself. It is quite possible, against the backdrop of the unprecedented growth of the industrial working class, we will see here the emergence of new militant organizations of working people. The irony of history, though, is that any action against the logic of capitalism will push the labor movement into a conflict with the party, which still calls itself 'communist'.

The historic defeat of social democracy was less dramatic and spectacular, but no less tragic. Social democratic parties, even when maintaining their positions in the electoral system, turned – using the expression of Antonio Gramsci – into empty shells, structures devoid of any political content. It would be unjust, therefore, to accuse the Social Democrats of today of reformism. Most of these parties have long forgotten what a reform is. Only the color of their banners, if that, distinguishes them from liberals and conservatives. The regimes created by national liberation movements have become bourgeois and corrupt so much that, at times, they are worse than the old colonial state for the populations of people they control.

Therefore, we see that the crisis of capitalism and the crisis of anti-capitalist alternatives go hand in hand. Worse, it was the collapse of all revolutionary and reformist alternatives to the rule of capital that became the most important factor in the destruction of the bourgeois order in the long run. The existence of these alternatives (even with all their negative aspects) disciplined and restrained the ruling classes, forcing capital not only to make concessions to the workers, but also to be more demanding and sober about themselves and not to completely believe in their own ideology and propaganda.

The global defeat of the left has stimulated rapid corruption and degradation of the capitalist classes and, as a result, has aggravated all the contradictions and problems that the system faces. The collapse of the left movement has given rise to a more acute need for a socialist alternative than ever before in the past 50 years. Moreover, this need, regardless of what intellectuals say and write, is acutely felt by the masses spontaneously taking to the streets – in India, in France, in Arab countries.

However, the need for transformation does not directly translate into a possibility of successful transformation. Existence of revolutionaries is not an absolute requirement for the destruction of the system: the system can perfectly destroy itself. However, in order to get out of the crisis, in order to find new ways of social development, we need conscious social forces, organizations and leaders.

In this sense, Samir Amin's call for a new International sounds quite timely. The only question is: should we take this appeal literally? Do we need to try to create international organizational structures, hold congresses, and write a program? I think that for this, the moment has yet to come.

The First International was necessary in order to formalize the very idea of a workers' socialist organization. It could neither fight for power, nor it could even conduct mass agitation – local structures for this were lacking. It was naturally replaced by the Second International, which united massive political parties. It is well known that German social democrats formed the core of the organization. For some time German social democratic movement was a model organization, and everyone else at least looked up to it, if was not aligned with it. The collapse of the Second International was associated not only with the opportunism of its leadership and with the split of almost all parties into the left and the right wings, but also with the appearance of a new successful model of political organization represented by Russian Bolshevism. It was completely natural to create the Third (communist) International on its basis.

The rejection of the global revolutionary project by the Soviet leadership under Stalin naturally led to the liquidation of the Comintern. Leon Trotsky tried to revive the revolutionary tradition under the banner of the Fourth International, but nothing came of it. In part, this happened because the sociopolitical niches where the new radical project could take root were already occupied in most countries. Trotskyism could not find a new mass base for itself without taking away the supporters of the already existing social democratic and communist parties and thereby undermining the already existing and functioning left movement. This movement was by no means free of the vices pointed out by Trotsky and his comrades. It still worked and its existence was still important to protect the interests and the rights of workers. Therefore, the politicians of the official workers' parties, who considered the Trotskyists not so much as critics, but rather as a kind of subversive element within the labor movement, were right in their own way. The ideological criticism of the Trotskyists in relation to the leadership of social democracy and the communist parties was often justified. However, Trotskyism as a political project was rejected not only by the leaders, but also by the working masses, who reasonably did not want to exchange a barely visible revolutionary crane in the sky for the opportunist bird in their hands.

The situation is completely different in the beginning of the 21st century. Most countries do not have strong and massive left parties. The old left parties have lost their organic connection with the masses, their authority and trust, even among their own voters. The space is objectively clear for new political forces. In addition, the changes that capitalism has undergone dictate the need for an emergence of new forms of the left-wing movement. Under new conditions, reviving the forms of revolutionary organization perfectly justified in the past is as meaningless as trying to form a Macedonian phalanx to fight against tanks. Each new stage of the evolution of capitalism requires a corresponding transformation of the anti-capitalist forces. The stiffness of the structures of the 'old left' that hindered this transformation was one of the reasons for its collapse.

Nevertheless, a new political alternative can be neither invented nor constructed artificially or mechanically. Our task today is to collect and integrate the experience of the struggle (including the political one) accumulated in different countries. We are entering a period when bold strategic experimentation is needed. Jeremy Corbyn and his supporters are trying to recreate the Labor Party of Great Britain. At the same time, we see how 'yellow vests', putting forward essentially the same slogans and demands, are avoiding political parties. The trade unions are politicizing in India, while in Spain, the left-wing activists are trying to create a new populist party from below. All these numerous and diverse experiments must still demonstrate their potential before a kind of common vision is formed on this basis, which would allow building of a more or less stable global coalition.

It would have to be a coalition, because the new era does not give us reason to hope that we will have a monolithic and homogeneous party with a clear ideology, united leadership, and unambiguous political decisions.

Translated by Natalie Minkovsky

Disclosure statement

No potential conflict of interest was reported by the author.

Sweeping the world clean of capitalism: Samir Amin, Abdullah Ocalan and the world of autonomous regions

Andrej Grubacic

ABSTRACT
This paper will attempt to rethink Samir Amin's concept of delinking in terms of selective delinking and selective engagement. The notion of delinking is perhaps Samir Amin's most distinctive contribution to alternative development, as well as to a vision of a new kind of politics. Inspired by the ideas of Abdullah Ocalan, this talk will focus on stateless (con)federalism seen as an active dialectical engagement with the modern capitalist world-system, an active process of (dis)engagement capable of modifying the conditions of capitalist world-economy.

Samir Amin, a leading scholar and co-founder of the world-systems tradition, died on August 12, 2018. Just before his death, he published, along with close allies, a call for 'workers and the people' to establish a 'fifth international' [https://www.pambazuka.org/global-south/letter-intent-inaugural-meeting-international-workers-and-peoples] *to coordinate support to progressive movements. To honor Samir Amin's invaluable contribution to world-systems scholarship, we are pleased to present readers with a selection of essays responding to Amin's final message for today's anti-systemic movements. This forum is being co-published between* Globalizations [https://www.tandfonline.com/rglo], *the* Journal of World-Systems Research [http://jwsr.pitt.edu/ojs/index.php/jwsr/issue/view/75] *and* Pambazuka News [https://www.pambazuka.org/]. *Additional essays and commentary can be found in these outlets.*

Several years ago, Arturo Escobar proposed that we should rethink Samir Amin's concept of delinking in terms of selective delinking and selective engagement (Escobar, 2004). I find this proposal very compelling. It is important to note that the notion of delinking was never closed to adaptation. This intriguing strategic proposal was open to various interpretations, change and innovation. The notion of delinking is perhaps Samir Amin's most distinctive contribution to alternative development, as well as to a vision of a new kind of politics. The prospect of autocentric development, a refusal to submit to the demands of the worldwide law of value, has been proposed as a positive part of his dependency argument. In its first iteration, delinking was firmly based on the institution of the nation-state. Amin believed that the creative strength of the first phase in the history of the national liberation movement, the one that manifested itself in the nonaligned movement and anti-colonization struggles, has been exhausted. The new phase of the national liberation project requires a fresh logic of emancipation. The main actor in the strategy of delinking is the popular alliance forged by the revolutionary intelligentsia and gathered around the nation state, seen as 'the means to national protection and assertion, the instrument of what we have called "delinking"' (Amin, 1990b, p. 181). If enough peripheral countries were to come together and pressure world capitalism from outside, the capitalist world system would shrink (Amin, 1990a). Amin was keenly aware of the cultural dimensions of the strategy and averse to any kind of cultural chauvinist nationalism; some of the most exciting pages of *Eurocentrism* (1989) were dedicated to this problem. Nor was delinking a form of autarky: 'Delinking is neither commercial autarky, nor chauvinist culturalist nationalism (1990b, p. 231). In his later works, he spoke of delinking at the level of world regions or a network of world regions. Delinking was suggested as a part of the polycentric world of autonomous regions (1990b, p. 231). Regional delinking, thus defined, implies active dialectical relationship with the capitalist world-system, a process of selective cutting off and selective engagement, an active insertion capable of modifying the conditions of capitalist globalization. Refusing worldwide capitalist expansion does not necessitate isolation, but rather re-articulation of economic and political development in terms relevant to localized needs and concerns. I believe that delinking on a regional level offers an alternative project for the world left that should be further refined to fit new conditions. The place to start is the non-state space of Kurdish Rojava, and the theory behind the Rojava revolution. I do not know if Abdullah Ocalan has read Samir Amin in his Turkish prison cell. I suspect that he might have, as his ideas of delinking and regionalism bear a striking resemblance to those advocated by the great sociologist of unequal exchange.

Like Samir Amin, Ocalan believes that we live in the time when it is necessary to (re) invent a new kind of national liberation project. In Ocalan's formulation, 'when society and civilization meet, the main contradiction is between the state and democracy' (2016, p. 63). In this collective effort to reinvent social emancipation, we need to recover, excavate and reinvent emancipatory energies and subjectivities of what he calls democratic modernity (Ocalan, 2011a, 2011b, 2015, 2016, 2017). Democratic modernity, a process and a project, is conceived not just as an alternative to capitalist accumulation, but as an entirely different civilization. The trialectics of democratic modernity includes liberation of nature from capitalism, liberation of democracy from the state, and liberation of women from masculine domination. Another defining element of democratic modernity is 'democratic nation'. For Ocalan, the main problem of modernity is the coupling of power and state with the nation, 'the most tyrannical aspect of modernity'. Nationalism is not just an obstacle, but a form of religious attachment imposed by the nation-state (Ocalan, 2017). The revolutionaries in Rojava speak of democratic nation as an alternative to statist nation. It is an 'organization of life detached from the state', as well as the 'right of society to construct itself' (2016, p. 21). Democratic nation is a a collective based on free agreement and plural identity. Instead of an ethno-statist nation, an inevitable product of a network of suppression and exploitation, we encounter an innovative conceptualization of a form of collective life

> that is not bound by rigid political boundaries, one language, culture, religion and interpretation of history, that signifies lurality and communities as well as free and equal citizens existing together and in solidarity. The democratic nation allows the people to become a nation themselves, without resting on power and state … (2016, p. 21)

Thus defined, democratic nation does not require dominant ethnicity or a dominant language. The organization of collective life is based not on a homeland or a market, but on freedom and solidarity . Territory is important, and sense of belonging to a place is only natural, but as place-based (not place-bound) 'tool for life'.

As Ocalan suggests,

the democratic nation is the model of a nation that is the least exposed to such illnesses of being a state nation. It does not sacralize its government. Governance is a simple phenomenon that is at the service of daily life. Anyone who meets the requirements can become a public servant and govern. Leadership is valuable, but not sacred. Its understanding of national identity is open-ended, not fixed like being a believer or a member of a religion. Belonging to a nation is neither a privilege nor a flaw. One can belong to more than one nation. To be more precise, one can experience inter-twined and different nationalities … With all these characteristics, the democratic nation is once again taking its place in history as a robust alternative to capitalist modernity's maddening instrument of war: nation-statism. (2016, p. 27)

The political expression of is democratic confederalism with democratic autonomy, which is a pol-itical expression of democratic nation, conceptualized as a pluricultural model of communal self-governance and democratic socialism.[1] He provides an elegant definition of democracy as 'a practice and process of self-governance in a non-state society … Democracy is governance that is not state; it is the power of communities to govern themselves without the state' (2016, p. 62).

There is nothing permanent or fixed about the process of direct democracy and democratic autonomy. Democracy abhors timelines. As Ocalan writes in one of his most moving passages, the democratic nation

represents a truth that requires devotion at the level of real love. Just as there is no room for false love in this voyage, there is also no room for uncommitted travelers. In this voyage, the question of when the construction of the democratic nation will be completed is a redundant one. This is a construction that will never be finished: it is an ongoing process. The construction of democratic nation has the freedom to re-create itself at every instant. In societal terms, there can be no utopia or reality that is more ambitious than this. (2016, p. 60)[2]

Abdullah Ocalan has a keen interest in history. He rejects the liberal belief in 'natural perversity of mankind'. State and capitalism were a radical departure from natural tendencies towards democracy and cooperation, and they developed by crushing cooperative solidarities (Grubacic & O'Hearn, 2016). However, the state could never prevent people from relating differently to each other and to nature. Furthermore, history has demonstrated that capitalism and the state are inseparable facts and concepts that were developed in order to prevent direct association among people. In his view, democracy without state is not a new order, but a reconstitution of something that has always been present, that is always in existence, laid waste alongside the state. Democracy as self-gov-ernment was a constructive force that flourished when small parts of humanity broke down the power of their rulers and re-assumed their freedoms in 'vibrant interstices', relatively autonomous from the intrusive power of the nation-state.

Therefore, progress assumes a different meaning in the conceptual language of democratic mod-ernity.[3] In this view, capitalist modernity suggests an experience of time as inevitable and linear pro-gress with an attendant division between nature and culture, and an imagined and imposed international spatial hierarchical model (Konishi, 2015; Ocalan, 2011b).

He calls for radical overturning of the social Darwinism widely promoted by liberal intellectuals and state-centered social sciences. Against the civilization fueled by rationality, possessive individu-alism, and nation-states, he advocates a democratic civilization created by acts of everyday commun-ism, self-organization, mutual interdependence and association. Against the utopian finality of a nation state, he emphasizes actually existing cooperative practices of mutual aid and voluntary association, as democratic practices retrieved from both past and present (Konishi, 2015; Ocalan, 2017). In agreement with the ideas of Marxist geographer Henri Lefebvre (2014; also Konishi, 2015), Ocalan speaks of the 'power of everyday life'.

It is in this space of everyday life that cooperative society must be re-invented and recovered, power socialized and evenly re-distributed, as a democratic nation becomes 'once again' a restorative and creative historical force that 're-democratizes those societal relations that have been shattered by nation-statism'. Here, Ocalan's thought discloses a curious affinity with the historical sociology of Reinhardt Koselleck (2004) and his notion of the temporality of lived time, or the temporality of possible futures and futures past. Society without the state is not society without history, but it is antagonistic to the capitalist present, resisting what Ocalan terms 'society-cide (2017)'. Society becomes ecological society, predicated on the liberation of women, referred to as the 'first colony' in the 5000 years long history of domination.

Progress is spontaneous and free experimentation with new social forms. He opposes the idea of progress and temporality that defined the imagined territorial utopia of liberal modernity. The resist-ance comes from the places and peoples least exposed to violence of the modern capitalist world-sys-tem. It points to the direction of delinking, or decentralization, both territorial and functional, as a way to encourage radical new forms of self-government that would return decision-making to local communities in democratic federal institutions (Grubacic & O'Hearn 2016).[4] Decentralization, for Ocalan, is a form of social organization; it does not involve geographical isolation but a particular sociological use of geography. For Ocalan, democracy without a state presumes an interwoven net-work composed of an infinite variety of groups and federations of all sizes and degrees. Federalism is seen as a basic principle of human organization. Defined as such, democratic confederalism is not a program for political change but an act of social self-determination.

This form of delinking from the world of capitalist modernity is effected through the pro-duction of alternative and oppositional conceptions of a non-state space, a recovery/invention of the new/old world that would consist of multiple autonomous micro-societies bound together within mutually agreed federal structures (Grubacic, 2011). Ocalan suggests a world-federation as a successor to the hierarchical inter-state organization of the capitalist world-system (Ocalan, 2011a, 2011b, 2017).[5] The statist nation would be replaced by a geographical confederation of confederations, in which all affairs would be settled by mutual agreement, contract, and arbitration.

Ocalan maintains that the conditions 'are ripe in the twenty-first century to avoid the fate of con-federal structures which were eliminated by the nation-states in the mid-nineteenth century, and to achieve the victory of democratic confederalism' (2016, p. 61). If the Kurds are today at the forefront of the struggle for the global democratization of society, that is because the liberation of Kurds is inextricably linked to the liberation of life, to the emancipation of humanity and nature:

> In accordance with their historical and societal reality, the Kurds have vigorously turned towards the construction of a democratic nation. As a matter of fact, they have lost nothing by ridding themselves of a nation-state god in which they never believed; they are rid of a very heavy burden, a burden that brought them to the brink of annihilation. Instead, they have gained the opportunity to become a demo-cratic nation. (2016, p. 60)

Indeed, who could be better poised to pave the way to a state-free modernity than stateless people engaged in a bitter anti-fascist struggle for dignity and life? The no-state socialism of Syrian Rojava becomes, in his words, a model for another Middle East, and another possible world of autonomous regions.

Weaving all these different threads together, he arrives at a definition of democratic modernity as an integral organization of democratic nation, communality and ecology. This 'system of liberated life' stands in stark opposition to the capitalist trinity of nation-state, capitalism, and industrialism.

Taken together, a utopian vision promoted by Ocalan, a vision of planetary delinking and planetary confederation, of nature in humanity and humanity and nature, of liberation of women, colonies and nature, of democratic socialism without a state, of democratic nation without nationalism, constitutes an insurgent and integral ecology of hope that should be placed in dialogue with the ideas of Samir Amin. Would Samir Amin be in favor of Ocalan's proposals? I have to say that I have my doubts. One of his more cherished ideas was a proposal for the fifth international, a global political party of the left. While he was a proponent of autonomous national projects, they were based on the concept of a statist-nation and worker/peasant -controlled states in the Global South. I suspect that Samir would have detected a disconcerting similarity with the ideas of the Zapatistas and the 'new' antiglobalization anarchists. We should not shy away from disagreements. If Amin was correct in his analysis of the crisis of the capitalist world-economy, we need to have as many creative disagreements as we can possibly afford. I won't attempt to hide my agreement with Ocalan's project of democratic autonomy. I think that an attempt to institute a global political party would be a mistake. The left needs to recover a part of its' history that was suppressed by various forms of Leninist internationalism. As Edward Thompson was fond of saying, history is forever unresolved: it is a field of unfinished possibilities. We reach back to refuse some possibilities and we reach back to select and develop others. That is what we need to do today. We need to refuse some historical possibilities. By this I refer to liberal vision of civilization and progress. But I would also mean refusing Lenin's vision of party-centered and state-centered internationalism and socialism. National liberation should be understood as democratic liberation from the statist-nation. Socialism should reinterpreted as movement against the state/party form. We should select and develop other unfinished possibilities. We should, as one Japanese exile had said, wake the people from their utopian dream of nation states, and sweep the world clean of capitalism, by reviving the old democratic project of libertarian communist modernity.

Notes

1. There is no doubt that Ocalan's thinking follows, and further develops, the (con)federalist project of other theorists of democratic modernity, including Peter Kropotkin and Murray Bookchin. Ocalan was mainly familiar with Bookchin, whom he read, and actively corresponded with, during his incarceration.
2. The alternative to capitalist modernity is democratic modernity, with the democratic nation at its core, and 'the economic, ecological and peaceful society it has woven within and outside of the democratic nation' (2016, p. 28). In opposition to nation-statism, democratic nation, "detaches" itself from the nation-state as a core institution of capitalist modernity (2011b). This would imply a deliberate fragmentation of the nation-state into non-state communities and townships linked together in complex new federal structures wherein the mutual relations of its members would be regulated by mutual agreement and social custom.
3. This is the real meaning of the curious formulation according to which 'The solution to the Kurdish question, therefore, needs to be found in an approach that weakens capitalist modernity or pushes it back' (2011b, p. 20). Ocalan's interpretation of history, just like Kropotkin's, is modern in a very peculiar sense: it is nonlinear and restoratively historical. History is projected into the future, and the present is seen as a product of backward capitalist modernity (Konishi, 2015).
4. For an in-depth conversation on de-linking as a strategy of democratic space-making see Grubacic and O'Hearn (2016).
5. Ocalan is quite clear that he sees Kurdish democratic autonomy as a model for the Middle East and the world, as 'an emerging entity' that 'expands dynamically into neighboring countries' (2011b, p. 36). The name of this emerging entity is democratic confederalism, a project that 'promises to advance the democratization of the Middle East in general' (2011b, p. 20).

Disclosure statement

No potential conflict of interest was reported by the author.

References

Amin, S. (1989). *Eurocentrism*. London: Zed Books.
Amin, S. (1990a). *Delinking: Towards a polycentric world*. London: Zed Books.
Amin, S. (1990b). *Maldevelopment: Anatomy of a global failure*. London: Zed Books.
Escobar, A. (2004). Beyond the third world: Imperial globality, global coloniality and anti-globalisation social movements. *Third World Quarterly, 25*(1), 207–230.
Grubacic, A. (2011). *Don't mourn, Balkanize: Essays after Yugoslavia*. Oakland, CA: PM Press.
Grubacic, A., & O'Hearn, D. (2016). *Living at the edges of capitalism: Adventures in exile and mutual aid*. Berkeley: University of California Press.
Konishi, S. (2015). *Anarchist modernity: Cooperatism and Japanese-Russian intellectual relations in modern Japan*. Cambridge: Harvard University Press.
Koselleck, R. (2004). *Futures past*. New York, NY: Columbia University Press.
Lefebvre, H. (2014). *Critique of everyday life*. London: Verso.
Ocalan, A. (2011a). *The road map to negotiations*. Berlin: Mesopotamien.
Ocalan, A. (2011b). *Democratic federalism*. Cologne: International Initiative Edition.
Ocalan, A. (2015). *Manifesto for a democratic civilization, I*. Porsgrun: New Compass Press.
Ocalan, A. (2016). *Democratic nation*. Cologne, Germany: Neuss International Initiative. Retrieved from http://ocalan-books.com/english/democratic-nation.html
Ocalan, A. (2017). *Manifesto for a democratic civilization, II*. Porsgrun: New Compass Press.

Needed: a new international for a just transition and against fascism

Francine Mestrum

ABSTRACT
We urgently need a new global solidarity movement, but it will not be shaped like the old ones, with failing solidarity when it is most needed or at the service of anti-imperialist regimes. What we need, urgently, is a global movement for a just transition, combining social and environmental justice, as well as a strong movement against re-emerging fascism, in North and South.

Samir Amin, a leading scholar and co-founder of the world-systems tradition, died on August 12, 2018. Just before his death, he published, along with close allies, a call for 'workers and the people' to establish a 'fifth international' [https://www.pambazuka.org/global-south/letter-intent-inaugural-meeting-international-workers-and-peoples] *to coordinate support to progressive movements. To honor Samir Amin's invaluable contribution to world-systems scholarship, we are pleased to present readers with a selection of essays responding to Amin's final message for today's anti-systemic movements. This forum is being co-published between* Globalizations [https://www.tandfonline.com/rglo], *the* Journal of World-Systems Research [http://jwsr.pitt.edu/ojs/index.php/jwsr/issue/view/75] *and* Pambazuka News [https://www.pambazuka.org/]. *Additional essays and commentary can be found in these outlets.*

Some years ago, during the Greek crisis, I was asked to speak on 'solidarity' for a European audience. I started to explain where the concept came from and how and why it is necessarily based on reciprocity. This is what makes it different from charity, a unilateral gift inevitably leading to a demand for gratitude. Solidarity, on the contrary, is always at least bilateral and based on mutual respect.

This is the reason why all demands and programmes for solidarity among workers and peoples all over the world are always met with a lot of sympathy. Isn't it obvious that whenever Greek workers are in trouble, workers from other countries in the European Union come to their help? Is it not as obvious that whenever people have serious problems, because of a natural catastrophe, for instance, people from other countries in the world try to assist? And in that same logic, is it not self-evident that victims of one same system, workers in capitalism, victims of exploitation of their labour force and of their environment, forge solidarity links to fight that one and only enemy?

Well, it is not. History tells us about the many failures of the left in trying to shape global organisations and struggles. Even in the recent past, most attempts for long-term transnational solidarity have bitterly failed, and there are lessons to learn from it.

In this contribution, I would like to look at some of the reasons for these failures and examine some of the conditions that will have to be met if we want to start what is now called a 'new international', as was proposed by the late Samir Amin. This will require some serious and honest self-criticism and a downright rejection of all romanticism and naive utopianism. The world is what it is, and people are what they are, all different even if they have common demands. In other words, we have to look for solutions beyond the easy slogans and assumptions.

Knowledge and perspectives

It is stating the obvious to say that knowledge about the world is not uniformly spread across this world. People in wealthy countries with more or less decent media may get every day their portion of world news, but that certainly does not mean they know what precisely is going on in Egypt, Myanmar or Venezuela. People in poorer countries, and certainly people with limited education, may not even have heard of Myanmar or Venezuela. And even in the best of circumstances, one has to admit that knowledge and interest in world happenings is limited indeed. An earthquake in Haiti may speak to all and open the purse for help, but a coup in Venezuela is much harder to convince people in France or India that they have to react. Not only do they not know Venezuelan history, they may also believe that if people go hungry, one should be grateful to the United States if it is ready to give so-called humanitarian aid.

These are very simple examples, but they clearly show that it is not so easy to organise solidarity. Surely, popular education programmes can help. But just imagine what happens when people learn their aid to Haiti was not well spent or has not arrived at all … with the next earth quake, help will diminish.

It is, then, in the first place a lack of knowledge and a lack of awareness that we are all humans, part of a single interdependent humankind that binds us together. When seeing a homeless hungry child in Africa on television, there is no one in Europe or America to think, this might happen to my child tomorrow, let us help …

One might think this solidarity is easier to organise when circumstances are more comparable, let us say amongst workers exploited by a brutal capitalist and neoliberal system? Well, again, it is not.

Workers in rich countries of the North know very well that their working conditions are far better than those of their colleagues in the South, and they will gladly support their trade unions when actions are set up to go and support unions in the South. At least, that was the case before the huge wave of globalization in the 1990s. When factories threaten to move to the East or to the South, workers more often than not agree with lowering wages or extending working time than with a move to give their colleagues in the South more jobs. In fact, solidarity did only flourish as long as workers in the North did not have to pay for it themselves. Even within Europe, we have seen many cases of strikes against company relocations where workers of the receiving European country refused to show any solidarity with the workers of the sending country, within the same company. Fortunately, this is not a general rule nor is it a way of criticizing workers, because after all, what is at stake is their livelihood, their jobs.

But as was brilliantly explained by the Belgian philosopher Jaap Kruithof, many years ago, the fact remains that in most cases, workers will more easily show their solidarity with their capitalist bosses than with workers in the South that might take their jobs. This is a very sad but understandable reality. Working conditions between the North and the South have become so hugely different, and profit-making often so easy in the South, that bosses have a ready-made tool in their hands – relocation – to blackmail their workers. The unity of workers, North and South, then, is not a given.

Add to this the difficulty of showing solidarity. Textile production has almost completely moved to the South, and we know how difficult the working conditions of mainly women in these factories are. Just think of the horrible accident in Rana Plaza, Bangladesh, some years ago. Trade unions in the North have set up a campaign to fight for 'clean clothes', which is fine. But it is no easy job to convince consumers in the North to not buy the 'made in Bangladesh'. Nor is it easy to make trade agreements that easily sanction countries in breach with ILO conventions. Today, we know that solidarity from abroad can only help when there is already a strong activism inside the country. That is why the cooperation between trade unions is so very important, though difficult as well.

A third difficulty is to define the agents of solidarity. Again, it is easy to state a global class struggle is going on, and workers are losing. But we now also want a broader struggle of 'people', all those who are not workers. It is a small step away from Marx and back to Flora Tristan, who insisted on organising all lower classes, women and men, workers and beggars and crippled ones. Sounds like a good idea, though we might wonder if the lower classes are the major agents of change in today's world.

What is confirmed once again in the current movement of the 'yellow jackets' in France is that anti-capitalism is as much in the hands of the right as it is in the hands of the left. Most progressive forces, in large parts of the world, can be found also in the urban middle classes and even in the top wealthy class. The anti-capitalist lower class and the left are no longer coterminous, even if they are the major victims of capitalism and neoliberalism. Who then to organise? Do we want to shape 'a people', as the French philosopher Chantal Mouffe proposes, or do we want to reject populism and work with progressive forces only? In my understanding, if a solidarity movement has to shape a better world, it will not be enough to look at the lower classes.

Ideological problems

Early 2019 The Economist published an interesting article on 'millennial socialism'. What it showed was that many young people easily speak of and organise for socialism, but their socialism is far from that of their parents and grand-parents. They do want public services, tax justice and more equality in society, but they do not dream of a planned economy. They do speak of capitalism, but their dreams are less to abolish capitalism than to start with the protection of the environment and the fight against climate change. They certainly want to limit the power of corporations but seem less likely to try and nationalise them. In other words, not only should we reflect on who to organise but also with what objective? Metanarratives and totalising analyses about 'capitalism' have been very useful, but they have also paralysed whole generations who did not know where to start and who rejected all intermediate, 'reformist' steps. In other words, anti-capitalism and socialism may look different in the future. The difficult task of defining a clear and feasible objective is certainly not made easier by the lack of successful socialist models to follow.

Secondly, in spite of thirty years of globalisation, the North South divide has not gone away, though the world has changed. Geo-politically speaking, there is still a totally powerless South with countries who have no real voice at the international level, excluded from the UN Security Council and with hardly any votes in the Bretton Woods institutions. However, Asian countries, and most importantly China are on the rise and are close to dethrone the US, Europe and Japan, the countries Samir Amin puts in 'the triad'. Hegemonic countries rarely let this happen without a war, and the near future does look rather grim when we look at the new arms race and the struggles at corporate level, such as with Huawei. What it means for our desired 'international' is that we need a very careful analysis of the new emerging powers, since they risk to not necessarily only bring improvements. Global political categories are changing, Trump's US is not the open liberal country it claims to be, while capitalist China or oil-dependent Venezuela are not on their way to become liberal democracies. Again, a 'new international against imperialism and capitalism' will require delicate choices.

Finally, and as has already been pointed at, the left right divide is still as lively as ever, in spite of all attempts to ignore it. Yes, wealthy countries and more and more middle-income countries have large middle classes, but these are threatened. While old divides as between workers and capitalists may be waning – many of the ultra-rich also living on wages -, new ones between urban and rural populations, migrants and natives, young and old, anti-globalists and cosmopolites are rising. The left and progressive forces can no longer be identified within the lower classes alone. It means that all attempts at global organisation will require careful analysis and in fact a very different kind of organisation.

Beyond slogans

Finally, what we will have to learn is … to learn. We have no socialist models to follow and social movements of the recent past have not been very successful. Clearly, there are some very good NGOs, working on the environment, on tax justice, on food and rural problems, but they remain one issue groups. We have not succeeded in bringing them together. We have international trade union organisations, which do very useful work at the level of our international institutions but are limited in terms of organising solidarity.

The World Social Forum (WSF) has been a failure, for political and organisational reasons. The European Social Forum and the Forum of the Americas have failed because of intra-left-wing bickering. Occupy, Nuits Debout, Indignados and other 'yellow jackets' have slowly disappeared, mostly because of their lack of organisation. The new slogan today is 'horizontalism', away from 'old-fashioned' vertical and hierarchical movements, with which more often than not trade unions and political parties are identified.

However, as I have been a close witness in the WSF of how this 'horizontalism' can be used to mask real power relations, and how a lack of transparency and accountability help to foster distrust, I can only warn for these 'easy' and 'new' solutions. A lack of clear rules and responsibilities inevitably will harm the possibilities for clear political analyses and hinder the identification of concrete objectives. The WSF has ended up as a totally apolitical gathering, without any direction or steering. Or, to sum up, it has become a toothless tiger.

Conclusion

The lack of awareness of our single humankind, the lack of concrete solidarity with workers that are perceived as competitors, the difficulty of identifying the current agents of change on the one hand, the shifting North South and left right divides and the difficult definition of a socialist objective are all serious obstacles for a 'new international', however broad we define it. Add to this the failures of the recent social movements for lack of organisation, and one can see how very difficult it will be to build something new.

However, not all hope is lost, and we do need a new international. We are indeed living in the autumn of capitalism, and the 'revolt of peoples' is, once again, on the agenda. But the way Samir Amin describes it cannot be the solution for the future. Surely, there still are 'dominated peripheries' and the Venezuelan people is experiencing right now what 'imperialism' means. But the struggles of the future will necessarily have to be global or regional struggles. It is difficult to see what the victory of the yellow jackets in France could mean, or what the fall of right-wing populist regimes in Central Europe would bring in terms of 'another world'. As Heikki Patomäki states, we are fundamentally connected and interdependent. We need to look beyond our borders and open them. I am not sure this is what Samir Amin also wanted to achieve. His project was still rooted in the movement of Bandung, of national development and of 'solidarity' movements at the service of these national regimes. This is what is happening now with the 'ALBA movement' and the 'International assembly' organised in Caracas.

Many current progressive movements are turning inwards, working mainly at the local level, exulting the power of 'municipalism' and the new 'commons'. This may be very useful but the risk, then, is that too much attention goes to individual successes and structural solutions remain out of sight. It can lead to a simple and heroic though useless collective withdrawal from society, such as happened with the neo-zapatistas in Chiapas, Mexico. They are autonomous, they reject modernity and development, but continue to live in extreme poverty.

New initiatives are being taken: a transnational political movement with one single progressive programme in Europe, Diem25, the result of Yanis Varoufakis' failure as minister of finance in Greece; an 'agora of inhabitants', a first gathering to reflect on a legal status for humankind and make all people 'citizens of the world', an initiative of Riccardo Petrella; a World Social Forum on Health and Social Protection, with a clear political input and the ambition to reach out to movements working on the environment, democracy or development; Heikki Patomäki's promotion of a global political party …

A new international is needed indeed, but it will not just be 'anti-imperialist' or be geared towards 'de-linking'. On the contrary, it will try to link countries and people as well as different issues: from social justice to climate justice, from democracy to just trade and tax justice. It will have to be, literally, alter-globalist.

What we need, then, is a movement for a 'just transition', linking social and environmental justice, necessarily based on democracy. And what we also need, urgently, is a strong global movement against re-emerging fascism, in North and South.

If each movement can identify its primary and secondary objectives, a common ground can certainly be found, not on abstract solidarities, but on concrete action and campaigning points. The second thing movements will have to learn is to articulate their struggles at the local, national, regional and global levels. This is not easy but extremely important.

Most of all, what movements will have to learn if they want to mobilize young people, is that 'anti-capitalism' cannot be the over-arching slogan, in spite of the on-going class war. Looking at the 'millennial socialists', working on tax or social justice and other concrete demands, it is obvious that with what I have called in the past 'obstinate coherency' one does change the system. Objectives need to be very concrete and have to be perceived as perfectly feasible. Campaign issues have to be interconnected, since no single campaign will be able to overthrow the system.

Finally, all movements will have to be political, which means they have to be emancipatory and transformative, geared towards the full realisation of individual and collective human rights for all, and, in the end, system change. There is one slogan that remains valid throughout: freedom, equality and solidarity, the keywords of the Enlightenment, with respect for universalism and diversity, the major victories of modernity. In spite of modernity's failure, having separated humankind and nature in its thinking, its basic philosophy remains valid and has to be defended if we also want to fight fascism.

Being political also means not to reject professional politics, but adding to it, extending it, shaping a global public sphere, making all individuals and movements indeed citizens of the world. This is not traditional socialism, we will not have to go in search of ideological purity while getting lost between left and right, but of tolerant, progressive forces, able and willing to cooperate and search for common objectives. This may – hopefully – lead to a more fruitful strategy for the immediate future, making and end to our losing all of our too fragmented struggles.

Disclosure statement

No potential conflict of interest was reported by the author.

Capital has an Internationale and it is going fascist: time for an international of the global popular classes

William I. Robinson

ABSTRACT

Global capitalism is approaching a general crisis of capitalist rule. It is urgent to renovate a popular revolutionary project and refound the state if we are to combat the onslaught of the neo-fascist right. Amin's call for a new Internationale is a timely move in that direction, notwithstanding the many challenges of organizing such an Internationale. Developing an umbrella program must engage political and theoretical debate on the nature of the new global capitalism, learn from the failures of Syriza in Greece and the Pink Tide in Latin America, and reconceive the three-way relationship between states, parties, and social movements. The downward mobility and destabilization of working classes in the former First World and the destruction of the old labor aristocracies provides the recruiting grounds for 21st century fascism but also new opportunities for transnational North-South solidarities. A new Internationale must identify and prioritize the class antagonisms within and across countries and regions over core-periphery or Global North-South contradictions.

Samir Amin, a leading scholar and co-founder of the world-systems tradition, died on August 12, 2018. Just before his death, he published, along with close allies, a call for 'workers and the people' to establish a 'fifth international' [https://www.pambazuka.org/global-south/letter-intent-inaugural-meeting-international-workers-and-peoples] *to coordinate support to progressive movements. To honor Samir Amin's invaluable contribution to world-systems scholarship, we are pleased to present readers with a selection of essays responding to Amin's final message for today's anti-systemic movements. This forum is being co-published between* Globalizations [https://www.tandfonline.com/rglo], *the* Journal of World-Systems Research [http://jwsr.pitt.edu/ojs/index.php/jwsr/issue/view/75] *and* Pambazuka News [https://www.pambazuka.org/]. *Additional essays and commentary can be found in these outlets.*

Samir Amin's call for an 'Internationale of workers and peoples' could not be timelier. If we are to face the onslaught of the neo-fascist right, the left worldwide must urgently renovate a revolutionary project and a plan for refounding the state. It must do so across borders under an umbrella organization that puts forth a minimum program around which popular and working-class forces can unite, and that establishes mechanisms for transnational struggle. While I concur with much of Amin's call I also have some significant differences as well as specifications with respect to the call that I will attempt to explicate below.

Global capitalism is facing a spiraling crisis of hegemony that appears to be approaching a general crisis of capitalist rule. In the face of this crisis there has been a sharp polarization in global society between insurgent left and popular forces, on the one hand, and an insurgent far right, on the other, at whose fringe are openly fascist tendencies (Robinson, 2019). Yet the far-right has been more effective in the past few years than the left in mobilizing disaffected populations around the world and has made significant political and institutional inroads. It would seem that Rosa Luxemburg's dire warning at the start of the World War I that we face 'socialism or barbarism' is as or even more relevant today than when she issued it, given the magnitude of the means of violence worldwide and the threat of ecological holocaust. If left, popular, and working-class forces are to regain the initiative and beat back barbarism they need a transnational umbrella organization with a minimum program against global capitalism around which they can coordinate national and regional struggles and *transnationalize* the fightback.

The international of capital and the specter of 21st century fascism

The theme of transnational struggles from below has been discussed at great length for several decades now. Capital has achieved a newfound transnational mobility yet labor remains territorially bound by the nation-state. In the wake of the structural crisis of the 1970s, emergent transnational capital went global as a strategy to reconstitute its social power by breaking free of nation-state constraints to accumulation, to do away with Fordist-Keynesian redistributive arrangements, and to beat back the tide of revolution in the Third World.

The corporate class and its agents identified the mass struggles and demands of popular and working classes and state regulation as fetters to its freedom to make profits and accumulate wealth as the rate of profit declined in the 1970s. As an emergent transnational capitalist class (TCC) congealed, it put in place a new transnational corporate order and went on the offensive in its class warfare against working and popular classes. Globalization enhanced the structural power of transnational capital over states and popular classes worldwide. Behind this alleged 'loss of state sovereignty', capitalist globalization changed the correlation of class forces worldwide in favor of the TCC. Transnational capital has been able to exercise a newfound structural power over states and territorially bound working classes, which has undermined the ability of states to capture and redistribute surpluses, and with it, the logic and basis for social democratic projects. This is the backdrop to what Amin identifies as the political neutering of traditional unions and left-wing parties and their organizations.

We should be clear that, despite nationalist and populist rhetoric, the forces of 21st century fascism do not constitute a departure from global capitalism but, to the contrary, their program advances the interests of transnational capital in the face of overaccumulation and stagnation in the global economy, as I have discussed at length elsewhere (see, inter-alia, Robinson, 2014, 2018). The fight against fascism is necessarily a fight against the TCC. The core of 21st century fascism is the triangulation of transnational capital with reactionary and repressive political power in the state and neo-fascist forces in civil society. Emergent 21st century fascist projects are a response to the crisis. Escalating inequalities and the inability of global capitalism to assure the survival of billions of people have thrown states into crises of legitimacy and now push the system towards more openly repressive means of social control and domination that exacerbate political and social conflict and international tensions. Neo-fascist projects are a contradictory attempt to refound state legitimacy under the destabilizing conditions of capitalist globalization.

Trumpism in the United States, Bolsonarism in Brazil, and to varying degrees other far-right movements around the world, represent the extension of capitalist globalization by other means, namely by an expanding global police state and a neo-fascist mobilization. They seek to create a new balance of political forces in the face of the breakdown of the short-lived global capitalist historic bloc. What is emerging is an Internationale of 21st century fascism. Far-right and neo-fascist groups around the world, for instance, celebrated the October 2018 electoral victory of Brazilian fascist Jair Bolsonaro. Former Trump advisor and neo-fascist organizer Steven Bannon served as an adviser to the Bolsonaro campaign (Telesur, 2018), while Italy's extreme-right interior minister Matteo Salvini declared in an exuberant tweet that was shared by U.S. neo-Nazi leader Richard Spencer that 'even in Brazil, the citizens have sent the left packing'. *The Guardian* of London warned in its headline coverage that 'Trump joy over Bolsonaro suggests new rightwing axis in Americas and beyond' (The Guardian, 2018).

Beyond such political agents of a 21st century fascism as Bannon or Salvini, the TCC had banked (literally) on Bolsonaro and was delighted with his victory. As in the United States under Trump, Bolsonaro proposed the wholesale privatization and deregulation of the economy, opening up the amazon to lumber, mining and transnational agribusiness interests, regressive taxation and general austerity, alongside mass repression and criminalization of social movements and vulnerable communities that may oppose this program. As Johnson (2018) noted the day after Bolsonaro's victory, the 'world's capitalists are salivating over the new investment opportunities' that Bolsonaro promises. Capital markets and Brazilian funds spiked on the world's stock exchanges the day after his electoral victory. Here we see the 'wages of fascism' for a global capitalism in crisis.

A new Internationale and a united front against 21st century fascism

The right has drawn on the well-known nationalist, populist, xenophobic, and racist repertoire to channel rising anxieties and transform mass anti-systemic sentiment into support for its neo-fascist program. We should be clear, however, that it has been the inability of the left to confront global capitalism and to put forth a clear leftist alternative that has paved the way for the neo-fascist right. The case of Brazil is particularly indicative. During its 14 years in power the Workers Party courted national and transnational capital, overseeing a dramatic expansion of capitalist globalization in the country (Robinson, 2017). It demobilized the mass movements that had brought it to power and absorbed its leaders into the state. Its renowned social welfare programs depended entirely on mild redistribution during the boom period of high prices for the country's commodities exports. Once the prices collapsed in 2014 and the economy tanked, the far-right, with the backing of the TCC in Brazil and abroad, moved on the offensive (see Fogel, 2018; Robinson, 2017).

The lessons from Brazil, Latin America, the United States, and elsewhere are clear. When faced with the inability of moderate reform to stabilize capitalism or neo-fascism, the political and economic elite will embrace the latter. And when a program of mild reform alongside capitalist globalization fails to resolve the plight of masses of people, some of these masses will embrace the fascist alternative. This is why the new Internationale that Amin calls for must stake out a clear position in frontal attack against global capitalism.

These lessons have been particularly painful in Latin America, where the Pink Tide (left turn) starting in the new century raised great hopes and expectations. As has now been discussed at some length by many, myself included, the left in state power (with the partial exception of Venezuela and, to a lesser extent, Bolivia) did not undertake structural transformations; it did not challenge the prevailing property relations and class structure. Social assistance programs depended on the whims of the global market controlled by the TCC. When the price of the region's commodities exports collapsed, starting in 2011, the left lost the very basis for its mildly reformist project.

The popular masses were clamoring for more substantial transformations. But under the pretext of attracting transnational corporate investment to bring about development, the demands from below for deeper transformation were often suppressed. Social movements were demobilized, their leaders absorbed by the institutional left in government and the capitalist state, and their mass bases subordinated to the left parties' electoralism. There is now an evident disjuncture throughout Latin America between mass social movements that are at this time resurgent, and the institutional and party left that is losing power and influence by the day. This disjuncture must be closed and the relationship between political organizations and social movements needs to be clarified as part of the work of a new Internationale.

Here is where we need a new Internationale that puts forth a unified minimal program coordinated across borders and across regions. The World Social Forum (WSF) explicitly rejected a political program and thus contributed to the separation of left political parties from mass social movements. For a fightback to be successful, we need to build a united front against fascism and a program around which such a united front can be organized. Infighting within the ruling groups is escalating as the global capitalist historic bloc constructed in the heyday of neo-liberalism from the 1990s until the financial collapse of 2008 now unravels (more broadly, the whole post-WWII international system is collapsing, but that is a discussion to take up elsewhere). Such infighting may present opportunities for the popular classes to build broad political alliances in the struggle against fascism.

Historically such fronts have subordinated the left to the reform-oriented and 'democratic' bourgeoisie. This time around, in my view, any strategy of broad anti-fascist alliances must foreground a clear and sharp analysis of global capitalism and its crisis and strive for popular and working-class forces to exercise their hegemony over such alliances. For this we need an Internationale with a program. Amin notes that such an Internationale would require several years before giving any tangible results. We should not be under any illusions that a new Internationale as called for by Amin will be free of conflict. All to the contrary, we will push forward in the midst of sharp debate among many different and even antagonistic positions. In the real course of history this is inevitable.

The challenge of Amin's call for an Internationale of workers and peoples

But the construction of programs must also involve debate over the analysis of global capitalism that is at once political and theoretical. It is here that I have significant disagreements with Amin. He correctly, in my view, notes the extreme concentration of capital worldwide and the centralization of power. However, I disagree with his confused insistence on a territorial (rather than a class/social) concentration of that capital and power, and with his insistence on a 'triad' (United States, Europe, Japan) framework that ignores the worldwide transnationalization of capital and the rise of powerful contingents of the TCC in the former Third World.

Amin is blind-sighted by his nation-state/triad framework. It is illustrative anecdotally that the most recent report issued by the Swiss bank UBS on the world's rich notes that most of the world's billionaires are in the United States but the number of ultra-wealthy people is growing fastest throughout Asia. In China, which now accounts for one in five of the world's billionaires, two new billionaires are minted every week (Neate, 2018). China's economic role in Africa, Asia, and Latin America now appears structurally the same as the traditional triad countries. Brazilian, Mexican, Indian, Saudi, Egyptian, and other capitalists who belong to the TCC now also invest worldwide in these same structures, including extensive investment *in* the triad countries. Another report by *Forbes* noted that wealth is growing faster among the super-rich in the former Third World than elsewhere. 'Between 2012 and 2017, Bangladesh saw its ultra-rich club grow by 17.3%', it noted. 'Over the same time period, growth in China was 13.4% while in Vietnam it was 12.7%. Kenya and India were among the other nations recording double-digit growth of 11.7 and 10.7% respectively. The U.S. came tenth overall for UHNWI [ultra-high net worth individuals] population growth at 8.1% from 2012 to 2017' (McCarthy, 2018). Amin is simply wrong when he asserts that 'the oligarchs of the triad are the only ones that count'.

Amin's tenacious nation-state/interstate framework of analysis of world political dynamics ignores both the 'Thirdworldization' of significant sectors of the First World working classes and the rise of TCC contingents in the former Third World that are now globally active and part of the global investor class. It is in fact the downward mobility and destabilization of working classes in the former First World, the destruction of the old labor aristocracies, that provides the recruiting grounds for 21st century fascism *but also* establishes fertile new opportunities for transnational North-South solidarities (yet another reason why Amin's call for a new Internationale is so urgent).

These are not merely analytical or theoretical differences. They have political implications insofar as we must banish any lingering illusions about a 'progressive' or 'nationalist' bourgeoisie in the former Third World with which one could ally against global capital. There may have been one in the bygone era of colonialism and the heyday of national liberation struggles in the 20th century but the interests of the leading contingents of capital and their political representatives in the former Third World now lie in the defense and consolidation of global capitalism. The 're-colonization' of the world by what Amin refers to as the 'collective imperialism' of the triad countries is in actuality a re-colonization by transnational capital, by the TCC, not by some nation-states of other nation-states, notwithstanding that the most powerful contingents of the TCC are still located in the old triad countries and now in China as well.

The worldwide struggle from below of a new Internationale – which *must* be *simultaneously national and transnational* – must identify and prioritize the class antagonisms within and across countries and regions over core-periphery or Global North-South contradictions, *even though* these latter contradictions are still very much relevant, if increasingly secondary. The irony is that Amin's 'triad against the Global South' framework of analysis is in direct contradiction with his entirely correct assertion that 'the possibility of substantial progressive reforms of capitalism in its current stage is only an illusion'.

Of course, the First, Second, Third, and Fourth Internationals were all umbrella international organizations for socialist political parties, whereas the WSF prohibited political parties from participating. I concur fully with Amin that we need to 'establish a new Organization and not just a "movement"' or a 'discussion forum'. At this time, in my view, it is necessary for a new Internationale to incorporate both social movements and left political organizations and parties. This is to say that a new Internationale would be quite distinct from the first four and also from the WSF, which was an international of social movements only. Commitment to a 'minimum program' and to joining forces around such a program with political parties may be tough for social movements to swallow. It is absolutely true that the vanguardist model of revolution in the 20th century (as an aside – this was less due to Lenin's approach than to a fetishization of that approach) involved control of social movements from below by political parties that sought to snuff out their autonomy, and moreover, that some left political organizations in and out of the state in the new century continue to seek such control over social movements from below.

Clearly, a new Internationale must put forth a model of revolutionary struggle in which social movements from below exercise complete autonomy from political parties and from states that may be captured by such parties. If the Left attempts to control or place brakes on mass mobilization and on autonomous social movements from below, if it suppresses the demands of the popular masses in the name of 'governance' or electoral strategies, it will be betraying what it means to be left. It is only such mobilization from below that can impose a counterweight to the control that transnational capital and the global market exercise from above over capitalist states around the world.

Finally, any new Internationale will have to deal with the matter of elections and of the capitalist state. We have learned that subordinating the popular agenda to winning elections will only set us up for defeat even if we must participate in electoral processes when possible and expedient. But we have also learned from recent experience of Syriza in Greece and the Pink Tide governments in Latin America, as well as social democratic governments that came to office around the world in the late 20th century, that once a left force wins government office (which is *not the same as state power … state power is imposed structurally by transnational capital*) it is tasked with administering the capitalist state and its crisis and is pushed into defending that state and its dependence on transnational capital for its reproduction, which places it at odds with the same popular classes and social movements that brought it to power.

There is no ready solution to this (these) dilemma(s). But certainly, a new Internationale of workers and peoples that entails 'an actual organization with statutes and a renovated socialist project' is integral to a solution. Amin is right that 'we are now in the phase of the 'autumn of capitalism' without this being strengthened by the emergence of 'the people's spring' and a socialist perspective.'

Disclosure statement

No potential conflict of interest was reported by the author.

References

Fogel, B. (2018). Brazil's never-ending crisis. *Catalyst*, 3(2), 73–99.
Johnson, J. (2018). After win by Brazilian fascist Jair Bolsonaro, world's capitalists salivate over 'new investment opportunities'. *Common Dreams*, 29 October. Retrieved from https://www.commondreams.org/news/2018/10/29/after-win-brazilian-fascist-jair-bolsonaro-worlds-capitalists-salivate-over-new
McCarthy, N. (2018). Where super rich populations are growing fastest. *Forbes*, 27 September. Retrieved from https://www.forbes.com/sites/niallmccarthy/2018/09/27/where-super-rich-populations-are-growing-fastest-infographic/#17ac328e4ce3
Neate, R. (2018). World's billionaires became 20% richer in 2017, report reveals. *The Guardian*, 26 October. Retrieved from https://www.theguardian.com/news/2018/oct/26/worlds-billionaires-became-20-richer-in-2017-report-reveals
Robinson, W. I. (2014). *Global capitalism and the crisis of humanity*. New York, NY: Cambridge.
Robinson, W. I. (2017). Passive revolution: The transnational capitalist class unravels Latin America's pink tide. *Truthout*, 6 June. Retrieved from https://truthout.org/articles/passive-revolution-the-transnational-capitalist-class-unravels-latin-america-s-pink-tide/
Robinson, W. I. (2018). The next economic crisis: Digital capitalism and global police state. *Race and Class*, 60 (1), 77–92.

Robinson, W. I. (2019). Global capitalist crisis and twenty-first century fascism: Beyond the Trump hype. *Science and Society*, *83*(2), 481–509.

Telesur. (2018). Brazil: Steve Bannon to advise Bolsonaro Presidential Campaign. 15 August 2018. Retrieved from https://www.telesurenglish.net/news/Brazil-Steve-Bannon-to-Advise-Bolsonaro-Presidential-Campaign-20180815-0003.html

The Guardian. (2018). Trump joy over Bolsonaro suggests new rightwing axis in Americas and beyond. 29 October 2018. Retrieved from https://www.theguardian.com/world/2018/oct/29/jair-bolsonaro-brazil-trump-rightwing-axis

On heeding the lessons of the past and adapting them to the present: a strategy for an effective Fifth International

Michael Tyrala

ABSTRACT

The establishment of a Fifth International that would coordinate and provide support to progressive forces from around the world as proposed by the late Samir Amin is long overdue, but its effectiveness will hinge on its ability to heed the lessons of the past and adapt them to the present. This essay argues that an effective Fifth International should move beyond the simplistic and exaggerated interpretations of the capitalist ruling classes wielding absolute power over the world system that leave the revolutionary shortcut as the only viable path forward, and should instead embrace the path of incremental progress and focus on providing support in educating, organizing, and agitating with the specific aim of securing electoral gains. These activities should be oriented globally, but priority should be given to the core, as it is in the core that the key disciplinary structures of capitalist power reside, and without progress against them, progress anywhere else can only be limited. Finally, an effective Fifth International should be organized around a long-term agenda which is at once inspiring and ambitious, broad and flexible, but also safe and familiar, as well as a short and medium term agenda made up of specific policy objectives that not only noticeably improve the lot of the masses, but also undermine the ideological and material bases of power of the capitalist ruling classes.

Samir Amin, a leading scholar and co-founder of the world-systems tradition, died on August 12, 2018. Just before his death, he published, along with close allies, a call for 'workers and the people' to establish a 'fifth international' [https://www.pambazuka.org/global-south/letter-intent-inaugural-meeting-international-workers-and-peoples] *to coordinate support to progressive movements. To honor Samir Amin's invaluable contribution to world-systems scholarship, we are pleased to present readers with a selection of essays responding to Amin's final message for today's anti-systemic movements. This forum is being co-published between* Globalizations [https://www.tandfonline.com/rglo], *the* Journal of World-Systems Research [http://jwsr.pitt.edu/ojs/index.php/jwsr/issue/view/75] *and* Pambazuka News [https://www.pambazuka.org/]. *Additional essays and commentary can be found in these outlets.*

1. Introduction

Writing in the early days of 2019, it is no longer controversial even among mainstream audiences to assert that the capitalist system is facing an unprecedented crisis of legitimacy so severe that it could threaten its very future. It is no longer just a case of radical leftist wishful thinking, but a reality felt across the power structures of the center and the right. And both centrists and rightists are preparing organizationally and institutionally to manage the inevitable transformation in line with their respective reactionary visions. For that reason alone, the establishment of a Fifth International that would coordinate and provide support to progressive forces from around the world as proposed by the late Samir Amin (2018) is in my view long overdue.

The more interesting and more divisive questions are those concerned with how exactly a Fifth International should go about doing this, and to what immediate or intermediate ends, other than of course the ultimate end of overthrowing the capitalist system and replacing it with a more democratic, more egalitarian, and more liberating alternative. Amin (2018) left these questions up for discussion at the end of his proposal's accompanying analysis of the global status quo, but not before indirectly providing his take on them by expressing belief in several key premises that, despite their popularity among certain segments of the radical left, I have long disagreed with, and which I believe warrant serious scrutiny on this occasion. As such, in the three sections that follow, I first provide a brief summary of his position and highlight these key premises, I then elaborate on why I disagree with them, and finally I offer my own take on these questions by proposing a three-point strategy for what would make for an effective Fifth International.

2. The global status quo according to Samir Amin

Amin (2018) conceived of contemporary capitalism as a 'completely closed system', in which some thousand corporate and financial oligarchies centered in a relatively few countries of the historical imperialist core (United States, Europe, and Japan) use their 'absolute political power as well as power over the media', military alliances, and a variety of systematic strategies 'to maintain their "historical privilege" and to prevent all the other nations from extricating themselves from the status of dominated peripheries'. Multi-partyism has been 'annihilated' and replaced by what is 'almost a one-party system, controlled by capital', with representative democracy thus having 'lost all its meaning' and 'its legitimacy'. The logical conclusion from all this is not left up to interpretation either, with Amin outright declaring that 'the possibility of substantial progressive reforms of capitalism in its current stage is only an illusion', and that there is thus 'no other alternative' than the 'renewal of the international radical left, capable of carrying out – and not just imagining – socialist advances', which can be achieved through the construction of 'an international front of workers and peoples of the whole world' once we figure out how to 'overcome' the 'political strategies' employed by the capitalist ruling classes to fragment this 'gigantic proletariat' into manageable fractions.

There is of course a lot of truth in this account, but several of its key premises are overly simplistic and exaggerated to the point of absurdity, boxing the radical left and any potential Fifth International into an unnecessarily rigid if not outright delusional, revolutionary TINA scenario. Somehow, Amin manages to at once overestimate and underestimate both the capitalist ruling classes and the masses. As for the capitalist ruling classes, they apparently preside over a 'completely closed system' within which they wield 'absolute' power over politics, media, and representative democracy, but the implication appears to be that aside from the use of divisive 'political strategies' they would be unable to effectively respond to organizational efforts aimed at bringing the masses together and fomenting global syndical or revolutionary action. As for the masses, they apparently have no way of effecting 'substantial progressive reforms of capitalism' through representative democracy as it is almost completely 'controlled by capital' and has thus 'lost all its meaning', but the implication is that once the divisive 'political strategies' employed against them are in some unspecified way 'overcome', the masses will be able to effect just such reforms by coming together and engaging in global syndical or revolutionary action.

I find this logic thoroughly unpersuasive and would instead offer an alternative interpretation of these key premises. Contemporary capitalism is not exactly an open system but it is far from 'completely closed'. The capitalist ruling classes wield immense structural power but it is far from 'absolute'. Representative democracy is stacked in favor of capital, but it is far from 'having lost all its meaning'. And figuring out how to 'overcome' the divisive 'political strategies' employed against the masses is necessary, but far from enough for uniting the peoples and having them engage in global syndical or revolutionary action. In fact, I would go a step further to argue that the capitalist system and its ruling classes are today more vulnerable than ever before, that this vulnerability offers unique electoral opportunities unavailable at any point during the past several decades, and that, at least in the circumstances of the short and medium term, these opportunities have a much higher likelihood of delivering 'substantial progressive reforms of capitalism' than any revolutionary shortcuts.

3. Systemic vulnerabilities, electoral opportunities, and revolutionary realities

To understand the systemic vulnerabilities of contemporary capitalism and its ruling classes, we must first understand the context of the contemporary crisis and what led to it. And to understand that, we must take a brief detour to a distant past, specifically to the world revolution of 1848, when organized class struggle at last began making its mark on the world. It took various forms, from the occasional revolutionary attempts to cast down the capitalist ruling classes from their positions of power outright, to more gradual, more moderate, but also more lasting efforts to steadily improve the lot of the masses by constantly demanding, fighting for, and eventually securing ever higher standards not only in terms of material wellbeing and a variety of individual and collective rights, protections, and entitlements, but also in terms of the quality of the institutions of representative democracy, which the radical left began using extensively. The only possible responses to these relentless pressures have been repression, relocation, or concessions, and while each has been deployed extensively and relatively effectively by the capitalist ruling classes over the centuries, each has also come at a significant cost, and each has been approaching its limits.

With the specter of communism looming ever larger, the capitalist ruling classes recognized that measured concessions were the least disruptive and thus most profitable way to keep the masses of the global core manageable.[1] The concessions came in the form of what Wallerstein (1995, p. 25) calls the 'three-part package: suffrage, welfare state, and double nationalism (of the states and of the White world, that is, racism)', and for a time it successfully transformed the 'dangerous classes' of much of the core into a 'responsible opposition'.

It was two unavoidable developments that put insurmountable pressure on this profitable stability. Firstly, the 'dangerous classes' of the semiperiphery and the periphery also began to assert themselves, laying claim to a larger piece of the global economic pie. Attempts were made to appease them with an augmented, scaled down version of the 'three-part package', offering national independence as a low-cost substitute for suffrage, and development aid as a low-cost substitute for the welfare state, but this was understandably not enough, and anything more than that was unacceptable to the capitalist ruling classes, as cutting in several billion semiperipheral and peripheral workers and farmers would threaten further capital accumulation. Secondly, the workers of the core, sold on the idea that they now constituted the middle class, continued to demand more as well, asserting their right to a middle class lifestyle, with 'automobiles, college education for their children, vacations in the sun, and adequate health facilities' all expected as the norm.

With the global bill beginning to add up, the capitalist ruling classes fully embraced the scorched earth option of neoliberalism to try to claw back what they had lost, thrusting capitalism into overdrive and straight toward several crucial socio-economic and natural limits through the excessive commodification of what Karl Polanyi (1944, pp. 68–76) referred to as the three 'fictitious commodities': (1) money; (2) labor; and (3) land (or nature).

(1) The excessive commodification of money pertains to the liberalization of capital flows, the private production and marketization of money, and the attempts by the capitalist ruling classes to restore growth and profitability through a seemingly limitless supply of cheap credit, leading to the continued ballooning of public and private debt. Despite the shock of the global financial crisis, the process appears to be nowhere near over, with too big to fail institutions and too big to jail perpetrators growing bigger and becoming too big to save in the case of another failure, which is more than likely forthcoming. Meanwhile, this pathological growth has been occurring in stark contrast to what most people have been experiencing in the rest of the economy, which continues to trudge along on what is often described as the slowest recovery in modern history.

(2) The excessive commodification of labor pertains to the proletarianized precariat of the unemployed, underemployed, underpaid, and unpaid, which has been steadily growing as a result of the continuing deregulation of labor markets, assaults on labor standards, social welfare cuts, and technological progress eliminating entire job categories, with scarcely any regard for how this affects aggregate demand. Instead, we are witnessing unfathomable levels of inequality, with the wealthiest 1% owning more wealth than the bottom 99% of the planet.

(3) The excessive commodification of land pertains to the mismatch between the capitalist logic of infinite expansion and the finite amount of planetary space and natural resources, and although the world has mostly come to terms with the need to reorient the global economy towards more environmentally sustainable outcomes, the actions taken thus far have been inadequate, and the crucial need to significantly lower global consumption has been avoided altogether, because it clashes with the fundamentals of capitalism. As a result, we are resigned to a potentially cataclysmic race between the total exhaustion and degradation of our natural habitat, and blind faith in messianic technological progress that is supposed to make continuation of ever-growing global consumption possible.

As Harvey (2003), Wallerstein (2006 [2004]), Streeck (2016), and a handful of others have long argued, the contemporary crisis context is not confined solely to global finance, but includes the succession of major systemic switching crises that have been appearing with greater frequency and increasing viciousness since around the 1970s. While it may be tempting to see the imposition of neoliberalism as nothing less than the total victory of the capitalist ruling classes over the masses, in world historical perspective the entire project reeks of reactionary desperation. We should not be blind to the fact that through the imposition of neoliberalism, the capitalist ruling classes have temporarily succeeded in vilifying and domesticating most of their radical leftist opponents while making themselves materially more well off than perhaps ever before. But we should also keep in mind that the capitalists made these gains only at the steep cost of undermining the legitimacy of their own structures of power, and not only in the vast reaches of the semiperiphery and the periphery, but increasingly, and arguably more dangerously, also in the core, including among some of their own technocratic cadres.

Whether it is because of the ever more frequent financial and debt crises, the looming prospect of mass unemployment and aggregate demand crises, or the already unavoidable crises associated with climate change, support for capitalism is slowly and irreversibly eroding, and the traditional responses of the capitalist ruling classes also face increasing constraints. Repression still takes place, but with advances in democratic rights and standards of conduct, not to mention the broadcasting capabilities of the smart phone era, this response is politically more costly and less acceptable than in the past, especially when attempted in the core and against a white demographic. Relocation is still widely used, but with most of the world already integrated into the capitalist system and most of the workers of the world not only proletarianized, but also increasingly more educated, more aware of what is happening beyond their borders, and thus more demanding, this response is nowhere near as profitable and effective as it was in the past either. What remains then are concessions – a strategic retreat done in the hope of buying time for the further prolongation of capitalist exploitation – but this is one of the goals, if not quite the ultimate goal, of class struggle, and while the masses of the semiperiphery and the periphery can still be temporarily appeased at a relatively low cost compared with those of the core, it is a cost that keeps rising everywhere. The capitalist system and its ruling classes undoubtedly remain powerful, but they are also more vulnerable than ever before, and this has clear implications for the struggles to come.

These systemic vulnerabilities offer unique electoral opportunities, but thus far it has only been the extreme right that has taken advantage of them, making electoral gains all around the world, and slowly pulling the centers of entire political spectrums in their direction. Today, the extreme right can showcase its victories by pointing to nothing less than the former and the current hegemons (Great Britain and the United States) and their successful campaigns for Brexit and the election of Donald Trump, as well as significant political party or leadership presence not only in nearly every European country, but far beyond as well, including the Philippines and most recently even Brazil. The contemporary extreme right is not anticapitalist, but it faced uphill battles against powerful segments of the capitalist ruling classes and their media empires, and nevertheless came out on top. So much then for contemporary capitalism being a 'completely closed system' with the capitalist ruling classes wielding 'absolute power' and representative democracy having 'lost all its meaning'.

Meanwhile, despite a solid historical track record of electoral and union gains having resulted in clear improvements in the lives of a significant segment of the core working classes, the radical left has been absent from most of the recent contests and so its gains of the past few years thus pale in comparison to those of the extreme right. As for the former hegemon, we can point to a clever use of entryism, though merely to secure Jeremy Corbyn an unstable leadership position in what despite the chaos around Brexit still remains the minority party. As for the current hegemon, we can only point to a handful of popular members of Congress like Bernie Sanders and more recently Alexandria Ocasio-Cortez. And as for the rest of the world, other than in the two most crisis-ravaged countries of the core, Greece and Spain, there have scarcely been any political party or leadership gains at all that could qualify as taking advantage of the contemporary systemic vulnerabilities.

What is especially frustrating is that this chasm between the electoral effectiveness of the extreme right and the radical left is to a significant degree self-inflicted, having to do with the rigid attitude running throughout Amin's analysis, according to which working through the system, even when it is clearly vulnerable, is somehow futile by default. In other popular varieties of this attitude, often feeding off each other, it is not that working through the system is necessarily futile, but rather that it is unethical, as it can be construed as legitimizing what are essentially capitalist structures, or that it blunts revolutionary potential, as competing in what are essentially rigged races wastes resources and breeds complacency. However, the alternative of working outside the system to overcome the divisive political strategies of the capitalist ruling classes, unite the workers and peoples of the world, and effect substantial progressive reforms of capitalism through syndical or revolutionary action has thus far served the anticapitalist cause poorly, and this is unlikely to change anytime in the short and medium term due to several harsh realities surrounding this monumental undertaking.

To start with, even if we did find some way to overcome the divisive political strategies of the capitalist ruling classes, a great many from among the world's masses are still perfectly capable of rampant racism, sexism, and other kinds of bigotry all on their own, so uniting the workers and peoples of the world is more complicated than just overcoming the coercive and persuasive power of capital. As for organizing these diverse masses to effect substantial progressive reforms of capitalism through syndical or revolutionary action, whether at the global or merely at the country level, let us not overstate the number of people actually willing to risk the little they have, their freedom, or even their life, let alone those of their families, to stand up to what would likely be armed opposition. Similar odds have been overcome in the past in Russia, China, Vietnam, Cuba, and a number of other countries, but it has never happened in the core, and without that crucial step, none of the past examples have really led to desirable outcomes, so let us not overstate the value of adding a few more semiperipheral or peripheral countries to the anticapitalist fold without first significantly weakening the immense disciplinary capacities of the core and its institutions of global governance (IMF, World Bank, OECD, etc.). One could argue that the contemporary systemic vulnerabilities finally make the revolutionary shortcut a possibility even in the core, but with revolutionary means generally considered less legitimate than democratic ones, and the capitalist ruling classes still as powerful as they are, success would be unlikely, and failure would be utterly devastating for the entire global radical left.

No matter which way one looks at it, at least in the short and medium term, the deck is stacked infinitely more against the revolutionary shortcut than against incremental progress. We should of course never abandon efforts to unite the workers and peoples of the world against the capitalist system and its ruling classes, and should the opportunity arise, we should also be ready for the revolutionary shortcut, but the former can be pursued through the institutions of representative democracy as well, and the latter is much easier to carry out while holding some political office. In the meantime, we are already witnessing what happens when we abandon efforts to pursue incremental progress through the system, with the capitalist ruling classes not only continuing to profit from ravaging the planet and immiserating the masses, but thanks to the escalating inroads made by the extreme right, they may soon be doing so in a more authoritarian, more hierarchical, and more divisive way than ever before, and all this at least in part because we are shutting ourselves off from a number of avenues for effective action, avenues which were ironically in many cases opened up through past class struggles spearheaded by the radical left. As tempting and gratifying as the revolutionary shortcut may seem, it could be decades before it becomes feasible. The electoral opportunities are feasible now.

4. A strategy for an effective Fifth International

Having demonstrated the main systemic vulnerabilities of contemporary capitalism and the most feasible opportunities they present us with, let me now translate all this into a three-point strategy for what I believe would make for an effective Fifth International.

(1) As a matter of method, an effective Fifth International should embrace incremental progress as its primary mode of conduct, with a focus on providing support in educating, organizing, and agitating with the specific aim of securing electoral gains in every country where this is an option and at every level of power, be it federal or national, state or regional, city, town, or even more local than that, including judges, attorneys general, members of school boards, and any other positions with a modicum of influence. The United States is particularly vulnerable in this regard, with a lot of positions being decided in elections instead of by appointment, incumbents especially at the lower levels of power often running unopposed, and even when opposed, voter turnouts being so low that votes are counted in the thousands or even just hundreds. To these ends, entryism as a political strategy should be revived, adapted to the present era, and utilized to transform every relevant political party that is at least nominally leftist. Lessons and inspiration should be drawn not just from the original Trotskyist and other radical leftist experiences, but also from those of the opposition forces, such as the neoliberal movement (Mirowski & Plehwe, 2009) or the conservative legal movement (Teles, 2010 [2008]), among others.

(2) As a matter of geographical focus, an effective Fifth International should of course be oriented globally, but its priority should be the core, especially the United States and the dominant members of the European Union. I realize this could make many understandably uncomfortable as it smacks of Eurocentrism, something Samir Amin would likely be the first to vehemently object to and would get my full support if it really was the case, but there are at least two genuinely good reasons for this.

The first reason is a matter of necessity and pertains to the fact that the power of the capitalist system and its ruling classes is centered in the core. Without significant progress in the core, progress anywhere else can only be severely limited, because the core not only can, but indeed historically has, served as a very effective spoiler in such situations in order to maintain its dominance and privilege, either directly, or indirectly through the various institutions of global governance. Despite persistent belief from some corners of the radical left that there is essentially no difference between mainstream political parties, there is demonstrably a world of difference between for instance a United States fully controlled by the Republican Party and a United States fully controlled by the Democratic Party, and it would be a whole other United States with the Presidency held by the likes of Bernie Sanders and a Congress held by a Democratic Party with a powerful progressive caucus led by someone like Alexandria Ocasio-Cortez. The latter kind of outcome is nowadays not at all an unrealistic prospect anywhere in the core, and since it is the core which has the decisive say in the staffing and general direction of the institutions of global governance and the EU's Brussels institutions, the impact would be far reaching, opening up new and more radical avenues for effective action.

The second reason is a matter of practicality and pertains to the fact that despite its crucial importance, the core nowadays generally makes for an easier target than much of the semiperiphery and the periphery because of the stark differences between the three in the levels of relative and absolute deprivation, and in the levels of openness and responsiveness of their political systems. After all, although the core masses have been exploited by the capitalist ruling classes as well, they have historically benefitted considerably more from capitalist exploitation than the masses of the semiperiphery and the periphery, enabling them to enjoy, and get used to, considerably higher material and democratic standards. With the bars for what is expected and acceptable thus raised higher than anywhere else, and the contemporary crisis context having produced, in the core, the first generation that is noticeably worse off than the previous one while offering nothing but bleak prospects, rage and resentment fill the air, bringing unique electoral opportunities. The masses of the semiperiphery and the periphery are comparatively worse off in absolute terms, but whatever rage and resentment they may harbor can still be dealt with relatively easily. Either their developmental starting position is low enough that whatever growth and redistribution there is still succeeds in generating an optimistic outlook among a sufficient amount of them, or it does not, but when push comes to shove, unlike in the core, repression is still relatively acceptable, and should that fail, appeasement through concessions is still relatively affordable for at least some time to come.

(3) As a matter of form and substance, an effective Fifth International should exercise extreme caution with regards to its messaging and conduct, presenting its long-term agenda through a manifesto which is at once inspiring and ambitious, broad and flexible, but also safe and familiar, and its short and medium term agenda through specific policy objectives that are achievable and clearly articulated, aimed not only at directly and noticeably improving the lot of the masses, but also at undermining the ideological and material bases of power of the capitalist ruling classes.

To elaborate on form, it is important to keep in mind that especially over the course of the last few decades, the capitalist propaganda machine has succeeded in tying the radical left as a whole to a variety of vicious totalitarian regimes both past and present, and portraying it as not only autocratic and dangerous, but perhaps even more damagingly, as hopelessly naïve, profligate, irresponsible, and incompetent. And even though concepts like socialism are once again becoming increasingly more acceptable and popular while the concept of capitalism heads in exactly the opposite direction, we are still operating from a position of weakness. As such, we should be confident but also measured, and especially when it pertains to the long-term agenda, the manifesto should check three important boxes. It should be inspiring and ambitious enough to attract most of those craving genuine change, broad and flexible enough so as not to repel those from among the radical left who already have a very refined idea about their ideal future society, and safe and familiar enough so as not to repel too large a segment of the center, which can serve a useful role in spreading the long-term agenda to a larger and more diverse audience, effectively normalizing it. In time, the long-term agenda can be crystallized and radicalized as appropriate, but its initial form should not needlessly alienate any potential allies, even if they are to be allies for only a part of the journey. There is less room for such strategizing with regards to the short and medium term agenda since specific policy objectives logically need to be clearly articulated, but even here in order to increase the chances of broader support, some care should be taken to present policy objectives in ways that make them more palatable to the people.

To elaborate on substance, one example of an existing manifesto that I believe fulfills all of the criteria set above is the #ACCELERATE Manifesto by Williams and Srnicek (2013),[2] but there are others worthy of consideration, and there should be a period set aside for studying them, debating them, and using them as inspiration for the drafting of an original document. As for the specific policy objectives, there is already a long list to choose from, including but far from limited to: reintroducing the separation of commercial and investment banking; tackling offshore tax dodging; overhauling the international tax system; making national tax systems more progressive; reforming antitrust legislation and breaking up monopolies and oligopolies; introducing a universal basic income; instituting the concepts of maximum wage and maximum wealth; expanding and improving public services; reforming media ownership and campaign financing laws; the list goes on and on. Some of them would be universally applicable, others more context-specific, and others still more experimental, although each would benefit from further research and debate on the ways in which they could or should be pursued and prioritized in different countries or regions. Fortunately, the radical left already has an unparalleled intellectual base from which to draw, and it should make full use of this unique advantage.

5. Conclusion

My only concluding remark would be that while this three-point strategy outline is unlikely to result in the demise of the capitalist system anytime soon, it does constitute small but important steps in that direction, so maybe we should try taking them instead of standing still and daydreaming about great leaps forward.

Notes

1. In the terminology of world-systems analysis, the Global North is called the core, and the Global South is divided into the semiperiphery and the periphery.
2. The #ACCELERATE Manifesto is a push toward an alternative modernity in which the existing material platform of capitalism and the productive forces of technology are appropriated and redirected from their current trajectories of endlessly developing new methods of financial chicanery and marginally better consumer gadgetry toward post-capitalist common ends that move humanity closer to the ultimate democratic holy grail of collective self-mastery. Three medium term goals are proposed. First, to build a radical leftist intellectual infrastructure mimicking the Mont Pèlerin Society. Second, to initiate a wide-scale media reform that would bring traditional media outlets as close as possible to popular control. And third, to reconstitute various forms of class power by knitting together the disparate array of proletarian and partially proletarian identities.

Disclosure statement

No potential conflict of interest was reported by the author.

References

Amin, S. (2018, July 3). *It is imperative to reconstruct the internationale of workers and peoples*. International Development Economics Associates. Retrieved from http://www.networkideas.org/featured-articles/2018/07/it-is-imperative-to-reconstruct-the-internationale-of-workers-and-peoples/
Harvey, D. (2003). *The new imperialism*. Oxford: Oxford University Press.
Mirowski, P., & Plehwe, D. (Eds.). (2009). *The road from Mont Pèlerin: The making of the neoliberal thought collective*. Cambridge: Harvard University Press.

Polanyi, K. (1944). *The great transformation: The political and economic origins of our time*. Boston, MA: Beacon Press.

Streeck, W. (2016). *How will capitalism end? Essays on a failing system*. London: Verso.

Teles, S. M. (2010 [2008]). *The rise of the conservative legal movement: The battle for control of the law*. Princeton, NJ: Princeton University Press.

Wallerstein, I. (1995). Response: Declining states, declining rights? *International Labor and Working-Class History, 47*, 24–27.

Wallerstein, I. (2006 [2004]). *World-systems analysis: An introduction*. Durham, NC: Duke University Press.

Williams, A., & Srnicek, N. (2013, May 14). *#ACCELERATE manifesto for an accelerationist politics*. Critical Legal Thinking. Retrieved from http://criticallegalthinking.com/2013/05/14/accelerate-manifesto-for-an-accelerationist-politics/

Eurocentrism, state-centrism and sexual self-determination in the construction of a global democratic organization

Teivo Teivainen

ABSTRACT
Based on conversations with and publications of Samir Amin, the article explores connections between his ideas on global political strategy and sexual self-determination. One of the questions is about struggles related to homosexuality in Africa. To what extent did he believe that some of the demands for sexual self-determination, including certain forms of feminism and LGBT rights, were so overly embedded in Eurocentrism that they were not fully suitable for popular struggles in many parts of the Global South? The question is framed in the context of state-centric conceptions of the political. Even if some of the analysis includes a critical tone toward his strategical options, it also highlights the continuing importance of Samir Amin as a point of reference for future struggles to create transnational and global instruments for democratic transformations.

Samir Amin, a leading scholar and co-founder of the world-systems tradition, died on August 12, 2018. Just before his death, he published, along with close allies, a call for 'workers and the people' to establish a 'fifth international' [https://www.pambazuka.org/global-south/letter-intent-inaugural-meeting-international-workers-and-peoples] *to coordinate support to progressive movements. To honor Samir Amin's invaluable contribution to world-systems scholarship, we are pleased to present readers with a selection of essays responding to Amin's final message for today's anti-systemic movements. This forum is being co-published between* Globalizations [https://www.tandfonline.com/rglo], *the* Journal of World-Systems Research [http://jwsr.pitt.edu/ojs/index.php/jwsr/issue/view/75] *and* Pambazuka News [https://www.pambazuka.org/]. *Additional essays and commentary can be found in these outlets.*

My first encounter with Samir Amin was through his texts in the late 1980s when I spent time at Binghamton University in the United States exploring debates about the capitalist world-system. Later, I have often used, and continue to use, his insightful analyses of Eurocentrism and his proposal to build a new organization, a Fifth International, in my classes in Finland and in Latin America.

During that time, I was particularly impressed by the books that Samir had written together with other members of the 'Gang of Four' that also included Giovanni Arrighi, Immanuel Wallerstein and Andre Gunder Frank. The books explored their coinciding interpretations of capitalism and social movements, but the most interesting chapters were the ones in which they laid out their divergences. In his own memory of Samir, Wallerstein (2018) said that of the four, Samir and him agreed the most. One difference between the four was about conquering state power, which Samir considered more advantageous for the struggles than his co-authors.

When I talked with Samir about these divergences, one particular comment seemed to make some of them clearer to me. We both agreed that Wallerstein was, and remains, one of the most important and insightful social scientists in the world. When I asked about where their theoretical and political differences might reside, Samir half-jokingly responded, after various caveats that expressed his basic agreements with a dear long-time friend: 'Do you know what my main problem with Immanuel is? He was never a communist'.

Compared to most intellectuals of his generation, Samir radiated politicizing energy that motivated him and many others to participate actively in multiple initiatives to realize the dreams that they mostly shared. 'Communist' is one expression he used to describe the roots of that motivation, though always making clear that one should not get stuck in dogmatic interpretations of the tradition. His communism and Marxism were explicitly rooted in the Global South,[1] focusing not only on the classical figure of the workers but emphatically also on the struggles of the peasants. For him, Western Marxism was a 'Marxism of the debating chamber and the university, with no social impact' (Amin, Arrighi, Frank, & Wallerstein, 1990, p. 135).

In order to honor Samir's memory as a public intellectual who did not shy away from debates, even with comrades, let me offer a few personal memories that highlight some aspects of his important work among social movements and also open some critical questions that may be useful for further debates about his legacy. The critical questions are about two seemingly different issues: state-centrism and struggles for sexual self-determination. In a sense, however, they are both about the meaning of the political.

In the early 2000s, I got to know Samir in person through various conversations and debates in the World Social Forum (WSF) and its International Council where he represented the World Forum for Alternatives. I always found him to be kind, generous and intellectually honest. His sense of humor was charming and disarming.

At the beginning of the WSF process, Samir thought that it should provide a forum for the creation of a 'global civil front' (see e.g. Amin, 2002). During the first forums in Porto Alegre, Brazil, Samir and I sometimes chatted and agreed on the importance of the Assembly of Social Movements as a 'legitimate trick', as Samir would sometimes call it, to create a political space within the WSF.

The WSF was, and continues to be, trapped in various dilemmas of being an open space that does not aim to become an organization that takes stands and calls for specific political actions. As is clear in Samir's later calls for a Fifth International, he emphasized the need for an Organization with a capital O. The Assembly of Social Movements that gathered inside the WSF events seemed like a possible solution to these dilemmas. Without claiming to represent the WSF as a whole, it consisted of movement organizations that would make various kinds of declarations and calls for action. In our conversations, Samir emphasized that the Assembly of Social Movements was the best available possibility to transgress the self-imposed limitations of the WSF Charter of Principles regarding political action.

Over the years, however, the role of the Assembly of Social Movements lost momentum inside the WSF. The reasons include the fear that some of the founders of the WSF, including most prominently Francisco Whitaker from Brazil, expressed about the Assembly of Social Movements wanting to 'hijack' the WSF process. For Whitaker, the WSF should remain a 'square without an owner', and attempts to transform it toward anything resembling an Organization were suspicious. As the Assembly of Social Movements became less visible, Samir grew increasingly frustrated with the WSF. My understanding is that Samir felt his warnings about the WSF being a 'mere discussion forum' or a 'bazaar' were ignored.

In 2006, the main event of the WSF that, until then, had been an annual gathering organized in one place, was for the first time organized in three different places on different continents. One of them was Caracas. During the Caracas WSF I was sitting with the Peruvian feminist scholar-activist Virginia Vargas and some other friends in the lobby of the hotel where the main activities took place. We were talking about how the political dimension of the forum should be understood.

The WSF had often been accused of not walking the walk, but simply talking the talk. Samir's conception of the WSF as a bazaar-like discussion forum had been one expression of the criticism. We thought that while the criticism was in many ways appropriate, there was something that it did not fully capture.

Three years earlier the biggest simultaneous street mobilizations in the history of the humankind had taken place during the global anti-war protests of February 2003. The social forums had played an important role in bringing about these protests. Yet, the WSF as a whole had never issued a statement against the U.S. invasion of Iraq. In this sense, the WSF had been walking the walk without talking the talk. Perhaps there was something innovative in the WSF method of not aiming to produce unified old-style declarations, but rather creating possibilities for political action to emerge out of its multiple meetings. Should the WSF become more political by strengthening these mechanisms of emergence, or should it become a more unified vanguard, perhaps in articulation with states that would resemble what Samir called a national popular construction?

During our Caracas coffee-table conversation, Samir walked by. He stopped to converse with us for a while and seemed to at least partially agree that new forms of doing politics might be emerging. Then he realized he had to leave. 'I have a meeting with Hugo Chávez', he said, and added smilingly: 'politics, you know'.

At that moment, during the peak period of the 'Pink Tide' Latin American left-leaning governments, the idea of allying the forum with these governments was gaining adherents among many forum participants. It was seen as a possibility that the WSF could finally become political. Others, including some around our table from the organization Articulación Feminista Marcosur, were skeptical and thought the WSF should keep more distance from these governments and focus on creating more autonomous options for becoming political. The debate was, or is, not merely about the desirability of a global political organization. It was more about different ways of prioritizing certain conceptions of the political. In Samir's 'politics, you know', articulating with state power seemed to be a key aspect of the political for the movements.

During that time, people with Samir's generational experience often referred to memories of Bandung. The Bandung Conference in 1955 had been a meeting of Asian and African political leaders. It had created great enthusiasm for a southern front of progressive states, many of which soon gained independence in Africa, that could change the world.

By the 1970s, some of this enthusiasm had faded away. Attempts to transform the rules of international organizations and the world-economy through concerted actions by a majority of the member states of the United Nations were met with strategies that transferred decision-making power to institutions using wealth-based systems of rule. During the 1980s, the powers of the International Monetary Fund and the World Bank were increased. Transnational corporations started playing an even more prominent role than before. South-based state-centric strategies for creating a more democratic world-system lost momentum. The emergence of the global justice protest movements and the World Social Forum at the turn of the millennium were one expression of a less state-centric approach.

Around 2006, ideals of Bandung had made a partial come-back. Beyond their differences, the government of Lula in Brazil and Chávez in Venezuela, together with other, mainly Latin American left-leaning governments such as that of the recently elected Evo Morales in Bolivia, reanimated these ideals. As made explicit in the concluding chapter of *Transforming the Revolution*, compared to many of his scholarly comrades such as Arrighi, Frank and Wallerstein, Samir had already earlier made a more optimistic assessments about the benefits of conquering state power (Amin et al., 1990, p. 183).

In Samir's analyses of the importance of national and popular construction of states, there is some similarity with Ernesto Laclau's conception of populism. Samir himself recognized this in his article 'The Democratic Fraud and the Universalist Alternative' in which he referred to Laclau's 'solid arguments that I will very largely make my own' (Amin, 2011). In the 1970s' debates on the nature of capitalism, Laclau was often considered to be opposed to the analyses of the world-economy made by Samir and the other members of the world-system school. At least in the case of Samir, the emergence of the left-leaning states in Latin America in the first decade of this century made some of these differences seem minor.

Samir's politics was by no means simply state-centric. He was also a true organic intellectual of the social movements. In 2006, one of the polycentric WSF events was organized in Bamako, Mali. Before the forum, a statement of intellectuals and social movement activists known as the *Bamako Appeal* (2006) was published and debated. It included an impressive list of demands that ranged from democratic control of the media to democratizing international institutions. It remains one of the boldest attempts of this century to synthesize various themes and demands that had been present in more scattered form in the WSF events until then. Samir and the Belgian liberation theologist François Houtard were the most visible architects of that creation, in tandem with various social movements. The appeal appeared almost exactly half a century after the Bandung Conference and it was often considered an attempt to create a 'new Bandung'.

Reading through the Bamako Appeal, I was impressed by how elegantly some of the multiple demands could be articulated together. I was also wondering about one particular omission, compared to the themes that were visible in the debates of the WSF and the global justice movements. Sexual diversity and demands for LBTG rights were missing. After all, for many WSF participants they had become an inseparable part of the multiplicity of demands. A decision not to highlight these demands in such an important document made me wonder.

In the WSF 2007 that was organized in Nairobi I participated in a panel with François Houtard. I asked him about the invisibility of gay rights in the Bamako Appeal. He responded that they had simply forgotten about it. Later, during the International Council meeting of the WSF in Nairobi, I asked Samir the same question. He gave a much longer answer, referring to the sensitivities of the Africans around homosexuality and how this meant that the theme could not be emphasized in a document produced in Africa.

We continued with a discussion about Eurocentrism and homosexuality in Africa. The president of Zimbabwe and a former hero of the national liberation struggles, Robert Mugabe, had famously argued that homosexuality was un-African. I mentioned the view according to which the most un-African thing about the Mugabe position was perhaps the colonial education that Mugabe himself had received, embedded with Victorian values about sexuality. Half-jokingly I asked Samir whether their appeal also had a Victorian dimension. Kind as always, he laughed. I wish we could still continue the conversation.

It seems clear to me that Samir was not opposed to rights of sexual self-determination. He repeatedly emphasized personal liberation as one dimension of a desirable future. He did condemn the 'liberal virus' and its celebration of diversity. When he spoke of the related belief that the established system allows 'the flourishing of the individual', he added, in parenthesis, that it really does not allow it (Amin, 2011). Nevertheless, there are parts of his work that may help make the invisibility of sexual self-determination and LGBT rights in the Bamako Appeal understandable.

In an analysis of the social movements in the periphery, Samir expressed some doubts about the ways that feminist and other contemporary movements sometimes approached family traditions (Amin et al., 1990, pp. 133–134, for a feminist critique of Samir's earlier ideas see Harris, 1992). He clearly spelled out that the overall impact of feminism was 'supremely progressive'. At the same time, in somewhat ambiguous sentences, he mentioned the risk of reinforcing 'negative attitudes toward popular national demands, like family-centeredness'. He associated this family-centeredness most strongly with the 'Confucian world', but my understanding is that he saw it as something relevant also in many parts of Africa. In the same text, he connected this negative attitude toward family-centeredness with 'the illusion of being able to do without the state level in the transformation of reality'.

It remains unclear to me to what extent this means that such demands that can seem to be in contradiction with family values might be, in Samir's interpretation, in contradiction with the task of moving toward construction of popular national states. My hypothesis, based on his texts and our conversations, is that he thought that some of the demands for sexual self-determination, including certain forms of feminism and LGBT rights, were so overly embedded in Eurocentrism that they were not fully suitable for popular struggles in many parts of the Global South.

It is obviously true that there exist contradictions between demands for sexual self-determination and important tendencies in popular cultures. This happens in most areas of the world-system and can surely be particularly relevant in some countries of the Global South. In this sense, Samir's description of these contradictions cannot be simply considered erroneous. The political usefulness of responding to these contradictions by leaving some struggles unattended in proposals to create civic fronts or new internationals is, however, more debatable (see e.g. Teivainen, 2016).

Shortly before his death, Samir wrote another version of his calls for a new global political Organization (Amin, 2018). He emphasized the 'inadequacy of the struggles being carried out by the victims of the system'. In his listing of weaknesses of the struggles, the first weakness was 'the extreme fragmentation of the struggles, whether at the local or world level, which are always specific and conducted in particular places and subject-matters (ecology, women's rights, social services, community demands, etc.)'. He warned about 'separating the defense of specific rights from the general fight against capitalism'.

In the movements for sexual self-determination, there are certainly tendencies that could not be comfortably considered parts of a broader anti-capitalist political organization. The same goes for a multitude of other movements. Environmentalism was another example sometimes mentioned by Samir. The World Social Forum has been a space where different concerns and struggles can meet and search for possibilities of political articulation and mutual learning. At least in some formal sense, the groups that participate in the forum already subscribe to the broad ideological guidelines of the WSF Charter of Principles, even if many may never have read it. According to the Charter, the forum participants are opposed to 'domination of the world by capital and any form of imperialism'.

Therefore, when we analyze presences and absences of struggles in calls for construction of global political organizations that are made with at least some linkage to the World Social Forum, one should not assume that some of the struggles are by definition so devoid of any anti-capitalist or anti-imperialist potential that they are made absent. As the Bamako Appeal was at least in some ways produced in the context of the World Social Forum, this kind of absence can be considered particularly intriguing. In future elaborations of similar appeals or calls, in which Samir's ideas are likely to remain an important source of inspiration, more careful attention should be paid to the representation and articulation of often silenced struggles.

In order to make democratic transformations of the world-system, there is a need to create transnational and global political instruments. Some of us have explored the idea of global political parties (Patomäki & Teivainen, 2007). The old ideals of numbered internationals is one way to approach this task. Samir has used the term Fifth International, and the tradition could certainly continue with new numbers. I have sometimes played with the idea of a *Penultimate International*, in order to emphasize the always unfinished task of creating transformational democratic organizations. Whatever terminology we use, one of the current theoretical and political challenges is to take matters of representation more seriously.

In the social movement activism of recent decades, there has sometimes been a tendency to regard 'political representation' as something that belongs to old politics of states and traditional parties or trade unions. For example, in the World Social Forum and occupy movements, ideals of direct participation and 'I can only represent myself' have been common. There has been a fear that taking political representation more seriously would lead back to such state-centric strategies that already led to various disappointments. Samir's 'politics you know in Caracas', that I referred to earlier in this article, had some aspects of this kind of return.

With Silke Trommer we have pointed to the need of cutting the umbilical cord between representation and the state (Teivainen & Trommer, 2017). Political representation should be seen as something that matters also in radical non-state politics. Perhaps transnational and global political organizations of the future will find novel strategies to integrate both state and non-state actors and help create a democratizable global political space. *The global political* should not consist only of the state-centric 'politics you know in Caracas'. Nor should it be approached through lenses that see social movements and other non-state actors as mere pressure groups or otherwise disconnected from real political action that involves political representation. Samir's work, with its strengths and weaknesses, is likely to continue as an important point of reference in these tasks.

Note

1. The terminology of the world-systems perspective normally divides the Global South into the periphery and the semiperiphery. The Global North is called the core.

Disclosure statement

No potential conflict of interest was reported by the author.

Funding

This work was supported by Academy of Finland [grant number 318240].

References

Amin, S. (2002). The priority of strengthening social movements on a global scale. In L. Rikkilä & K. Sehm-Patomäki (Eds.), *From a global market place to political spaces* (pp. 45–55). Helsinki: Network Institute for Global Democratization.

Amin, S. (2011, October). The democratic fraud and the Universalist alternative. *Monthly Review*. Retrieved from https://monthlyreview.org/2011/10/01/the-democratic-fraud-and-the-universalist-alternative/

Amin, S. (2018, August). It is imperative to reconstruct the Internationale of workers and peoples. *Monthly Review*. Retrieved from https://mronline.org/2018/08/23/it-is-imperative-to-reconstruct-the-internationale-of-workers-and-peoples/

Amin, S., Arrighi, G., Frank, A. G., & Wallerstein, I. (1990). *Transforming the revolution. Social movements and the world-system*. New York: Monthly Review Press.

Bamako Appeal. (2006). Retrieved from https://mronline.org/2006/01/17/the-bamako-appeal/

Harris, C. (1992). Samir Amin's maldevelopment: A feminist critique. *Socialism and Democracy, 8*(2-3), 257–290.

Patomäki, H., & Teivainen, T. (2007). Conclusion: Beyond the political party/civil society dichotomy. In K. Sehm-Patomäki & M. Ulvila (Eds.), *Democratic politics globally* (pp. 151–158). London: Zed Books.

Teivainen, T. (2016, February). Occupy representation and democratize prefiguration: Speaking for others in global justice movements. *Capital & Class, 40*(1), 19–36.

Teivainen, T., & Trommer, S. (2017). Representation beyond the state: Towards transnational democratic non-state politics. *Globalizations, 14*(1), 17–31.

Wallerstein, I. (2018, August 15). Samir Amin: Comrade in the struggle. *Commentary* 479. Retrieved from https://www.binghamton.edu/fbc/commentaries/archive-2018/479en.htm

Rethinking Samir Amin's legacy and the case for a political organization of the global justice movement

Bonn Juego 🄳

ABSTRACT
A case is made here for the desirability and viability of the late Samir Amin's call for a new International. However, the project to forge a political organization of the global justice movement must in the first instance draw lessons from the limitations of the recent network structure of new social movements, notably the World Social Forum, and rectify the failures of the old internationals of left-wing cadres. The actualization of such a radical idea also needs to observe the realpolitik of class formation and class struggle under conditions of the imperialistic globalization of capitalism today. Envisioned as a plural and participatory learning organization, the new International's progression should be evolutionary and its strategic engagements have to balance the imperatives of political realism with the ideals of democratic values.

Samir Amin, a leading scholar and co-founder of the world-systems tradition, died on August 12, 2018. Just before his death, he published, along with close allies, a call for 'workers and the people' to establish a 'fifth international' [https://www.pambazuka.org/global-south/letter-intent-inaugural-meeting-international-workers-and-peoples] to coordinate support to progressive movements. To honor Samir Amin's invaluable contribution to world-systems scholarship, we are pleased to present readers with a selection of essays responding to Amin's final message for today's anti-systemic movements. This forum is being co-published between Globalizations [https://www.tandfonline.com/rglo], the Journal of World-Systems Research [http://jwsr.pitt.edu/ojs/index.php/jwsr/issue/view/75] and Pambazuka News [https://www.pambazuka.org/]. Additional essays and commentary can be found in these outlets.

Introduction

Samir Amin's demise on 12 August 2018 is a great loss not only to the left intelligentsia but also to the global justice movement. It comes at a time when much critical thinking and progressive political work need to be done in order to prevent humankind from eventually falling into barbarism, chaos and environmental catastrophe. Amin devoted his intellectual life to unmasking the mechanisms of Eurocentrism and the historical evolution of world capitalism, so as to craft an effective resistance against these oppressive structures and build an alternative socialist future. He was unrivalled as a scholar-activist, with high degree of knowledge on geopolitical economy and active engagements in social movement struggles.

In one of his last writings addressed to activists, Amin (2018) argued for the necessity and poten-tiality of 'a new Internationale of workers and peoples' to counteract the social forces and ideology of capitalist imperialism. This proposal came from his perception of the 'political impotence' of pro-gressive movements vis-à-vis the dangers of the globalized capitalist system controlled by the Wes-tern bourgeoisie (Amin, 2018). Drawing upon his critical examination between the potential effectiveness and actual performance of social movements in the last thirty years of imperialist glo-balization, Amin problematized 'the extreme fragmentation of the struggles, whether at the local or world level' (Amin, 2018). He regretted that the counter-hegemonic movements had lost and aban-doned their originally global and anti-capitalist class orientations, largely due to coercion and coop-tation on them by vested interests in the Triad (i.e., the US, Western Europe, and Japan). Yet, he was relentless in his Marxist understanding of historical processes in the context of the conflictive world structure of 'generalized-monopoly capitalism' dominated by the Triad which, at the same time, cre-ated the precarious conditions of 'generalized proletarianization' of waged workers, salaried middle classes, and market-dependent peasants (see also, Amin, 2013, 2014). He envisioned the historical possibility of overcoming this structural contradiction through the mobilization and consolidation of the victims of the prevailing exploitative system into a radical worldwide organization. He was coherent in utilizing scientific Marxism as a theoretical tool to critique capitalism, analyze tendencies for historical change, and advance socialism as an essentially political project.

As expected, Amin's appeal for a new International to restore class politics of the left at the global scale is haunted by the specters of bitterness and successive defeats of the old internationals. This is despite the expressed vision for the new, Fifth International to be a democratic global movement led by a South-South solidarity of workers, peasants and peoples from peripheral countries in the con-tinents of Africa, Latin America, and Asia – which is intended to be different from the First, Second, Third, and Fourth Internationals that were directed by a leadership or committee of socialist and communist cadres from the Northern and Western countries, including Russia. Still, the project to establish a global political organization based on an anti-imperialist internationalism is both desir-able and viable. It is worthy of serious consideration also for activists who never let their usual intel-lectual pessimism get the better of their political will to make transformative strategies and alternative futures happen.

Public protests, civil disobedience, labor strikes, and political opposition against injustices can occur spontaneously in different countries with diverse socioeconomic regimes. The challenge, how-ever, is to sustain their revolutionary momentum, which a cohesive political organization of global justice movements can provide.

Amin was reaching out to left militants, including fellow travelers, to involve themselves in brain-storming about the agenda of forming a truly global and progressive organization against imperialist capitalism. Such gesture must be perceived as an openness to have a dialogue, even with skeptical and disgruntled sections of the left who have had disappointing experiences with international efforts at activist conferences and labor movement organizing. The novelty of the proposed project is that it starts with a humble admission of the mistakes of the left in the history of internationalizing people's struggles against the world capitalist system. It is substantively different from past initiatives where the questions 'what is the problem in the world' and 'what is to be done with it' were the starting points of the left's united front. Indeed, participants willing to contribute to the process of building an organization for the new International have to admit and learn from: [1] the limitations of recent global discussion forums of civil society and social movements, especially the once-promising World Social Forum (WSF); and [2] the need to rectify the organizational errors in the age-old workers' internationals.

Lessons from the World Social Forum

The routine in the conduct of social and people's forums from the 1990s on has become all too familiar. Almost the entire time schedule of their program of activities are allotted to talks, speeches and debates on wide-ranging thematic and sectoral issues. With the notable exception of the WSF, the main output of international activist gatherings like the Asia-Europe People's Forum (AEPF) is a consolidated final statement or declaration written for public consumption and policy advocacy. It is counter-intuitive, however, that there is hardly any session in these discussion forums where participants plan about organizational development. It also appears that there is scant regard for conducting at least interactive conversations about the inter-national and cross-thematic coordination of campaigns despite the recognition of the intersectionality of social problems and the interdependence of the needed solutions.

Take, for example, the AEPF, which holds interregional events biennially since 1996. Geographical representation is the usual emphasis on the composition of resource speakers in specific workshops within the forum. However, it may be more impactful if each workshop theme had participants from across all issue areas. Thus, instead of designing a workshop on food sovereignty for the simple purpose of articulating an Asian and a European view, this particular topic must also be tackled from the perspectives of fellow activists who have long singly focused on their respective thematic clusters. Such arrangement shall encourage, say, peace activists, human rights defenders, and labor unionists to think about the ways to link their campaigns and advocacies with the question of immigration, the problem of climate change, or the debates on inequality and economic reforms.

The experience, feedback, as well as frustrations, of activists in major discussion forums, especially in the WSF, should definitely inform the process of forming the new International. The WSF, notwithstanding its claim to be a horizontal and transversal organization, manifests the ubiquity of power relations (i.e. the relationship of dominance, both hidden and overt) even among progressive individuals and between social movements. Real existing differences based on gender, geography, educational attainment, status and class also define the inequalities in the assembly and interactions of activists. Nevertheless, despite differences in life circumstances and lived experiences, the strongest basis of unity of activists in the global justice movement is the shared consciousness against varied manifestations of oppression and exploitation.

Much has been said and written about the crucial shortcomings of the WSF, its affiliated regional forums and supported national campaigns to realize the objective of altering neoliberal globalization. Among the critiques of the history of the WSF, the most useful for organizational rethinking of the proponents of the new International are the specific observations on how this so-called 'movement of movements' has evolved into a mere talk shop, an apolitical group, a leaderless and fragmented opposition, and a non-global formation with ahistorical worldview (see, for example, Hanin & Afaya, 2016; Mestrum, 2017; Wallerstein, 2016). But it is also important for the new International to fully appreciate the WSF phenomenon as a concrete representation of present-day realities in organizing emancipatory struggles at the global level. In particular, recall how its origins as a transnational open space had inspired confidence in civil society and social movements to participate actively in envisioning alternative futures through a multiplicity of thematic issues on a cosmopolitan structure (see Santos, 2005, 2006).

There is a real danger for the new International project to be captured by ideological hardliners who may easily denounce most participants in the WSF as at best 'passive victims' of capitalist globalization, or at worst active agents of 'false' popular consciousness. If the new International had to act consistently based on the precepts of political realism and democratic values, then its strategies for organizing must draw lessons from the WSF experience. The pluralist composition of the WSF, alongside other characteristics of new social movements, is a real eye-opener for contemporary left politics. The reality of pluralism in the global justice movement does not only present a difficult challenge for working-class formation, but it also demands deep reflections about the limitations, if not failures, of traditional working-class organization and ideology.

Class formation and class struggle under imperialism

Since the new International would ascribe primacy to class struggle, in which the workers are principal actors of global and social change, it is most appropriate for the organization to regard existing resources from the WSF and the like as a challenge for their consciousness building programs. Class formation is neither static nor predetermined, but subject to a historical process and thus to political currents. This is not to suggest limiting the horizon of the global struggle, but it is to emphasize the need to improve on the resources and insights from *new* social movements. Here, Ellen Meiksins Wood's perspective about pluralism, in line with the theoretical agenda of renewing classical Marxist's historical materialism, remains compelling for the new International's socialist project:

> What is needed is a pluralism that does indeed acknowledge diversity and difference … that recognizes the systemic unity of capitalism and can distinguish the constitutive relations of capitalism from other inequalities and oppressions … . We should not confuse respect for the plurality of human experience and social struggles with a complete dissolution of historical causality, where there is nothing but diversity, difference and contingency, no unifying structures, no logic of process, no capitalism and therefore no negation of it, no universal project of human emancipation. (Wood, 1995, p. 263)

The process of class formation is already a tough ideological conflict to be resolved internally between progressives. But the most difficult and dangerous political war for the international left to confront are the specific externally-generated historical circumstances that limit class struggle within and across nations. Beyond trite sloganeering and ungrounded idealism, the left's strategies must account for the global context of imperialism on which social changes, let alone socialist revolutions, would take place.

There is no doubt that Amin had convincingly provided a comprehensive analysis of the contradictory structure of the crisis-ridden capitalist globalization. By identifying the cracks within contemporary imperialism to signify its own unviability, he also pointed to them as political opportunities where social forces of resistance can arise, namely: [i] the reformist responses to economic crises and stagnation in the Triad that are always geared at protecting the interests of transnational oligarchs, rather than the well-being of ordinary citizens; [ii] the violent propensity of the core Triad to not peacefully give up their dominance to peripheral countries – particularly from Asia – even though these economies have actually gained considerably from liberalization policies and technological advances under conditions of neoliberal globalization during the post-Cold War period; and [iii] the ecological disasters that entail the capitalist accumulation process (Amin, 2018; cf. Juego, 2018a). These contradictions, indeed, constitute the objective stimulus in the current conjuncture, providing the rational and necessary conditions for the global left to forge a radical counter-hegemonic bloc.

However, taking into consideration class struggle in the real world, the left should not only downplay what they deem to be weaknesses of the capitalist system, but must not also forget the historical record of the imperial oppressors. This means that the struggle of the international left needs to exert more attention to imperialist capitalism's tendency to interfere in the socio-economic evolution of sovereign states, and its interventionist capacity in weakening national-level social revolutions.

The history of contemporary world politics suggests that there have been no revolutionary states, no alternative regionalism projects, and no militant social movements that have freely operated and organized without them getting subjected to imperialist pressures and the often-violent intervention-ism of the US-led Triad.

Against this background, Amin's well-known idea of 'de-linking' or 'de-connexion' can be aptly deployed at this historic juncture by regarding it as a concrete geo-political and geo-economic strat-egy of the global South to bypass the structure of mal-development under imperialism, if not surpass the level of capitalist development of the core countries. This particular method of struggle would aim to realize at least three national goals for developing countries: firstly, the development of pro-ductive forces so as to improve the social conditions and quality of life of the population; secondly, the defense of state sovereignty; and thirdly, the creation of a socio-economy of the commons where economic modernity in the manufacturing, agriculture, and service sectors also allows for human flourishing in sustainable communities, creative arts and other alternative ways of living (Juego, 2016). Some may argue that this is currently what China and Russia are attempting to do in their economic modernization and social development strategies to compete with US hegemony. But the fundamental idea is not for the South-South solidarity to engage in an inter-imperialist rivalry with the Triad; it is to break away from the logic of imperialism altogether.

On solidarity and the learning organization

Operating in the spirit of transnational solidarity, the new International's primary organizational function should be the global coordination of actions of progressive grassroots movements from country to country. For pragmatic and strategic purposes, resistance against imperialist relations and capitalist accumulation processes must give greater focus on the level of local communities and nation-states, where these dominating structures are well-rooted and close to homes of the oppressed multitude. Yet, the new International shall never lose sight of the dynamics in the inter-state system of globalized capitalism, within which different societies, nations and states are fully but unevenly integrated.

The new International can offer itself as an umbrella organization of social movements, labor unions, political parties, progressive politicians, and individual activists pursuing different forms of struggle – ranging from pressure politics and policy lobbying, to formal engagements in demo-cratic elections and state representation – for a just, humane and ecological world. It shall coexist with already established socio-political movements, particularly those well organized by the sectors of labor and peasantry (i.e., the global union federations and the international peasant's movement La Via Campesina), and on the issues of migration, ecology, trade and taxation. At its formative stage, the new International may operate as a loose organization. Subjection to organizational disci-pline must depend on the consent and willingness of members. An observer or affiliate status should be open to those not yet ready for the duties and obligations required of a full member.

While the agenda of building 'new' solidarities has become a popular theme in today's global acti-vist networks, there is also a need to rediscover 'old' solidarities, specifically with the working class and the peace movement. Historically, these two progressive formations had been at the forefront of international resistance against capitalist globalization and imperialist wars. Thus, they were the first targets of demolition by the coercive forces of capitalism and imperialism. Contemporary social movements organized around egalitarian principles (e.g., the Occupy movement) and liberal identity politics (e.g., human rights activism, pro-refugee campaigns, and the #MeToo movement) can advance their causes more effectively and meaningfully with the simultaneous mobilization of labor unions and anti-war activists. The new International must be able to take a holistic perspective that understands the connections and underlying causes of all forms of oppression and exploitation based on class, race, gender and sexual orientation. For instance, in addressing the recent mass immigration phenomenon and refugee crisis, campaigns to stop wars of encroachment and reparations for victim countries of these crimes against humanity, combined with concrete policy proposals to resolve the causes of underdevelopment in the developing world, might have much more discursive power for popular mobilization than the usual activist positions against right-wing xenophobia and Islamophobia (Juego, 2018b).

As a 'learning organization', the new International must observe a continuous dialogue between bottom-up and top-down approaches to decision-making. Akin to a global coordinating council, it has the responsibility of keeping into perspective the varying initiatives, campaigns and mass actions at all geographical levels of membership. It must have an open mind, in which its idealism is grounded on a pragmatic understanding of *realpolitik* especially in struggles at national and local scales. This requires an appreciation of the dialectics between reform and revolution, and of the expected political necessity of forging tactical alliances and strategic compromises as particular circumstances arise.

Solidarity in this relationship is not only revolutionary, but also evolutionary, whereby the development of the global organization and local movements is understood through a process of their co-evolution. They all learn from and with each other's perspectives and experiences. The intended result is a powerful synergy between global, regional, national and local struggles.

Past internationals, democracy and the audacity of struggle

The new International will have to guard against the predisposition of the organization's leadership to counter-revolutionary attitudes. It ought to be mindful of the importance of avoiding the vices that plagued the bitter splits and historical enmities in the last four Internationals: sectarianism, centralism, vanguardism and intellectual elitism (recall, for example, Trotsky, 1935). Democracy, or democratic decision-making, is the unifying virtue that most modern-day activists and old-timers hope for a progressive socio-political organization.

By nature of its composition as a broad-based coalition of multiple activist movements around the world, the new International needs to embody a progressive kind of representational politics, where pluralism, diversity and inclusiveness are inherent. In a very diverse formation, the foremost concern of a democratic organization is not to definitively problematize who a participant speaks for, but to mainly ensure both the freedom and equality of speech of every member. Whether a participant represents oneself, a membership, or a constituency in deliberations and decision-making process must not be the basis for determining the power of an argument and the legitimacy of an idea (cf. Teivainen, 2016). Participatory democracy guarantees full rights to every member, and enjoins all representatives to voice out and express themselves without threats and intimidation from fellow members. Decisions over positions on pressing issues and plans of action will still have to be made through dialogue, research, and discussion based on reasoned judgement, progressive principles, and calibrated strategies in the interest of the common good. Yet democratic decisions on courses of action will depend on social contexts, historical specificities, and organizational capabilities.

Of course, it is never easy to establish and manage a genuinely democratic and progressive global organization. Amin's call was not made out of academic naiveté. Up to his death, he kept his revolutionary idealism and optimism. He had an inimitable can-do attitude and determination to carry on with the struggle, and remained hopeful about the capacity of collective and coordinated action of committed militants to lead the global transformation. Indeed, Samir Amin left an intellectual and political legacy for activists contemplating to bring to life a new International for the intensified struggles at this historic moment: the audacity to lose, but not without trying.

Disclosure statement

No potential conflict of interest was reported by the author.

ORCID

Bonn Juego 🄳 http://orcid.org/0000-0001-9894-0129

References

Amin, S. (2013). *The implosion of contemporary capitalism*. New York, NY: Monthly Review Press.

Amin, S. (2014). Popular movements toward socialism: Their unity and diversity. *Monthly Review*, 66(2), 1–31.

Amin, S. (2018, July 3). It is imperative to construct the Internationale of workers and peoples. *Network IDEAS*. Retrieved from http://www.networkideas.org/featured-articles/2018/07/it-is-imperative-to-reconstruct-the-internationale-of-workers-and-peoples/

Hanin, M., & Afaya, K. (2016, September 21). For the purpose of preserving the trace of hope: Let us rethink together about the future of the World Social Forum. *intercoll.net*. Retrieved from https://intercoll.net/For-the-purpose-of-preserving-the-trace-of-hope

Juego, B. (2016). A commons perspective on human-nature relations: Analysis, visions, and strategies for alternative futures. In *Humanity and nature: Traditional, cultural & alternative perspectives* (pp. 62–67). Bangkok: Focus on the Global South, The Sombath Initiative, and Heinrich-Böll-Stiftung Southeast Asia.

Juego, B. (2018a). Authoritarian neoliberalism: Its ideological antecedents and policy manifestations from Carl Schmitt's political economy of governance. *Administrative Culture*, 19(1), 105–136.

Juego, B. (2018b). Nationalism that violates the dignity of human beings deserves condemnation (an interview with Bonn Juego by Ella Soesanto and Fabian Heppe). In *Perspectives Asia: Nationalisms and Populisms in Asia* (Issue 7, pp. 4–8). Berlin: Heinrich Böll Stiftung.

Mestrum, F. (2017, November 18). Reinventing the World Social Forum: How powerful an idea can be. Open Democracy / ISA RC-47: Open Movements. Retrieved from https://opendemocracy.net/francine-mestrum/reinventing-world-social-forum-how-powerful-idea-can-be

Santos, B. (2005). The future of the World Social Forum: The work of translation. *Development*, 48(2), 15–22.

Santos, B. (2006). *The rise of the global left: The World Social Forum and beyond*. London: Zed Books.

Teivainen, T. (2016). Occupy representation and democratise prefiguration: Speaking for others in global justice movements. *Capital & Class*, 40(1), 19–36.

Trotsky, L. (1935, October 22). *Sectarianism, centrism and the fourth international*. Retrieved from https://www.marxists.org/archive/trotsky/1935/10/sect.htm

Wallerstein, I. (2016, November 1). *The World Social Forum still matters*. Commentary No. 436. Retrieved from https://www.iwallerstein.com/the-world-social-forum-still-matters/

Wood, E. M. (1995). *Democracy against capitalism: Renewing historical materialism*. Cambridge: Cambridge University Press.

Building a new international is necessary and urgent

Carlos Serrano Ferreira

ABSTRACT

Samir Amin was one of the most creative Marxists, but also an orthodox, as his appeal for a new international proves, consistent with his defense of the socialist revolution against a decaying capitalist system, which threatens with the extinction of human civilization. However, in a contradictory way, if in the past the material conditions did not exist, they exist today, materializing in a distorted manner by capitalism, the organization of a revolutionary international leadership has never been so non-existent. This article begins by demonstrating the systemic conditions that require the proletariat to build a new International, the reasons for the current difficulty in achieving it; and, from the analysis of the most successful experience to date, the Third International, lessons are drawn for a future Fifth International.

Samir Amin, a leading scholar and co-founder of the world-systems tradition, died on August 12, 2018. Just before his death, he published, along with close allies, a call for 'workers and the people to establish a 'fifth international' [https://www.pambazuka.org/global-south/letter-intent-inaugural-meeting-international-workers-and-peoples] *to coordinate support to progressive movements. To honor Samir Amin's invaluable contribution to world-systems scholarship, we are pleased to present readers with a selection of essays responding to Amin's final message for today's anti-systemic movements. This forum is being co-published between* Globalizations [https://www.tandfonline.com/rglo], *the* Journal of World-Systems Research [http://jwsr.pitt.edu/ojs/index.php/jwsr/issue/view/75] *and* Pambazuka News [https://www.pambazuka.org/]. *Additional essays and commentary can be found in these outlets.*

Samir Amin was one of the great Marxist theorists of the twentieth century, with a creative application of Marxism, but demonstrated in his commitment to revolution a fidelity to the basic assumptions of this current. The Marxist tripod is composed of the dialectical method, the labour theory of value and the revolution, as several have pointed out. Contrary to an anti-Marxist version of Marxism, which removes the element of revolution, as if this were only an epistemological current and not the scientific theory of social transformation, Amin has always articulated the three.

In one of his later writings he proves this once more by stating that 'It is imperative to reconstruct the Internationale of workers and peoples'. There is no way of thinking of the dialectical overcoming (*aufhebung*) of capitalism without a vision of totality that only a proletarian international organization can build. The smallest international organization has a perspective that a national organization lacks. Nor is it possible to overcome the process of global dissemination of the overex-ploitation of labour without a unitary articulation of a socialist offensive that has as its horizon the overcoming of material labour, of the limits imposed by capitalist production relations, and the open-ing of a kingdom of abundance, out of the world of need that humanity has been forced to live in.

This horizon is a possibility that the Scientific and Technological Revolution (STR) opened since the middle of the last century, by engendering globalization, which is, in fact, the definitive contra-diction between the limits of capitalist relations of production and the socialized and internationalized productive forces. Thus, this process 'confronts the capitalist mode of production and its legal-political and ideological superstructure with a structure of productive forces that it can not fully absorb' (Martins, 2011, p. 113).[1] In this way, the STR poses the possibility of realizing the wishes of the Marx-ists of the early 20th century, who believed that this transition was possible when, in fact, the material conditions were not placed. The misunderstanding of imperialism as a decadent form of capitalism, and not as its mature form, blurred the capacity for analysis to differentiate conjunctural crises from the structural crisis of capitalism, and served 'to justify the oblivion of the material conditions of possibility of communist revolution' (Veraza, 2012, p. 125). This explains the impossibility of a socialist transition at that time, but it posits the possibility and necessity of it today.

At that time, material conditions were not given, but there were capable national revolutionary directions and the Third International was built. Nowadays these material conditions are not only posed, but are rotting, paraphrasing what was stated by Leon Trotsky in 1936, but with the wrong timing. But there are no subjective conditions for revolution. The social and environmental crisis we face, which threatens even the possibility of human survival, demonstrates the enormity of the challenge posed by this deadly contradiction.

However, contrary to tendentially subjectivist interpretations, in particular trotskyists and anar-chists, which point out all responsibility to class leaderships, we must remember, as Karl Marx claimed, that it is necessary to 'educate the educator himself' (Marx, 2002, n.p.). The leader of the class must be educated in leadership, not a product of oneself. The popular leaders are neither what they are by themselves, by subjective impulses; nor are they merely a reflection of circum-stances. It is obligatory in this question to rescue the process of dialectical co-constitution, 'the coincidence of the changing of circumstances and of human activity or self-changing can be con-ceived and rationally understood only as revolutionary practice' (Marx, 2002, n.p.). That is, it is necessary to re-establish the necessary understanding of the correlation between subjective and objective elements of analysis, including on the formation of the workers' directions, and avoid mor-alistic judgments that explain the phenomena based on 'betrayals'. If leaders help to shape class organizations, these and the circumstances of class existence and consciousness shape the leaders. Liberation is 'not a gift, not a self-achievement, but a mutual process' (Freire, 2005, p. 7).

It is not possible to imagine that our era of immense objective and especially subjective setbacks would not be reflected in the class and in its directions. This is an element that can not be ruled out in the constitution of a new International, and must be taken into account, as it will be one of the great-est obstacles to its realization. It should guide its practice in relation to the national leaderships and organizations of the International, but mainly its relation to the great oppressed and exploited human masses, so that it does not fall into a sectarian dynamic that marks many groups mistakenly called Marxists. A dialogue must be established.

Attempting to liberate the oppressed without their reflective participation in the act of liberation is to treat them as objects which must be saved from a burning building; it is to lead them into the populist pitfall and transform them into masses which can be manipulated. (Freire, 2005, p. 65)

This relationship, based on manipulation, on the dissolution of the organized and self-organized class into masses of individuals followers of demagogues, which pseudo-fulfill themselves in the heteronomy of the leader, serves towards fascism, to the counter-revolution, never to the revolution socialism and progress. As the growth of the far right around the world demonstrates, neoliberal hegemony has engendered, with the economic destruction of class organizations, the fertile field of misery and existential despair where these forces can develop, and also generated the ultraindividualist ideological environment that let the dilution of the class in mass, which can easily become a fascist mass.

However, the creation of an International is also a necessity for other reasons. Above all, it is not possible to think of revolution as a local or particular process, but rather as an international articulation, although having national moments, de-linkages and new linkages. It has specific national paths, which reflect correlations of forces and peculiarities of each social formation, both for the victory of proletarian power and after in the socialist transition. This view was defended even by those accused of denying the overriding necessity of this international process, such as Josef Stalin Although he later changed his perspective, stated in 1924:

> But the overthrow of the power of the bourgeoisie and establishment of the power of the proletariat in one country does not yet mean that the complete victory of socialism has been ensured. [...] No, it does not. [...] the revolution which has been victorious in one country must regard itself not as a self-sufficient entity, but as an aid, as a means for hastening the victory of the proletariat in other countries. (Stalin, 2008, n.p.)

We now know from past experiences that a socialist transition 'proves to be more complex and tortuous as less developed the country in which it develops is and the more unfavorable and dramatic is the international context in which it operates' (Losurdo, 2007, p. 24). Hence the importance of concerted international action to support these transitions and to create a more peaceful and supportive environment.

The imperative of the formation of a new International is expressed by the new phase of an imperialism that advances with radical processes of recolonization and colonization, as it happens in the global periphery, including in the south and east of Europe. The setback in the socialist field in the last decades has opened space for a reactionary offensive on a large scale, giving new impetus to capitalism. The contradictions of capital, insoluble by capital itself, impose neoliberalism, financerization and mass unemployment as an instrument of preservation against the productive forces that it can not control and to dismantle the organizations of the popular sectors. It is the end of the 'Golden Age' of reformism and the possibility of achievements, albeit minimal, of rights and better living conditions for the masses. As a result we see the suffocation of popular and national sovereignty, preventing the accomplishment of bourgeois revolutions' tasks not yet realized in peripheral countries, such as Agrarian Reform or the right to self-determination. Imperialism will play an important role in the almost eternal affairs of Palestine and Western Sahara, and it will breed new ones, such as the Libyan collapse or the Bosnia and Herzegovina and Kosovar protectorates.

The globalization of the productive forces has created new forms of capitalist organization that enable large transnational imperialist conglomerates to crush the organization of workers, promote massive relocations and exert a blackmail power that benefits from the inability of international workers' articulation. Regardless of how great the local and national economic struggles of the working class can be, as Marx warned

> past experience has shown how disregard of that bond of brotherhood which ought to exist between the workmen of different countries, and incite them to stand firmly by each other in all their

struggles for emancipation, will be chastised by the common discomfiture of their incoherent efforts. (Marx, 2000, n.p.)

Therefore, it is necessary that these converge, not only in economic perspective, but also in politics, even at a world level, with the experience already have taught

> [...] the working classes the duty to master themselves the mysteries of international politics; to watch the diplomatic acts of their respective governments; to counteract them, if necessary, by all means in their power; when unable to prevent, to combine in simultaneous denunciations [...]. (Marx, 2000, n.p.)

Only an international organization is able to convert the working class' great power of the '[...] numbers; but numbers weigh in the balance only if united by combination and led by knowledge' (Marx, 2000, n.p.). Because '[...] the emancipation of the working classes requires their fraternal concurrence [...]' (Marx, 2000, n.p.).

This becomes even more imperative when we compare the state of fragmentation and disorganization of our class at the international level with the ruling class's organizations of various natures and objectives: UN, NATO, World Bank, G7, IMF, World Economic Forum, EU, OECD, Bilderberg Club; Socialist International, etc. There are even organizations that congregate only fascists, such as the former World Anti-Communist League, now ironically called World League for Freedom and Democracy. There is the action of many organizations of the imperialist powers, in particular those of the US hegemonic power, such as the CIA, and its various so-called non-governmental organizations, but which are in reality parastatals, e.g. the National Endowment for Democracy. There are even oligarchs who operate worldwide, such as Georges Soros and his foundation. Faced with this dispersion, and even contradiction in the action between these various bourgeois poles, as well as the nonexistence of a bourgeois international central committee, why would the situation of workers be different? Why can we not maintain the present reality of dispersion of proletarian organizations?

These questions overlook a fundamental fact: the intrinsic difference between the tasks of the bourgeois class and those of the working class. An organization should reflect in the most appropriate way the needs imposed by the tasks that are placed. The bourgeoisie as the ruling class doesn't need to produce a concerted transformation of the world. This is positive for this class, because its internal divisions, both sectoral or national and international, would make such unity impossible. For the bourgeoisie it is enough to maintain the status quo. Disputes between them can alter the correlation between their fractions and representative political sectors, but not the whole system, which is even strengthened by this appearance of plurality, even though these disputes can produce disastrous consequences for the peoples, such as successive wars, as the carnage of the two great wars. This multi-dimensional action produced by different groups and organizations generates a myriad of effects such that it becomes omnipresent, working to solidify the political, economic and, above all, ideological structures of domination. Some spaces of international institutionalization can be produced to answer specific questions, and this will suffice.

The task of the proletariat, however, is of a different nature. The international proletariat must destroy the status quo, the whole system. Therefore, if the normal functioning benefits the bourgeoisie, it is necessary for the proletariat to constitute and maximize its energies for the purpose of articulating, first in several national spheres, then on a world scale, the overcoming of bourgeois power. This task is far more demanding than that of the rising bourgeoisie in the past, for two reasons. First, by the breadth of the scale, which is now international, when before, due to the reach of the productive forces, it was national. Second, due to the depth of the transformation. As antagonistic as the bourgeoisie was in some cases to the Old Regime, what was at stake was the mere substitution of one exploiting class for another, not the enormous historical novelty of replacing an exploitin_ class by an exploited class which in turn can only carry out its complete emancipation with th end of all classes. While the capitalist state has culminated the prior development of capitalism ir the economic field, the embryos of socialism can not develop within capitalism, except in its degen erate capitalist expressions. For example, the possibility of overcoming the material labour that auto mation poses, the material basis of socialism, cannot generate human liberation in capitalism anc ends up creating massive structural unemployment. Hence, it is only through political victory, th_ destruction of the bourgeois state and the construction of a broad set of proletarian states, tha workers can break the straitjacket of capitalist production relations and develop the socialis seeds. This last fact also implies a greater challenge, since the bourgeoisie as a privileged class alread had resources to prepare itself for the task of the future management of its society, even before reach ing political power. The proletariat, on the other hand, does not possess it naturally; on the contrary the normal functioning of the system forces its withdrawal and apathy. So, the International woulc also serve to train the cadres and the masses in the tasks of future management of the proletariar states, a mass school of revolution and socialist management. Therefore, it should develop in it: internal functioning a democratic socialist dynamic, so that it was a school not only theoretical but also practical.

If it is necessary to build a proletarian International, an executive committee for the world revolu tion, what traits should it have? History is always the best master. Instead of establishing a reflectior on utopian perspectives, we must return to past experiences in order to avoid the mistakes and tc reproduce the successes in this new International. The civilizational decadence that we have already achieved does not give us wide margins of errors. There is no room for experimentalism. It is necess ary to incorporate the

> decades and decades of a particularly intense historical period, which includes the October revolution, the Chinese, and Cuban revolution, etc. [... which cannot be] classified as simple misunderstandings, without meaning and without relevance to the 'authentic' revolutionary theory, [... which would have been] definitively delivered in texts that we should only rediscover and rethink! (Losurdo, 2007, p. 18)

These are part of the heritage of the world proletariat in its history of struggle. For having been the main experience, we will make an analysis of the Third International to extract the possible lessons, presented on theses at the end.

Its importance and success can be measured in multiple ways. Between its years of existence (1919–1943) the Communist International reached practically the entire world, to a great extent not reached before or after by any world class, political or ideological organization or movement. Even the successful Second International focused mainly on Europe, e.g. in Latin America it had par- ties only in Argentina and Uruguay. The Third International lasted only less than the Second Inter- national (1889–1916), and had much more time and vitality than other experiences. The Third International was involved in the most important events of its period, as in the solidarity with the Spanish Revolution and the struggle against Nazi-Fascism. One of its main achievements was to be able to build, even with more or less success, a whole constellation of organizations, such as Kres- tintern (Peasant International); the Young Communist International; the Profintern (Red Inter- national of Labour Unions) and the International Red Aid.

Unlike the First International, which emerged after initiatives of solidarity with the defeated Pol- ish Revolt (1863), or the Second, which emerged from small victories in the expansion of socialist space in the late nineteenth century, with the formation of socialist parties in several European countries, the Third International came about thanks to the greatest victory of the workers until today, the October Revolution. The impact of this would be even greater as it came a few years after the break-up of the Second International in 1916, but which had already collapsed in 1914, in Lenin's words, when war credits were voted by almost all the socialist parties of the belligerent countries – with the notable exceptions of Russia and Serbia.

With the Second International, we can see the emergence of an element that will be extremely negative also in the Comintern: the existence of a dominant party. The Social Democratic Party of Germany (SPD) was to be the model and main reference because it was the most successful party, had Engels in its origins, and the presence of a great theoretician such as Karl Kautsky. The Comintern will follow, in turn, the Bolshevik Party.

It was in Russia, in the midst of the civil war and under the leadership of Lenin, that in January 1919 the Central Committee of the Russian Communist Party together with foreign directions issued a call for the formation of a Revolutionary International. Its most important achievement was that it became a revolutionary pole that brought together in its orbit activists from all over the world, leading to the formation of communist parties, whether coming from divisions of opportunist socialist parties or from anarchist organizations (as in Portugal and Brazil).

Ideologically, the greatest successes were to have defeated the two opposing tendencies that emerged within: first opportunism, then ultra-leftism. The first suffered a major defeat already in the Second Congress (June 1920). Until then there were no clear boundaries and the parties were mostly poorly formed. Important definitions were missing, such as the relationship with the unions, the internal working regime, etc. As is often in processes of this nature, the opportunists began to flock in droves. This was especially serious where the parties came from splits of opportunist socialist parties. That is why the 21 conditions of admission were established, which separated the wheat from the chaff. However, the rigidity of these norms, adding to the necessary decisions that could be left to local decision, such as the name of the party, prevented an institutional adaptation that should exist in front of different realities.

Perhaps this rigidity, which imposed, for example, an almost automatic purge of parties, without safeguarding the necessary times that the class struggle and the internal party life in each country demanded, was responsible, in the then existing conjuncture, for the emergence of the ultra-leftism that found answer in the Third (1921) and Fourth (1922) congresses. A tough action was required against those who had not understood the shift from the revolutionary conjuncture to the reactionary, not understanding the need to adapt the tactics. However, it is undeniable that the imposition of a sudden and total break with the opportunists determined at the previous congress, helped to build a sectarian culture that wanted to extend this rupture to organisms like the unions and saw opportunism in what should be the communist practice of agitate partial demands of the masses, even if not only for the fulfillment of these, but for the advancement of class consciousness and organization.

In these first four congresses, one success was the elaboration of theses on central themes: the question of the woman, the black and the national and colonial question, affirming the correct Bolshevik defense of the right to self-determination of the peoples. Nevertheless mistakes were made in this respect, such as the rejection of the request for help of the Catalan independence leader, Francesc Macià i Llussà, to overthrow the dictatorship of Miguel Primo de Rivera in 1926.

There were other failures. For example, the failure of the 1935 uprising in Brazil. It may also be noted in the wrong directions given to Tito, that if he had followed them he would have been swallowed up by the reaction. These errors express in the first case the tendencies of imposition of politics to the local parties, disregarding the analyzes of the militants of their own countries; in the second case, by placing the interests of the dominant party, even more so, of the interests of the dominant state over the local revolutionary interests.

However, the biggest mistake was the refusal to establish a front with the German social-democracy against Nazism, equating both with the pseudo-concept of 'social-fascism', which allowed the fascist victory. This defeat signified the harbinger of the Comintern disintegration.

Six theses for a new international:

Briefly, from the analysis of the Comintern, we will point out six initial theses, which should be developed in the future. The new International would have to:

(1) Undertake a broader organization of all the oppressed and exploited, especially among the most attacked, creating trade union fronts and fighting against all oppressions (chauvinism, racism, fascism, homophobia, national opression, among others). It must carry out a relentless defense of peoples' self-determination.

(2) Theoretical plurality. The end of the USSR made the polemics of the second half of the twentieth century useless and outdated. We return to the controversy that occurred in the Second International, with the disjunctive reform or revolution. Therefore, the new International needs to embrace all revolutionaries, independent of their origins: Stalinists, Trotskyists, Maoists, etc.[2] It is necessary to the peaceful coexistence of broadest theoretical differences, but the political decisions have to be accepted by all after being voted. Only in this way can it be an agglutinator of all revolutionary sectors.

(3) To perform the above, must permanently carry out a theoretical-ideological battle against opportunist and ultra-leftist deviations.

(4) From the organizational point of view, the International should take priority over national parties. However, without discarding the opinions of those, who should have autonomy to the most important decisions, such as the action for taking power. The International must have an educational role, but cannot substitute national directions or intervene.

(5) It will also have to avoid the tendency to establish a dominant party, ensuring equality between the parties in the direction of the international and creating counterbalancing mechanisms against the strongest ones, with balanced composition, not by the effective of the parties. Only in this way will it prevent an international direction from becoming a transmission belt. Among other measures, congresses and headquarters should be done and chosen in a rotating system.

(6) It must have a complete material and political separation from the Proletarian States. This is fundamental so that the International does not become a transmission belt for national interests. However, the International must unconditionally defend these states against imperialism, but from an autonomous position that allows even criticism when necessary.

Proletarians of all countries, unite!

Notes

1. All quotations were freely translated into English by the author.
2. As stated by the most important historical leader of communism in Portugal, Cunhal (2008, n.p.), when addressing the theme of the international communist movement:

> The international communist movement and its component parties have undergone profound changes as a result of the collapse of the USSR and other socialist countries [...]. There were parties that denied his past struggle, their class nature, its goal of a socialist society and its revolutionary theory [...]. This new situation in the international communist movement has opened in

society a vacant space in which other revolutionary parties have taken particular importance, which, in the concrete conditions of their countries, have identified with the communist parties in important and sometimes fundamental aspects of their objectives and action. That is why, when speaking today of the international communist movement, one cannot, as was once done, put a border between communist parties and any other revolutionary parties. The communist movement now has a new composition and new limits in motion.

Disclosure statement

No potential conflict of interest was reported by the author.

References

Cunhal, A. (2008). *As Seis Características Fundamentais de um Partido Comunista*. Marxists Internet Archive. Retrieved from https://www.marxists.org/portugues/cunhal/2001/09/15.htm

Freire, P. (2005). *Pedagogy of the oppressed*. New York, NY: Continuum.

Losurdo, D. (2007). Marx, Cristóvão Colombo e a Revolução de Outubro. *Princípios, 92*, 17–31.

Martins, C. E. (2011). *Globalização, dependência e neoliberalismo na América Latina*. São Paulo: Boitempo.

Marx, K. (2000). *Inaugural address of the international working men's association*. Marxists Internet Archive. Retrieved from https://www.marxists.org/archive/marx/works/1864/10/27.htm

Marx, K. (2002). *Theses On Feuerbach*. Marxists Internet Archive. Retrieved from https://www.marxists.org/archive/marx/works/1845/theses/theses.htm

Stalin, J. (2008). *Foundations of Leninism*. Marxists Internet Archive. Retrieved from https://www.marxists.org/reference/archive/stalin/works/1924/foundations-leninism/ch03.htm

Veraza, J. (2012). *Del Reencuentro de Marx con América Latina en la época de la degradación civilizatoria mundial*. Caracas: Ministerio del Poder Popular para la Cultura.

The kick off*

Mamdouh Habashi

ABSTRACT
Samir Amin's call for the establishing of a fifth international is timely, urgent and necessary. This essay explores some key questions that should be debated by those seeking to create the new international: including the appropriate organizational form; membership; and decision making procedures.

Samir Amin, a leading scholar and co-founder of the world-systems tradition, died on August 12, 2018. Just before his death, he published, along with close allies, a call for 'workers and the people' to establish a 'fifth international' [https://www.pambazuka.org/global-south/letter-intent-inaugural-meeting-international-workers-and-peoples] *to coordinate support to progressive movements. To honor Samir Amin's invaluable contribution to world-systems scholarship, we are pleased to present readers with a selection of essays responding to Amin's final message for today's anti-systemic movements. This forum is being co-published between* Globalizations [https://www.tandfonline.com/rglo], *the* Journal of World-Systems Research [http://jwsr.pitt.edu/ojs/index.php/jwsr/issue/view/75] *and* Pambazuka News [https://www.pambazuka.org/]. *Additional essays and commentary can be found in these outlets.*

PROLETARIER ALLER LÄNDER, VEREINIGT EUCH!
PROLETARIANS OF ALL COUNTRIES: UNITE!

Samir Amin's publication of his 'founding' paper on 17/7/17 was a historic event in every sense of the word. Not only because it summarizes the situation on the front of the struggle between imperialism and the forces of revolution at the global level with a high degree of precision and clarity, but because it launches a new phase in this struggle qualitatively different from all that preceded it.

Since the idea of the establishment of the Fifth International began to crystallize about a decade ago and my insistence on Samir Amin is increasing day by day to complete this paper, until the urgency in recent years reached the degree of a nerve saw. Samir Amin, always a perfectionist in his work, was not hesitant in his conviction of the idea itself but about the timing of its emergence.

For the first time in history, the forces of the global revolution begin to take the lead in their struggle against imperialism, armed with the experience and lessons of the history of former

---

*This paper was the contribution of Mamdouh Habashi in the Second World Congress on Marxism, organized by and held in the University of Peking, May 5th & 6th 2018 and can be only understood in connection with the paper of Samir Amin 'It is imperative to reconstruct the Internationale of workers and peoples' of 17.07.2017.

Internationals', moving from reaction to action, from defense to attack, … no exaggeration in this description.

The task is difficult, … difficult, complicated and complex, but it has no alternative for the real revolutionary forces. We are talking here about the 'process' of building the Fifth International, which may take years. For this process to begin with steady and constant steps, it must have a 'motor' or a steering committee.

This committee will be formed from 10 to 15 parties of those which are the first convinced of the task. It would start with a preparatory meeting to launch the first 'Brain Storming' among the attendees to consolidate:

(A) the points of agreement and disagreement, but more importantly
(B) the expected problems and obstacles of the process.

(A) The points of agreement and disagreement

- Do the participants of this very first meeting have to discuss the a.m. paper of Samir Amin first to find out all points of agreement or possibly disagreement of its analysis of our today's world?
- Would it be preferable for the process to have a preamble of the paper presenting a profile of the former Internationals with their successes and failures without losing the original goal of the process?
- The process should eliminate the opportunistic currents in the left – in the north and in the south – which still do not want to see imperialism in the policies of Europe and Japan and limit imperialism in the United States, not to mention the forces that do not see the existence of imperialism at all.
- After the political analysis of the current situation in the world of today on the paper, a road map to establish the 5th International has to be presented, at least for the first steps of putting the foundation; i.e. when, how, where and with whom the first meeting with the required BRAIN SRORMING will be held.
- The oligarchy of financial market capitalism and political oligopolies rule the world of today with a totalitarian dictatorship which is getting deeper and deeper. The new international is the most accurate expression that this crisis an L- and not U-shape one.
- The unwillingness or ability of the ruling bourgeoisie of the peripheries in general to have any degree of independence.
- The BRICS Group pursues pragmatic opportunistic policies that do not live up to the challenge, as they resist hegemony but not capitalism, not even its neoliberal form.
- The deepening of the crisis of global capitalism does not mean that it is nearing its demise, as much as it means the intensification of its violence and aggression.
- Due to its internal contradictions, the global financial system will face a new collapse in the coming years. The next collapse may be more severe than that of September 2008. The global left must prepare itself to confront this situation with the new International to put forward a global alternative and chart a roadmap out of capitalism rather than out of the Crisis of capitalism. The missing of an 'International' in 2008 has led to a decline in the performance of the global left in facing the crisis instead of getting the most benefit out of it.
- The great popular uprisings in the peripheries (Egypt is a clear example) are going back to what is worse. If the 5th International did exist and had been active and effective in January 2011, it would have changed the course of history.

- The left of the centers is in general lagging behind both, in its strength and in its discourse to face the globalization of the financial market.
- The differences between the attitudes and tactics of the left forces in the world vary deeply despite the high degree of agreement on understanding and analyzing the global situation.
- I do not see a moment more urgent than today to begin thinking about the creation of the new 'International'.

The mission is certainly tough but the journey of a thousand miles begins with a step and all the projects that have changed the world have started as dreams.

(B) The expected problems and obstacles of the process

- The differences between left-wing currents in the world will continue, but we must use them as enrichment and deepen the dialogue rather than fight it, if there is a solid basis for agreement on the strategic issues.
- Of course, the new International will not replace the local struggles, but it will definitely give it the compass and the necessary political support, which may increase the efficiency of these local and regional struggles.
- Collective imperialism has globalized its command since the middle of the twentieth century, while the forces of progress have abandoned this basic weapon.
- The World Social Forum WSF was an attempt to globalize the struggle, but despite all the successes it has achieved the struggle today needs something much more effective and structured.
- The relationship between the national and the international must be addressed and treated from a revolutionary perspective.
- What is the role of the 'revolutionary' party today in the peripheries and – especially – in the centers? And how this party would carry out its goals under the conditions of the Western 'parliamentarism'?
- The New International is the only way to universalize and globalize the struggle for the 'Common Good of Humanity' as a first step towards a socialist perspective, otherwise it would be just wishful thinking.
- In this concern, I have to emphasize that we are talking here about establishing an 'ORGANIZATION' and not any kind of forum or discussion collectives.
- I believe that the basic or most difficult task of the process 'Kick Off' is not primarily to prove the utmost necessity of establishing the International but to answer the unavoidable questions how to manage the organization in the new circumstances ... such as:

  o What is the most appropriate organizational form between the 'Forum' and the 'Com-Intern'?
  o Should it include Marxist parties only? Or also other kinds of organizations? How do we define selection criteria?
  o How do we deal with the presence of more than one Marxist party in a country?
  o How will decisions be taken, by consensus? unanimous? Or by voting?
  o How will it solve the problem of the political 'weight' of the different parties, organizations or countries? Will it be the same voice for each party; the Socialist Popular Alliance in Egypt and the Communist Party of China, for example?
  o The previous question leads us to the need to invent a mechanism to avoid the domination of a country or a party on the International ... How?

Dear Comrades and Friends,

This is my appeal to you all to contribute. We all need your active suggestions and innovative ideas to start the process. Please feel free to contact me, even with negative your critiques, which could be also quite constructive.

Disclosure statement

No potential conflict of interest was reported by the author.

Index

Michels, Robert 63
millennial socialism 115, 117
modern world system 2, 5n2, 15
Moghadam, Valentine 5
Moll, J. 25
Monthly Review 36, 84
Mont Pèlerin Society 134n2
Mouffe, Chantal 115
movement of movements 25–7, 69, 72n4, 145
The Movements of Movements (Sen) 34, 36
Mugabe, Robert 139
multi-centred world system 16
Multilateral Agreement on Investment 78
multi-partyism 127
Myanmar 114

National Endowment for Democracy 153
nationalism 4, 42, 68, 72, 99, 101, 108, 111
nation-states 1, 4, 10, 46–7, 97–101, 107–10, 111n2, 120, 122–3, 147
Navarro, Vicente 83
neo-fascism 17, 66–7, 72, 121
neo-fascist 4, 26, 67–8, 72, 73n13, 119–21
neoliberal globalization project 16, 62, 65
neoliberalism 7–8, 16, 34, 43, 62–3, 65, 79, 87, 90, 94, 100, 115, 129, 152
New Global Left 34–6, 62, 66–7
new international 3–5, 15–16, 40–1, 79, 81, 89, 96, 100, 104–5, 113–18, 144–8, 150–7
New York Tribune 54
Nkrumah, Kwame 56
non-capitalist society 49–51, 78
Nyerere, Julius 56

Obscolescent capitalism (2003) 15
Ocalan, Abdullah 4, 108–11, 111n5
O'Connor, James 8
Our Revolution 35

Pan African movement 57–8
Paris 2, 20, 28, 41, 77
Paris Climate Agreement 10
Patomäki, Heikki 5, 35–6, 117
Penultimate International 141
Peoples Global Action summit 78
Petrella, Riccardo 117
Piedmont-type function 23, 27
Pink Tide 2, 66–7, 78–9, 121, 124, 138
Pleyers, Geoffrey 63
Polanyi, Karl 21, 129
"political Islam" 36
Pol Pot regime 42
Pour la Cinquième Internationale 14
Prague 9, 78
prefiguration 66, 69
producer-consumer co-operatives (P-CC) 49–50, 52–3
Progressive International 36

Qatar 9

race-class-gender articulation 54–8
realpolitik 148
re-colonization 123
Red International of Labour Unions 154
Reese, E. 11
reformism 83–4, 105, 152
Reitan, Ruth 66
representative democracy 41, 127–8, 130–1
Republican Party 17, 132
right of neoliberal globalization 17
right-wing populism 34–6, 71
Robinson, William 3
Rodney, Walter 55
Rojava 21, 29n1, 35, 108, 110
Ross, Stephanie 34
Roundtable, Cavtat 32
Russia 2, 20, 80, 144

Sader, Emir 34
Sanbonmatsu, John 68
Sanders, Bernie 35
Schapper, Karl 25, 28
Schumacher, E. F. 49
Scientific and Technological Revolution (STR) 151
second Marxist century 27
self-organization 70
senile capitalism 14–17
senility 15, 17, 92–3
Sharzer, Greg 68
Sklair, Leslie 4–5
Slovo, Joe 57
Small is Beautiful: A Study of Economics as if People Mattered (Schumacher) 49
Smith, Jackie 35
social democracy 17, 51, 97, 104, 106
Social Democratic Party of Germany (SPD) 155
socialism 2, 4, 14, 16–17, 25, 41–2, 46–53, 83, 89–90, 97, 99–100, 110–11, 115, 120, 133, 144, 152, 154
Socialism and Democracy 32
socialist global society 48
Socialist International 22
socialist project 17, 124, 146
socialist revolution 4, 48, 51, 146
socially necessary labour time (SNLT) 53
social movements 16, 21, 27–8, 33–5, 37, 47, 50, 61–3, 65–6, 69–70, 72n5, 78–9, 83–4, 116, 121–4, 136–7, 139–40
social revolutions 23, 26–7
societas civilis (civil society) 34, 43
Société des saisons 28
society-cide 110
solidarity 25–6, 113, 117, 147–8
Soros, Georges 153
South Africa 56, 80–1, 85n8, 153
South African Communist Party (SACP) 57
South Africa's Treatment Action Campaign 81
sovereign projects 97
Soviet Union 3, 34, 42, 90
Spain 2–3, 66–7, 106
spontaneity 21–4
Srnicek, N. 133

For Product Safety Concerns and Information please contact our EU representative GPSR@taylorandfrancis.com Taylor & Francis Verlag GmbH, Kaufingerstraße 24, 80331 München, Germany